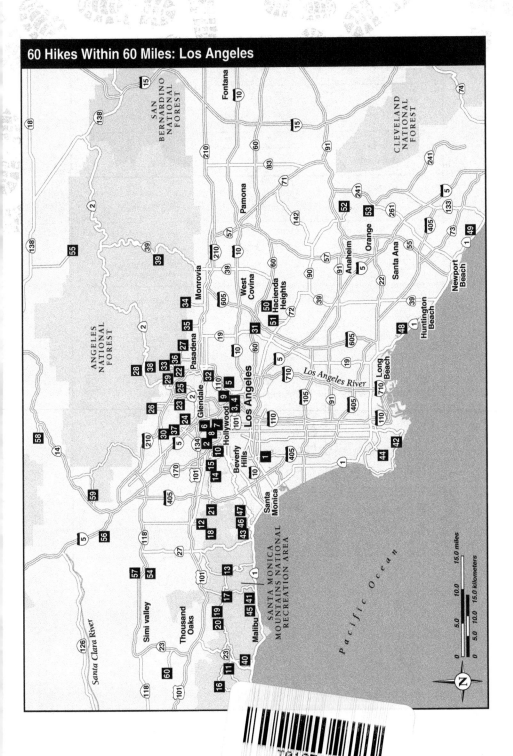

←→ →→	———————	···················
Directional arrows	Featured trail	Alternate trail
═══════════════	══════ ══════	———————————
Freeway	Highway w/bridge	Minor road
▭▭▭▭▭▭▭▭▭▭	··················	═══════════════
Boardwalk	Stairs	Unpaved road
Cliffs	┼┼┼┼┼┼┼┼┼┼┼┼	•—•—•—•—•—•—•
Cliffs	Railroad	Power line
Park/forest	Water body	River/creek/ intermittent stream

♨ Amphitheater	¶¶ Food service	🏛 Picnic shelter
🏃 Baseball field	⋈ Footbridge	🏠 Pit toilets
⊕ Basketball court	❋ Garden	☙ Playground
⊓ Bench	•—• Gate	▲ Primitive campsite
▲ Campground	● General point of interest	🗼 Radio tower
⛵ Canoe access	♀ Golf course	♟♟ Restrooms
✝ Cemetery/grave site	▲ Group campsite	M Scenic view
╱ Dam	⑦ Information kiosk	🏇 Stables
⛾ Drinking water	P Parking	🎾 Tennis court
♯ Electrical tower	🏠 Park office	🏃 Trailhead
$ Fee station	▲▲ Peak/hill	⌒ Tunnel (pedestrian)
⛺ Fire pit	☎ Phone access	⌒ Tunnel (railroad)
◢ Fishing access	⇞ Picnic area	∥ Waterfall/cascades

Overview Map Key

Other cities in the 60 Hikes Within 60 Miles series:

Albuquerque

Atlanta

Baltimore

Boston

Chicago

Cincinnati

Cleveland

Dallas and Fort Worth

Denver and Boulder

Harrisburg

Houston

Madison

Minneapolis and St. Paul

Nashville

New York

Philadelphia

Phoenix

Pittsburgh

Richmond

Sacramento

Salt Lake

San Antonio and Austin

San Diego

San Francisco

Seattle

St. Louis

Washington, D.C.

60 HIKES WITHIN 60 MILES

LOS ANGELES

Including
VENTURA and
ORANGE Counties

3RD EDITION

Laura Randall

MENASHA RIDGE PRESS
Birmingham, Alabama

60 Hikes Within 60 Miles: Los Angeles Including Ventura and Orange Counties

Cover design and cartography: Scott McGrew
Typesetting and text design: Annie Long
Cover photo: Malibu Creek State Park © Marek Zuk/Alamy
Back cover photos: Corriganville Park, Hellman Park, Deukmejian Wilderness Park,
and Ocean Trails Reserve
Back cover and interior photos: Laura Randall

Library of Congress Cataloging-in-Publication Data
Names: Randall, Laura, 1967-
Title: 60 hikes within 60 miles, Los Angeles : including Ventura and Orange counties / Laura Randall.
Description: 3rd Edition. | Birmingham, Alabama : Menasha Ridge Press, [2016]
   | "Distributed by Publishers Group West"—T.p. verso. | Includes index.
Identifiers: LCCN 2015043565 (print) | LCCN 2015045296 (ebook) | ISBN 9781634040365 (pbk.) |
   ISBN 9781634040372 (ebook) | ISBN 9781634041645 (hardcover)
Subjects: LCSH: Hiking—California—Los Angeles Region—Guidebooks. | Los Angeles Region
   (Calif.)—Guidebooks.
Classification: LCC GV199.42.C22 R357 2016 (print) | LCC GV199.42.C22 (ebook)
   | DDC 796.5109794/94—dc23
LC record available at http://lccn.loc.gov/2015043565

 MENASHA RIDGE PRESS
An imprint of AdventureKEEN
2204 First Ave. S, Ste. 102
Birmingham, Alabama 35233
menasharidge.com

Visit **menasharidge.com** for a complete listing of our books and for ordering information. Contact us at
our website, at **facebook.com/menasharidge,** or at **twitter.com/menasharidge** with questions or
comments.

DISCLAIMER

This book is meant only as a guide to select trails in the Los Angeles area and does not guarantee hiker
safety in any way—you hike at your own risk. Neither Menasha Ridge Press nor Laura Randall is liable for
property loss or damage, personal injury, or death that result in any way from accessing or hiking the trails
described in the following pages. Please be aware that hikers have been injured in the Los Angeles area. Be
especially cautious when walking on or near boulders, steep inclines, and drop-offs, and do not attempt to
explore terrain that may be beyond your abilities. To help ensure an uneventful hike, please read carefully
the introduction to this book, and perhaps get further safety information and guidance from other
sources. Familiarize yourself thoroughly with the areas you intend to visit before venturing out. Ask questions, and prepare for the unforeseen. Familiarize yourself with current weather reports, maps of the area
you intend to visit, and any relevant park regulations.

Table of Contents

FOR JACK AND THEO—LAURA RANDALL

Acknowledgments

A SPECIAL THANKS TO ALL THE PARK RANGERS AND DESK RECEPTIONISTS who patiently provided me with condition updates and described trails with the kind of detail and enthusiasm parents exhibit when they talk about their children. The volunteers who clean and maintain trails like Sam Merrill in Altadena and Amir's Garden in Griffith Park also deserve a singling out of gratitude for upholding the spirit of the departed nature lovers for whom the trails are named and making life on the trails better for the rest of us.

I couldn't have completed this third edition without the always ebullient companionship and limitless energy of my son Jack. He was generally up for joining me on any hike, at any time, and helped me to slow down and enjoy every cairn. My husband, John, and friends Kit Ross and Laura Witten were also welcome and encouraging companions who made me want to tackle any trail if it also involved their genial company.

In 2009 the worst fires in the history of Los Angeles County swept across more than 150,000 acres of the Angeles National Forest. On behalf of all hikers and outdoors enthusiasts who use and cherish its trails, creeks, and campgrounds, my deepest thanks go to the firefighters and other heroes who worked so hard and fearlessly to save it. As the third edition of this hiking guide goes to press, I'd also like to single out the volunteers and others who put so much effort into restoring native plant life and rebuilding entire trails that were destroyed by the Station Fire. Most of them are accessible to everyone once again and as lovely as ever.

—*Laura Randall*

Foreword

WELCOME TO MENASHA RIDGE PRESS'S *60 Hikes Within 60 Miles*, a series designed to provide hikers with the information they need to find and hike the very best trails surrounding metropolitan areas.

Our strategy was simple: First, find a hiker who knows the area and loves to hike. Second, ask that person to spend a year researching the most popular and very best trails around. And third, have that person describe each trail in terms of difficulty, scenery, condition, elevation change, and other categories of information that are important to hikers. "Pretend you've just completed a hike and met up with other hikers at the trailhead," we told each author. "Imagine their questions; be clear in your answers."

An experienced hiker and writer, author Laura Randall has selected 60 of the best hikes in and around the Los Angeles metropolitan area. From casual strolls through manicured gardens to history-rich explorations of old railway routes and early 20th-century movie sets, from birding excursions in coastal wetlands to backcountry treks through the Santa Monica Mountains, Randall provides hikers (and walkers and trail runners) with a great variety of routes—all within roughly 60 miles of Los Angeles.

You'll get more out of this book if you take a moment to read the Introduction, which explains how to read the trail listings. The "Maps" section will help you understand how useful topos are on a hike and will also tell you where to get them. And though this is a where-to, not a how-to, guide, readers who have not hiked extensively will find the Introduction of particular value.

As much for the opportunity to free the spirit as to free the body, let these hikes elevate you above the urban hurry.

All the best,
The Editors at Menasha Ridge Press

Preface

WHEN I SIGNED ON TO WRITE THIS BOOK, I thought I knew most everything about hiking in Los Angeles. I lived near the Hollywood Hills and hiked the canyons regularly both for exercise and as a quick escape from the chaos of living and working in a city teeming with millions of people. Whenever we had out-of-town guests, my husband and I tried to squeeze a hike into the sightseeing agenda, often one that included postcard-worthy coastal views, to show them there was more to L.A. than movie stars and freeway grid-lock. As I started to do research for this book, however, I realized I had only tapped the surface of the Los Angeles hiking experience. I discovered fabulous trails hidden behind freeway exits, amid tract developments, and next to airports. I stumbled onto treks through historic city neighborhoods I never knew existed. I scrambled over boulders and across fields that once served as a backdrop for John Wayne, Henry Fonda, and other movie stars. One of my favorite discoveries—the Devil's Punchbowl Natural Area near the San Andreas Fault—opened up a whole new side of Los Angeles County for me and offered an up close lesson on the region's vulnerability to earthquakes. Another favorite— the Peter Strauss Trail in the Santa Monica Mountains—impressed me with its seclusion and total surrender to nature.

I still love the busy canyon trails—Runyon Canyon remains one of my all-time favorites for its city-ocean-mountain views and people-watching opportunities. But now I know that when friends and family visit, they can choose from a long list of trails guaranteed to suit every mood and season.

For this revised edition, I added seven new hikes that complement the ones already in the book. I replaced a few of the easier hikes with more challenging treks, such as the Devil's Chair Trail in the Antelope Valley, and I updated trails that were extended, rerouted, or altered in some other way by fire or rain over the last five years. After reading Cheryl Strayed's Pacific Crest Trail memoir *Wild*, I was inspired to research the PCT's route in Southern California and found a wonderful 5-mile hike on the trail within 60 miles of Los Angeles. You'll find that hike in this edition (page 225)—I hope you enjoy it as much as I did.

The Trails

MOST OF L.A.'S PUBLIC HIKING TRAILS can be found north and west of downtown.

SANTA MONICA MOUNTAINS

The Santa Monica Mountains are probably the most popular and recognizable. Comprising more than 153,000 acres, the Santa Monica Recreation Area sprawls across the Hollywood Hills, Malibu, the San Fernando Valley, and the southwestern tip of Ventura County. It is the world's largest urban national park. The trails here have it all—waterfalls, volcanic-rock formations, dense woodland, and 100-mile coastal views. Anchoring the whole system is the Backbone Trail, an unfinished 60-plus-mile path that runs between Will Rogers State Historic Park in Pacific Palisades and Point Mugu State Park in Ventura County.

ANGELES NATIONAL FOREST

Established as a national forest in 1892, the 656,000-acre forest includes much of the San Gabriel Mountains and parts of the Santa Clarita and Antelope Valleys. It boasts more than 500 miles of hiking trails, including a stretch of the Pacific Crest Trail, 110 camping and picnic sites, and five lakes, and its elevations range from 1,200 to 10,064 feet. Dense chaparral and fir and pine trees blanket much of the forest; it is also home to volcanic rock formations, coastal sage scrub, and a cornucopia of spring wildflowers. In late 2014 President Barack Obama designated more than half of the forest as a national monument in an effort to preserve and protect the area, which draws an estimated 4 million annual visitors.

VERDUGO MOUNTAINS

A geologically detached piece of the San Gabriel Mountains, the Verdugos encompass 9,000 acres of chaparral, coastal sage scrub, southern willow scrub, coast live oak, and waterfalls. The mountains can be accessed via Burbank and Glendale in the San Fernando Valley and via Tujunga and La Tuna Canyon from La Crescenta Valley. A network of relatively new fire roads makes for excellent hiking and biking conditions.

OTHERS

Then there are the random parks that dot the city and bring their own unique scenery and style to the Southern California hiking experience—parks like Deukmejian Wilderness Park in Glendale, Wildwood Park in Thousand Oaks, and the Kenneth Hahn Recreation Area in Baldwin Hills. Griffith Park, a kingdom unto itself, has some excellent off-the-beaten-path trails and shouldn't be ignored. Besides 53 miles of trails, the park boasts an observatory, a merry-go-round, a zoo, an outdoor amphitheater, and countless picnic areas. Another great yet inexplicably unsung city park is Ernest E. Debs Regional Park, also known as Debs Park, in the eastern L.A. neighborhood of Highland Park. The trails are pristine, quiet, and home to grasslands, wildflowers, more than 130 species of birds, and a bucolic hilltop pond. Angelenos drive right past this park every day via the busy Pasadena freeway, yet few outside the neighborhood even know it exists.

TIPS

A few words of advice that may help your Southern California hiking experience.

> ➢ ALWAYS HAVE A BACKUP TRAIL IN MIND. Trails can be closed at a moment's notice due to damage or a special event, and reaching a ranger familiar with current conditions is sometimes challenging. Whenever I hiked the Santa Monica Mountains, I brought along a National Park Service (NPS) map of the entire

area, just in case the trail I wanted was closed. The maps are available at the park service headquarters in Thousand Oaks. Call 818-370-2301 to request one by mail, or visit **nps.gov/samo.**

➤ ROAM IF YOU WANT TO. Discovering new trails is one of the best parts of hiking in Southern California. It's difficult to get impossibly lost because many of the trails are well marked or cocooned by residential developments and freeways. Many of the parks listed in this book offer a variety of trails that cater to all ages and fitness levels. It's often easy to extend or shorten the trail described to fit your own needs.

➤ DON'T JUDGE A TRAILHEAD BY ITS COVER. Some of the best L.A. trails begin in or near crowded residential developments or unsightly debris basins. It never ceased to amaze me how quickly I would find myself surrounded by wilderness and natural beauty after leaving my car.

➤ CITING BUDGET CUTS AND OTHER CONSTRAINTS, more parks are charging visitors a hefty day-use fee to use their parking lots. If you park on nearby streets, make sure to check signs for restrictions. The Adventure Pass is a controversial fee program used by the Angeles, Cleveland, and Los Padres National Forests. This requires all hikers, bikers, and other visitors to purchase a vehicle pass— either $5 a day or $30 a year—to use the forest. Passes can be purchased at forest ranger offices and local sporting goods stores such as REI, Big 5, and Sport Chalet. For a detailed list of vendors that sell the pass, go to **www.fs.fed.us/r5 /sanbernardino/ap.vendors.php.**

60 Hikes by Category

Hike Categories

- Mileage
- Difficulty*
- Strenuous Climbs
- Water Features
- Waterfall
- Coastal Views

* Difficulty: **E** = easy, **M** = moderate, **D** = difficult, **S** = strenuous

REGION Hike Number/Hike Name	Page	Mileage	Difficulty	Strenuous Climbs	Water Features	Waterfall	Coastal Views
DOWNTOWN LOS ANGELES (including Griffith Park, Hollywood, Baldwin Hills)							
1 Baldwin Hills: Kenneth Hahn State Recreation Area Trails	12	2	E–M				
2 Burbank Peak to Mount Lee	16	3.2	M	✓			
3 Elysian Park: Angels Point to Bishops Canyon	20	3	M				
4 Elysian Park: Wildflower Trail	23	2.5	E				
5 Ernest E. Debs Regional Park: City View and Walnut Forest Trails	27	2.6	M		✓		
6 Griffith Park: Amir's Garden	31	1	M				
7 Griffith Park: Charlie Turner Trail	34	3	M				
8 Griffith Park: Hollyridge Trail	38	2.5	E				
9 Mount Washington: Jack Smith Trail	41	4.25	M–S				✓
10 Runyon Canyon	44	3.5	S	✓			
WEST (including San Fernando Valley, Verdugo Mountains, Santa Monica Mountains)							
11 Arroyo Sequit Trail	50	2	E				
12 Caballero Canyon Trail	53	3.1	M				
13 Calabasas Peak Motorway	56	3.8	D	✓			
14 Franklin Canyon: Ranch and Hastain Trails	59	4.9	M		✓		✓
15 Fryman Canyon Loop	63	2.6	M				
16 Grotto Trail	66	3	M		✓		
17 Malibu Creek State Park: M*A*S*H Trail	69	5	M		✓		

REGION Hike Number/Hike Name	Page	Mileage	Difficulty	Strenuous Climbs	Water Features	Waterfall	Coastal Views
WEST (including San Fernando Valley, Verdugo Mountains, Santa Monica Mountains) *(continued)*							
18 Marvin Braude Mulholland Gateway Park: Hub Junction Trail	72	5.5	M				
19 Paramount Ranch: Hacienda Trail to Backdrop Trail	75	3.6	E–M				
20 Peter Strauss Trail	79	1.5	E				
21 San Vicente Mountain: Old Nike Missile Site	83	3	E				
EAST (including Glendale, Pasadena, San Gabriel Mountains)							
22 Arroyo Seco: Gabrielino National Recreation Trail	88	5	E–M		✓		
23 Beaudry Loop	92	5.8	M–S	✓			
24 Brand Fire Road Trail	96	4.5	M–D	✓			
25 Cherry Canyon Park	99	3.5	M				
26 Deukmejian Wilderness Park Trails	103	2.6–6.5	M	✓			
27 Eaton Canyon Falls and Henninger Flats	107	3.6–7.4	M–S			✓	
28 Josephine Peak	111	8.2	S	✓			
29 La Cañada Fire Road to Gabrielino National Recreation Trail	114	3.4	M				
30 La Tuna Canyon	117	4.4	M	✓			
31 Legg Lake Loop Trail	120	2.2	E		✓		
32 Lower Arroyo Seco Trail	123	4	E		✓		
33 Millard Canyon: Sunset Ridge Trail	127	5	S	✓	✓		
34 Monrovia Canyon Park: Bill Cull and Falls Trails	131	2.6	M		✓	✓	
35 Mount Wilson Trail to Orchard Camp	135	7	S	✓			
36 Sam Merrill Trail to Echo Mountain	139	5.9	S	✓			
37 Stough Canyon Nature Center Trail	143	2.4	M	✓			
38 Switzer Falls via Bear Canyon Trail	146	3.9	M–S		✓	✓	
39 West Fork Trail	149	14	E		✓		
COAST (including Malibu, Pacific Palisades, Palos Verdes)							
40 Charmlee Wilderness Park Loop Trail	156	2.3	E				✓
41 Corral Canyon Loop	159	2.25	M				✓
42 Palos Verdes: Ocean Trails Reserve	162	4.6	E				✓

REGION Hike Number/Hike Name	Page	Mileage	Difficulty	Strenuous Climbs	Water Features	Waterfall	Coastal Views
43 Paseo Miramar Trail to Parker Mesa Overlook	166	5.5	M	✓			✓
44 Portuguese Bend Reserve: Burma Road Trail	170	4.6	S	✓			✓
45 Solstice Canyon and Rising Sun Trails	173	3	E–M		✓	✓	✓
46 Temescal Ridge Trail	176	4.6	S	✓			✓
47 Will Rogers State Historic Park: Inspiration Point Loop Trail	179	2.2	E				✓
ORANGE COUNTY AND LA PUENTE HILLS							
48 Bolsa Chica Ecological Reserve, Huntington Beach	186	3	E		✓		✓
49 Crystal Cove State Park: El Moro Canyon Trail	190	3.7	M				✓
50 Hacienda Hills Trail	194	3.4	M				
51 Hellman Park: Peppergrass Trail to Rattlesnake Ridge Trail	197	5.5	M	✓			
52 Oak Canyon Nature Center: Bluebird Lane and Wren Way	201	2	E				
53 Peters Canyon Regional Park: Lake View Trail	204	2.5	E–M		✓		
SIMI AND ANTELOPE VALLEYS							
54 Corriganville Park: Interpretive and Loop Trails	210	1.7	E				
55 Devil's Punchbowl Natural Area: Devil's Chair Trail	214	7.4	M–S				
56 Ed Davis Park in Towsley Canyon: Canyon View Loop Trail	218	2.2	S		✓		
57 Hummingbird Trail	221	2	S				
58 Pacific Crest Trail at Vasquez Rocks	225	5.5	M				
59 Placerita Canyon: Walker Ranch	229	4.4	M				
60 Wildwood Park: Lizard Rock	233	2.7	M	✓			

More Hike Categories

• Solitude	• Kid-Friendly
• Birding	• Wheelchair Accessible

• Running	• Wildflowers
• Historical Interest	

REGION Hike Number/Hike Name	Page	Solitude	Birding	Kid-Friendly	Wheelchair Accessible	Running	Historical Interest	Wildflowers
DOWNTOWN LOS ANGELES (including Griffith Park, Hollywood, Baldwin Hills)								
1 Baldwin Hills: Kenneth Hahn State Recreation Area Trails	12			✓	✓			
2 Burbank Peak to Mount Lee	16							
3 Elysian Park: Angels Point to Bishops Canyon	20							✓
4 Elysian Park: Wildflower Trail	23							✓
5 Ernest E. Debs Regional Park: City View and Walnut Forest Trails	27		✓	✓				
6 Griffith Park: Amir's Garden	31	✓		✓				
7 Griffith Park: Charlie Turner Trail	34							
8 Griffith Park: Hollyridge Trail	38							
9 Mount Washington: Jack Smith Trail	41	✓			✓		✓	
10 Runyon Canyon	44				✓		✓	
WEST (including San Fernando Valley, Verdugo Mountains, Santa Monica Mountains)								
11 Arroyo Sequit Trail	50	✓		✓				✓
12 Caballero Canyon Trail	53							
13 Calabasas Peak Motorway	56							
14 Franklin Canyon: Ranch and Hastain Trails	59				✓		✓	
15 Fryman Canyon Loop	63							
16 Grotto Trail	66						✓	
17 Malibu Creek State Park: M*A*S*H Trail	69						✓	
18 Marvin Braude Mulholland Gateway Park: Hub Junction Trail	72							
19 Paramount Ranch: Hacienda Trail to Backdrop Trail	75				✓		✓	
20 Peter Strauss Trail	79	✓		✓	✓			
21 San Vicente Mountain: Old Nike Missile Site	83	✓			✓		✓	

REGION Hike Number/Hike Name	Page	Solitude	Birding	Kid-Friendly	Wheelchair Accessible	Running	Historical Interest	Wildflowers
EAST (including Glendale, Pasadena, San Gabriel Mountains)								
22 Arroyo Seco: Gabrielino National Recreation Trail	88		✓		✓	✓		
23 Beaudry Loop	92	✓						
24 Brand Fire Road Trail	96				✓	✓		
25 Cherry Canyon Park	99				✓			
26 Deukmejian Wilderness Park Trails	103				✓			
27 Eaton Canyon Falls and Henninger Flats	107			✓				
28 Josephine Peak	111	✓						
29 La Cañada Fire Road to Gabrielino National Recreation Trail	114				✓			
30 La Tuna Canyon	117							
31 Legg Lake Loop Trail	120			✓	✓	✓		
32 Lower Arroyo Seco Trail	123				✓	✓		
33 Millard Canyon: Sunset Ridge Trail	127	✓			✓			
34 Monrovia Canyon Park: Bill Cull and Falls Trails	131							
35 Mount Wilson Trail to Orchard Camp	135						✓	
36 Sam Merrill Trail to Echo Mountain	139				✓		✓	
37 Stough Canyon Nature Center Trail	143							
38 Switzer Falls via Bear Canyon Trail	146				✓			
39 West Fork Trail	149			✓	✓	✓		
COAST (including Malibu, Pacific Palisades, Palos Verdes)								
40 Charmlee Wilderness Park Loop Trail	156			✓				✓
41 Corral Canyon Loop	159							
42 Palos Verdes: Ocean Trails Reserve	162			✓	✓	✓		✓
43 Paseo Miramar Trail to Parker Mesa Overlook	166							
44 Portuguese Bend Reserve: Burma Road Trail	170				✓			✓
45 Solstice Canyon and Rising Sun Trails	173			✓	✓			
46 Temescal Ridge Trail	176							
47 Will Rogers State Historic Park: Inspiration Point Loop Trail	179				✓		✓	

REGION Hike Number/Hike Name	Page	Solitude	Birding	Kid-Friendly	Wheelchair Accessible	Running	Historical Interest	Wildflowers
ORANGE COUNTY AND LA PUENTE HILLS								
48 Bolsa Chica Ecological Reserve, Huntington Beach	186		✓	✓	✓	✓		
49 Crystal Cove State Park: El Moro Canyon Trail	190							
50 Hacienda Hills Trail	194							
51 Hellman Park: Peppergrass Trail to Rattlesnake Ridge Trail	197				✓	✓		
52 Oak Canyon Nature Center: Bluebird Lane and Wren Way	201			✓	✓			
53 Peters Canyon Regional Park: Lake View Trail	204				✓	✓		
SIMI AND ANTELOPE VALLEYS								
54 Corriganville Park: Interpretive and Loop Trails	210				✓			
55 Devil's Punchbowl Natural Area: Devil's Chair Trail	214			✓	✓		✓	
56 Ed Davis Park in Towsley Canyon: Canyon View Loop Trail	218							
57 Hummingbird Trail	221	✓						✓
58 Pacific Crest Trail at Vasquez Rocks	225		✓	✓				
59 Placerita Canyon: Walker Ranch	229			✓	✓			
60 Wildwood Park: Lizard Rock	233	✓		✓				

Introduction

WELCOME TO *60 HIKES WITHIN 60 MILES: LOS ANGELES.* If you're new to hiking or even if you're a seasoned trekker, take a few minutes to read the following introduction. We'll explain how this book is organized and how to use it.

How to Use This Guidebook

THE OVERVIEW MAP, OVERVIEW MAP KEY, AND MAP LEGEND

Use the overview map on the inside front cover to assess the general location of each hike's primary trailhead. Each hike's number appears on the overview map, on the map key facing the overview map, and in the table of contents. As you flip through the book, a hike's full profile is easy to locate by watching for the hike number at the top of each page. The book is organized by region, as indicated in the table of contents. A map legend that details the symbols found on trail maps appears on the inside back cover.

REGIONAL MAPS

The book is divided into regions, and prefacing each regional section is an overview map of that region. The regional map provides more detail than the overview map does, bringing you closer to the hike.

Hike Profiles

Each hike contains seven or eight key items: a brief description of the trail, a key at-a-glance information box, GPS coordinates, directions to the trail, a trail map, an elevation profile (if the change in elevation is 100 feet or more), a trail description, and notes on things to see and do nearby. Combined, the maps and information provide a clear method to assess each trail from the comfort of your favorite reading chair.

IN BRIEF

Think of this section as a taste of the trail, a snapshot focused on the historical landmarks, beautiful vistas, and other sights you may encounter on the trail.

KEY AT-A-GLANCE INFORMATION

The information in the key at-a-glance boxes gives you a quick idea of the specifics of each hike.

DISTANCE & CONFIGURATION The length of the trail from start to finish (total distance traveled) and a description of what the trail might look like from overhead. Trails can be loops, out-and-backs (trails on which one enters and leaves along the same path), figure eights, or a combination of shapes. There may be options to shorten or extend the hikes, but the mileage corresponds to the described hike. Consult the hike description to help decide how to customize the hike for your ability or time constraints.

DIFFICULTY The degree of effort an average hiker should expect on a given hike. For simplicity, the trails are rated as easy, moderate, or difficult.

SCENERY A short summary of the attractions offered by the hike and what to expect in terms of plant life, wildlife, natural wonders, and historical features.

EXPOSURE A quick check of how much sun you can expect on your shoulders during the hike.

TRAFFIC Indicates how busy the trail might be on an average day. Trail traffic, of course, varies from day to day and season to season.

TRAIL SURFACE Indicates whether the trail is paved, rocky, smooth dirt, or a mixture of elements.

HIKING TIME The length of time it takes to hike the trail. A slow but steady hiker will average 2–3 miles an hour depending on the terrain.

ACCESS A notation of fees or permits needed to access the trail (if any), whether the trail has specific hours, and whether pets and other forms of trail use are permitted.

WHEELCHAIR ACCESSIBLE Notes whether the trail is wheelchair compatible.

MAPS A list of maps for the trail.

FACILITIES What to expect in terms of restrooms, water, and other amenities available at the trailhead or nearby.

CONTACT Phone numbers and websites, where applicable, for up-to-date information on trail conditions.

COMMENTS These comments cover little extra details that don't fit into any of the above categories. Here you'll find information on trail-hiking options and facts, or tips on how to get the most out of your hike.

DESCRIPTIONS

The trail description is the heart of each hike. Here, the author provides a summary of the trail's essence and highlights any special traits the hike offers. The route is clearly outlined, including landmarks, side trips, and possible alternate routes along the way. Ultimately, the hike description will help you choose which hikes are best for you.

NEARBY ACTIVITIES

Look here for information on nearby activities or points of interest.

TRAIL MAPS

A detailed map of each hike's route appears with its profile. On each of these maps, symbols indicate the trailhead, the complete route, significant features, facilities, and topographic landmarks such as creeks, overlooks, and peaks.

ELEVATION PROFILES

For trails with significant changes in elevation, the hike description will contain a detailed elevation profile that corresponds directly to the trail map. This graphical element provides a quick look at the trail from the side, enabling you to visualize how the trail rises and falls. On the diagram's vertical axis, or height scale, the number of feet indicated between each tick mark lets you visualize the climb. To avoid making flat hikes look steep and steep hikes appear flat, varying height scales provide an accurate image of each hike's climbing challenge. Elevation profiles for loop hikes show total distance; those for out-and-back hikes show only one-way distance.

GPS INFORMATION

In addition to highly specific trail outlines, this book also includes the latitude (north) and longitude (west) coordinates for each trailhead. The latitude–longitude grid system is likely quite familiar to you, but here's a refresher, pertinent to visualizing the coordinates.

Imaginary lines of latitude—called parallels and approximately 69 miles apart from each other—run horizontally around the globe. Each parallel is indicated by degrees from the equator (established to be 0°): up to 90°N at the North Pole and down to 90°S at the South Pole.

Imaginary lines of longitude—called meridians—run perpendicular to lines of latitude and are likewise indicated by degrees. Starting from 0° at the Prime Meridian in Greenwich, England, they continue to the east and west until they meet 180° later at the International Date Line in the Pacific Ocean. At the equator, longitude lines also are approximately 69 miles apart, but that distance narrows as the meridians converge toward the North and South Poles.

In this book, latitude and longitude are expressed in degree–decimal minute format. For example, the coordinates for Hike 1, Baldwin Hills (page 12), are as follows: N34° 0.761' W118° 22.238'. For more on GPS technology, visit **usgs.gov.**

TOPO MAPS

The maps in this book have been produced with great care. When used with the route directions in each profile, the maps are sufficient to direct you to the trail and guide you on it. However, you will find superior detail and valuable information in the United States Geological Survey's (USGS) 7.5-minute series topographic maps.

Topo maps are available online in many locations. At **mytopo.com,** for example, you can view and print topos of the entire Unites States free of charge. Online services, such as **trails.com,** charge annual fees for additional features such as shaded relief, which makes the topography stand out more. If you expect to print out many topo maps each year, it might be worth paying for shaded-relief topo maps. The downside to USGS topos is that most of them are outdated, having been created 20–30 years ago. But they still provide excellent topographic detail. Of course, **Google Earth** (**earth.google.com**) does away with topo maps and their inaccuracies—replacing them with satellite imagery and its inaccuracies. Regardless, what one lacks, the other augments. Google Earth is an excellent tool whether you have difficulty with topos or not.

If you're new to hiking, you might be wondering, "What's a topographic map?" A topo indicates not only linear distance but elevation as well, using contour lines. Contour lines spread across the map like dozens of intricate spiderwebs. Each line represents a particular elevation; at the base of each topo, a contour's interval designation is given. If the contour interval is 20 feet, then the distance between each contour line is 20 feet. Follow five contour lines up on the same map, and the elevation has increased by 100 feet.

Let's assume that the 7.5-minute series topo reads "Contour Interval 40 feet," that the short trail we'll be hiking is 2 inches in length on the map, and that it crosses five contour lines from beginning to end. What do we know? Well, because the linear scale of this series is 2,000 feet to the inch (roughly 2.75 inches representing 1 mile), we know that our trail is approximately 0.8 mile long (2 inches are 4,000 feet). But we also know that we'll be climbing or descending 200 vertical feet (five contour lines are 40 feet each) over that distance. And the elevation designations written on occasional contour lines will tell us if we're heading up or down.

In addition to the places listed in Appendixes A and B, you'll find topos at major universities and some public libraries, where you might try photocopying what you need. But if you want your own and can't find them locally, visit **nationalmap.gov** or **store.usgs.gov.**

Weather

AVERAGE DAILY TEMPERATURES BY MONTH					
	JAN	**FEB**	**MAR**	**APR**	**MAY**	**JUN**
HIGH	67°F	68°F	68°F	72°F	72°F	76°F
LOW	47°F	48°F	50°F	52°F	56°F	59°F
MEAN	57°F	58°F	59°F	59°F	64°F	67°F
	JUL	**AUG**	**SEP**	**OCT**	**NOV**	**DEC**
HIGH	80°F	81°F	81°F	77°F	71°F	67°F
LOW	62°F	63°F	62°F	58°F	52°F	47°F
MEAN	71°F	72°F	71°F	67°F	61°F	57°F

The climate in Los Angeles is mild and pleasant most of the year—though, contrary to popular belief, the region does have seasons. The rainy season is between December and April. Summer brings dry, hot weather, with temperatures reaching the triple digits in the San Fernando Valley and inland areas. Late spring usually means "June gloom," a few weeks during which the skies are overcast from early morning to midafternoon, especially in the coastal areas.

Choose your hiking locations wisely. The trails in the hot, shade-deprived Simi Valley are best visited in cooler months, whereas the coastal trails of Malibu, Laguna Beach, and Rancho Palos Verdes will yield the best weather and views in the late summer and early fall.

Allocating Time

On flat or lightly undulating terrain, the author averaged 2 miles per hour when hiking. That speed drops in direct proportion to the steepness of a path, and it does not reflect the many pauses and forays off trail in pursuit of yet another bird sighting, wildflower, or photograph. Give yourself plenty of time. Few people enjoy rushing through a hike, and fewer still take pleasure in bumping into trees after dark. Remember, too, that your pace may slow over the back half of a long trek.

Water

How much is enough? One bottle? Two? Three? Well, one simple physiological fact should convince you to err on the side of excess when it comes to deciding how much water to pack: A hiker working hard in 90°F heat needs approximately 10 quarts of fluid every day. That's 2.5 gallons—12 large water bottles or 16 small ones. In other words, pack along one or two bottles even for short hikes.

Some hikers and backpackers hit the trail prepared to purify water found along the route. This method, while less dangerous than drinking it untreated, comes with risks. Many hikers pack along the slightly distasteful tetraglycine hydroperiodide tablets (sold under the names Potable Aqua, Coughlan's, and others). Some invest in portable, lightweight purifiers that filter out the crud.

Probably the most common waterborne "bug" that hikers face is *Giardia,* which may not hit until one to four weeks after ingestion. It will have you living in the bathroom, passing noxious rotten-egg gas, vomiting, and shivering with chills. Other parasites to worry about include *E. coli* and *Cryptosporidium,* both of which are harder to kill than *Giardia.*

For most people, the pleasures of hiking make carrying water a relatively minor price to pay to remain healthy. If you're tempted to drink "found" water, do so only if you thoroughly understand the risks involved. Better yet, hydrate prior to your hike, carry (and drink) 6 ounces of water for every mile you plan to hike, and hydrate after the hike.

Clothing

There is a wide variety of clothing from which to choose. Basically, use common sense and be prepared for anything. If all you have are cotton clothes when a sudden rainstorm comes along, you'll be miserable, especially in cooler weather. It's a good idea to carry along a light wool sweater or some type of synthetic apparel (polypropylene, Capilene, Thermax, and so on) as well as a hat.

Be aware of the weather forecast and its tendency to be wrong. Always carry raingear. Thunderstorms can come on suddenly in the summer. Keep in mind that rainy days are as much a part of nature as those idyllic ones you desire. Besides, rainy days really cut down on the crowds. With appropriate raingear, a normally crowded trail can be a wonderful place of solitude. Do, however, remain aware of the dangers of lightning strikes.

Footwear is another concern. Though tennis shoes may be appropriate for paved areas, some trails are rocky and rough; tennis shoes may not offer enough support. Waterproofed or not, boots should be your footwear of choice. Sport sandals are more popular than ever, but these leave much of your foot exposed, leaving you vulnerable to hazardous plants and thorns or the occasional piece of glass.

The 10 Essentials

One of the first rules of hiking is to be prepared for anything. The simplest way to be prepared is to carry the "10 Essentials." In addition to carrying the items listed below, you need to know how to use them, especially navigational items. Always consider worst-case scenarios such as getting lost, hiking back in the dark, broken gear (for example, a broken hip strap on your pack or a water filter getting plugged), a twisted ankle, or a brutal thunderstorm. The items listed below don't cost a lot of money, don't take up much room in a pack, and don't weigh much, but they might just save your life.

Water: durable bottles and water treatment, such as iodine or a filter

Map: preferably a topo map and a trail map with a route description

Compass: a high-quality compass

First-Aid Kit: a good-quality kit including first-aid instructions

Knife: preferably a multitool device with pliers

Light: flashlight or headlamp with extra bulbs and batteries

Fire: windproof matches or lighter and fire starter

Extra Food: You should always have food in your pack when you've finished hiking.

Extra Clothes: rain protection, warm layers, gloves, warm hat

Sun Protection: sunglasses, lip balm, sunblock, sun hat

First-Aid Kit

A typical kit may contain more items than you might think necessary. These are just the basics. Prepackaged kits in waterproof bags (Atwater Carey and Adventure Medical Kits make a variety of kits) are available. Even though there are quite a few items listed here, they pack down into a small space:

➢ Ace bandages or Spenco joint wraps

➢ Antibiotic ointment (Neosporin or the generic equivalent)

- ➢ Aspirin or acetaminophen

- ➢ Band-Aids

- ➢ Benadryl or the generic equivalent diphenhydramine (an antihistamine, in case of allergic reactions)

- ➢ Butterfly-closure bandages

- ➢ Epinephrine in a prefilled syringe (for people known to have severe allergic reactions to such things as bee stings)

- ➢ Gauze (one roll and a half dozen 4-by-4-inch compress pads)

- ➢ Hydrogen peroxide or iodine

- ➢ Insect repellent

- ➢ Matches or pocket lighter

- ➢ Moleskin/Spenco Second Skin

- ➢ Snakebite kit

- ➢ Sunscreen

- ➢ Water-purification tablets or water filter (on longer hikes)

- ➢ Whistle (more effective in signaling rescuers than your voice)

Animal and Plant Hazards

SNAKES

Southern California has a variety of snakes—including gopher snakes, king snakes, and racers—most of which are benign. Rattlesnakes are the exception, and they dwell in every area of the state: mountains, foothills, valleys, and deserts. Species found in the region include the Western diamondback, sidewinder, speckled rattlesnake, red diamond rattlesnake, Southern Pacific rattlesnake, Great Basin rattlesnake, and Mojave rattlesnake, according to the state Department of Fish and Game.

When hiking, stick to well-used trails and wear over-the-ankle boots and loose-fitting long pants. Rattlesnakes like to bask in the sun and won't bite unless threatened. Do not step or put your hands where you cannot see, and avoid wandering in the dark. Step on logs and rocks, never over them, and be especially careful when climbing rocks or gathering firewood. Always avoid walking through dense brush or willow thickets. Hibernation season is November–February.

TICKS

Ticks are often found on brush and tall grass, waiting to hitch a ride on a warm-blooded passerby. They are most active in the Los Angeles area between April and October. Among the local varieties of ticks, the Western black-legged tick is the primary carrier of Lyme disease. Ticks may settle in shoes, socks, or hats, and they may take several hours to actually latch on. The best strategy is to visually check every half hour or so while hiking, do a thorough check before you get in the car, and then, when you take a post-hike shower, do an even more thorough check of your entire body. Also, throw clothes into the dryer for 10 minutes when you get home, and be sure to check your pet for any hitchhikers. Ticks that haven't attached are easily removed but not easily killed. If you pick off a tick in the woods, just toss it aside. If you find one on your body at home, dispatch it and then send it down the toilet. For ticks that have embedded, removal with tweezers is best.

POISON OAK

Poison oak is rampant in the shady canyons and riparian woodlands of Southern California. It grows in moist areas, favoring shade trees and water sources. Recognizing and avoiding the plant is the most effective way to prevent the painful, itchy rashes associated with it. Identify the plant by its three-leaf structure, with two leaves on opposite sides of the stem, and one extending from the center. Refrain from scratching because bacteria under fingernails can cause infection, and you will spread the rash to other parts of your body. Wash and dry the rash thoroughly, applying a calamine lotion or other product to help dry the rash. If itching or blistering is severe, seek medical attention. Remember that oil-contaminated garments, pets, or hiking equipment can easily cause an irritating rash on you or someone else, so wash not only any exposed parts of your body but also clothes, gear, and pets.

POODLE-DOG BUSH

This 3- to 8-foot-tall bush has numerous long, slender leaves and clusters of purple, funnel-shaped flowers. It thrives in areas recently disturbed by fire. Do *not* touch this plant. It can cause severe contact dermatitis.

MOSQUITOES

Though it's not a common occurrence, individuals can become infected with the West Nile virus from the bite of an infected mosquito. Culex mosquitoes, the primary varieties that can transmit West Nile virus to humans, thrive in urban rather than natural areas. They lay their eggs in stagnant water and can breed in any standing water that remains for more than five days. Most people infected with West Nile virus have no symptoms of illness, but some may become ill, usually 3–15 days after being bitten.

In the Los Angeles area, late February–October is likely to be the highest risk period for mosquitoes. At this time of year, you may want to wear protective clothing such as long sleeves, long pants, and socks. Loose-fitting, light-colored clothing is best. Spray clothing with insect repellent. Remember to follow the instructions on the repellent and take extra care with children.

Hiking with Children

No one is too young for a hike in the woods or through a city park. Be careful, though. Flat, short trails are probably best when traveling with an infant. Toddlers who have not quite mastered walking can still tag along, riding on an adult's back in a child carrier. Use common sense to judge a child's capacity to hike a particular trail, and always expect that the child will tire quickly and need to be carried.

When packing for the hike, remember the child's needs as well as your own. Make sure children are adequately clothed for the weather, have proper shoes, and are protected from the sun with sunscreen. Kids dehydrate quickly, so make sure you have plenty of fluid for everyone.

Hikes suitable for children are indicated in the table on pages xvi–xviii. Finally, when hiking with children, remember the trip is bound to be a compromise. A child's energy and enthusiasm alternate between bursts of speed and long stops to examine snails, sticks, dirt, and other attractions.

The Business Hiker

Whether you're in the Los Angeles area on business as a resident or visitor, these 60 hikes offer perfect, quick getaways from the busy demands of work and routine. Good hiking trails abound near LAX airport, Hollywood, and just off the exit ramps of major freeways. Instead of eating inside, pack a lunch and picnic in Griffith Park. Or take a small group of your business comrades on an easy ocean-view hike at Will Rogers State Historic Park or on one of the dozens of trails in the Santa Monica Mountains Recreation Area. A brief outdoor getaway is the perfect complement to a business trip to Los Angeles.

Trail Etiquette

Whether you're on a city, county, state, or national park trail, always remember that great care and resources (from nature as well as from your tax dollars) have gone into creating these trails. Treat the trail, wildlife, and fellow hikers with respect.

1. Hike on open trails only. Respect trail and road closures (ask if not sure), avoid possible trespassing on private land, and obtain all permits and authorization as required. Also, leave gates as you found them or as marked.

2. Leave only footprints. Be sensitive to the ground beneath you. This means staying on the existing trail and not creating any new ones. Be sure to pack out what you pack in. No one likes to see the trash that someone else has left behind.

3. Never spook animals. An unannounced approach, a sudden movement, or a loud noise startles most animals. A surprised snake or skunk can be dangerous for you, for others, and to themselves. Give animals extra room and time to adjust to your presence.

4. Plan ahead. Know your equipment, your ability, and the area where you are hiking—and prepare accordingly. Be self-sufficient at all times; carry necessary supplies for changes in weather or other conditions. A well-executed trip is a satisfaction to you and to others.

5. Be courteous to other hikers, bikers, or equestrians you meet on the trails.

DOWNTOWN LOS ANGELES

(INCLUDING GRIFFITH PARK, HOLLYWOOD, BALDWIN HILLS)

The Lake Hollywood Reservoir can be seen from Burbank Peak Trail (see page 16).

Downtown Los Angeles
(including Griffith Park, Hollywood, Baldwin Hills)

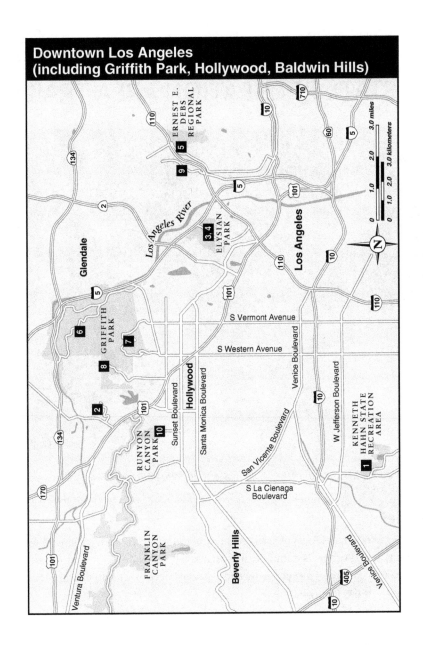

1 Baldwin Hills: KENNETH HAHN STATE RECREATION AREA TRAILS

The entrance to Kenneth Hahn State Recreation Area is surrounded by coast live oak trees and marsh.

In Brief

Following a well-maintained path to great city vistas, this accessible trail near Los Angeles International Airport is dotted with coastal sagebrush and prickly pear cactus. Picnic areas, several children's playgrounds, and a lake stocked with catfish make this a nice place for an all-day family outing.

Description

It's hard to believe that the area around this low-key trail was an active oil field in the first half of the 20th century. After an earthen dam on the oil field was breached in 1968 and flooded many homes in the surrounding neighborhood, the property was turned into the Kenneth Hahn State Recreation Area, named after a longtime member of the Los Angeles County Board of Supervisors. Little by little, conservationists and local volunteers turned it into a hillside haven despite the strip malls, traffic-choked roads, and active oil fields that surround it.

DISTANCE & CONFIGURATION: 2-mile out-and-back	Monday–Friday, free; Saturday–Sunday and holidays, $6 parking fee
DIFFICULTY: Easy-moderate	**MAPS:** USGS *Hollywood;* **file.lacounty**
SCENERY: Sagebrush, salamanders, California quail, jackrabbits, L.A. city views	**.gov/dpr/cms1_213796.pdf**
	WHEELCHAIR ACCESSIBLE: Partial access
EXPOSURE: Mostly sunny	
TRAFFIC: Light on weekdays; moderate on weekends	**FACILITIES:** Garbage cans at trailhead; restrooms and water fountains through- out park
TRAIL SURFACE: Packed dirt path	**CONTACT:** 323-298-3660; **parks.lacounty**
HIKING TIME: 1.25 hours	**.gov/wps/portal/dpr/Parks/Kenneth_Hahn**
ACCESS: Daily, sunrise–sunset;	**_State_Recreation_Area**

This hike combines several trails located within the park, including the Walk for Health Trail and the Bowl Loop that borders the east side. I usually begin on the western side, near the Cienega Boulevard entrance. There's a parking area to the left of the entrance kiosk; look for the trailhead marked Walk for Health.

The singletrack dirt path begins to climb uphill to a ridge. Despite its man-made origins, Baldwin Hills is one of the few places where coastal sage scrub and the gray fox thrive in an urban setting, according to conservationists. Western toads, prickly pear cactus, cottontail rabbits, quails, black-bellied salamanders, painted-lady butterflies, and more than 150 species of birds also make their home here.

A short, steep climb soon gives way to a ridge with panoramic vistas of southwest Los Angeles and the Santa Monica Bay (as well as those active oil pump–lined hills to the west). From here, the trail winds southeast, straddling views of the Hollywood Hills and downtown L.A. Follow the short trail to the left to a viewing pavilion called Autumn's Peak, one of the best places to soak up the views of downtown Los Angeles on a clear day. On a clear winter day, you can see the downtown Los Angeles skyline set against a stunning backdrop of snowcapped San Gabriel Mountains—a vision that is often captured (but rarely witnessed) on souvenir-shop postcards from L.A. Lest you forget that you're following the Walk for Health Trail, another sign gently lectures about the importance of eating nutritious foods.

From Autumn's Peak, follow the trail as it heads east and follows a gray wall that used to be a part of the doomed reservoir dam. This is the least attractive leg of the trail; it's relatively flat and flanked by electric transmission towers. Where the gray wall ends and a chain-link fence begins, the path is flanked by trees as it narrows and starts to meander downward; you'll see private homes on your left and the park facilities on your right.

At the 1-mile marker, the chain-link fence ends, and you'll come to a sign that marks the turnaround point for the Walk for Health Trail. From here, continue east down a flat, paved path to the Bowl Loop, which circles an expansive meadow called Janice's Green

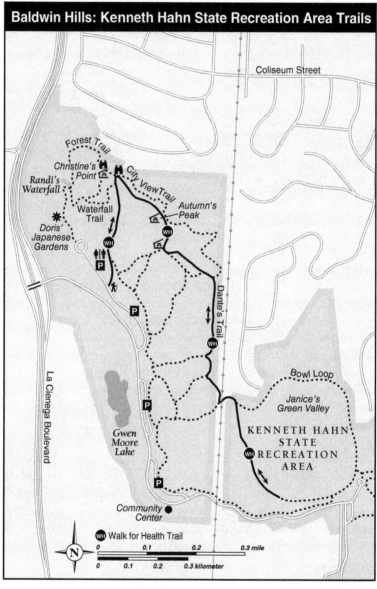

Baldwin Hills: Kenneth Hahn State Recreation Area Trails

Coliseum Street

Forest Trail

Christine's Point

Randi's Waterfall

City View Trail

Autumn's Peak

Waterfall Trail

Doris' Japanese Gardens

WH

Dante's Trail

WH

Bowl Loop

Janice's Green Valley

KENNETH HAHN STATE RECREATION AREA

WH

La Cienega Boulevard

Gwen Moore Lake

Community Center

WH Walk for Health Trail

N

0   0.1   0.2   0.3 mile

0   0.1   0.2   0.3 kilometer

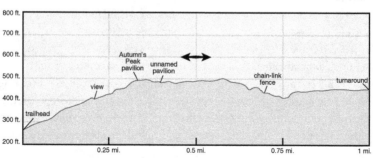

800 ft.				
700 ft.				
600 ft.	Autumn's Peak pavilion			
500 ft.	view	unnamed pavilion	chain-link fence	turnaround
400 ft.	trailhead			
300 ft.				
200 ft.				
	0.25 mi.	0.5 mi.	0.75 mi.	1 mi.

DISTANCE & CONFIGURATION: 3.2-mile out-and-back	**TRAIL SURFACE:** Packed and loose dirt
DIFFICULTY: Moderate	**HIKING TIME:** 1.5 hours
SCENERY: Chaparral, city-to-ocean views, Hollywood sign	**ACCESS:** Daily, sunrise–sunset; free
	WHEELCHAIR ACCESSIBLE: No
EXPOSURE: Sunny	**FACILITIES:** None
TRAFFIC: Light	**CONTACT:** 323-913-4688; **laparks.org /dos/parks/griffithpk**

from celebrities (Bugsy Siegel and Madonna have both called it home) to studio workers who like its easy access to Burbank and Universal City. Don't be surprised if you hear snippets of conversation on this trail about weekend box office results or Seth Rogen's weight loss. You're in the heart of L.A.'s entertainment industry, and soon you'll look down on the movie and TV studios that orchestrate it.

From Lake Hollywood Drive, begin walking east up the hill on Wonder View past a row of manicured homes. You will see the reservoir and the hillside homes that surround it, but even better views await. When you come to a fire-road gate at the end of the paved road, continue past that onto the wide gravel path for about 0.25 mile. Take the wide loose-dirt path on the right, and follow that until you come to a wooden post and stone marker. To the left of the post is a set of rustic wooden steps; take them up the mountain and continue on this singletrack trail for about 0.75 mile up to the ridge. You'll gain about 600 feet in elevation here and start to see some great views of the reservoir and Los Angeles basin. At the ridge, head left or west up a short hill to a clearing anchored by a lone tree. Known as the wisdom tree, it is the lone survivor of a wildfire that swept through the area in 2007; it even has its own Instagram account (**@the_wisdom_tree_la**). This is a good place to hydrate, have a snack, and take in the panoramic views of L.A. and the San Fernando Valley. You can see the studios of Walt Disney and Warner Bros. from here, as well as the neon-green lawns of Forest Lawn Cemetery and the San Gabriel Mountains.

From the clearing, retrace your steps down the hill and continue east along the ridge. The bulk of the uphill climbing is behind you, so relax and enjoy the views that stay with you along the trail. After about 0.4 mile, you will see a small, round U.S. Geological Survey marker that indicates you're at Cahuenga Peak. There's not much of a clearing here, so most hikers just continue on a slightly downward path toward Mount Lee. There is more brush and hints of shade along this part of the trail, and it requires some minor rock scrambling and attention to stay with it. Just before meeting up with the fire road that leads to Mount Lee, a short trail leads to overlooks with plaques honoring heiress Aileen Getty and *Playboy* mogul Hugh Hefner (two names you will probably never see in tandem again, but both helped make this trail happen).

From here, it's a short scramble to the fire road that rounds the bend to Mount Lee and the chain-link fence that separates it from the Hollywood sign. At this point, you can

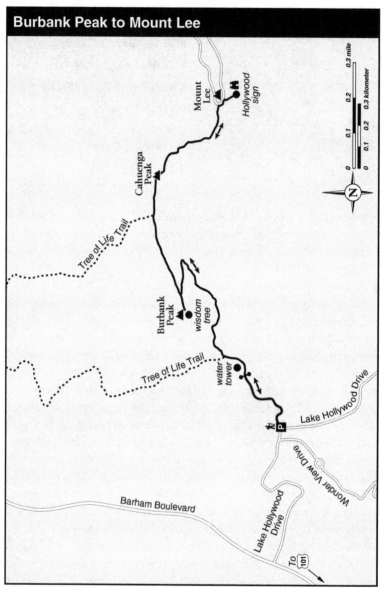

Burbank Peak to Mount Lee

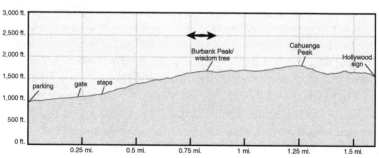

expect to see throngs of people who hiked to the sign from more popular trailheads. Take a selfie, or just admire the city views that unfold in front of the sign before retracing your steps back to Wonder View Drive.

Nearby Activities

The Lake Hollywood Reservoir is a popular 3.2-mile walking trail with scenic views of the Mulholland Dam and the Hollywood sign. Portions of it were closed for several years after heavy rainstorms caused mudslides that wiped out roads around the reservoir, but it's now fully reopened, much to the relief of local walkers and runners. It can be seen from Burbank Peak or accessed by pedestrians via Lake Hollywood Drive.

GPS TRAILHEAD COORDINATES
N34° 7.929' W118° 20.286'

From US 101, exit at Barham Boulevard and head east. In 0.3 mile, turn right onto Lake Hollywood Drive, and follow it up the hill as it winds through a residential neighborhood. Just after the intersection with Wonder View Drive, bear right as Lake Hollywood Drive descends toward the reservoir, and park on either side of the road.

---

3 Elysian Park: ANGELS POINT
TO BISHOPS CANYON

In Brief

A mix of paved road and rugged dirt path, this hike through L.A.'s oldest park leads to a bluff-top recreation area with sweeping views of Dodger Stadium and the San Gabriel Mountains.

Description

The 600-acre Elysian Park, which includes Dodger Stadium and the Los Angeles Police Academy, is the city's oldest park and second only in size to Griffith Park. No stranger to controversy, this park saw three of its communities uprooted to make room for the stadium in 1950, and later it was divided in half by the Pasadena Freeway.

Still, it's a great place for a solitary run or hike, though its lack of good trail maps can be confusing for those unfamiliar with the area. Birders also frequent the park; residents include red-tailed hawks, Western bluebirds, black-headed grosbeaks, and Lucy's warblers. On weekends, the park is full of picnicking families, exercise hounds, and nature lovers. If there happens to be a home baseball game, the area is even livelier; plan your visit so it doesn't coincide with the beginning or end of a game, or you will likely find yourself caught in a massive traffic jam.

The first time I hiked Elysian Park, I showed up without a plan, figuring the trail system was small enough to make that unnecessary. In reality, the park has many and varied trails spread over its 600 acres. A couple of trail maps are posted within the park, but it's hard to get a sense of how long or difficult they are. So my husband, a baseball fan, and I just decided to wander uphill in the direction of Dodger Stadium, where we figured (correctly) that we would find nice views of the venerable sports venue. The hike we cobbled together begins in the parking lot of Grace E. Simons Lodge. We crossed Stadium Way and headed uphill along Angels Point Road, a paved road that is blocked to car traffic during the week. At about 0.5 mile, you'll come to Angels Point, a clearing with a playground, picnic tables, and good views of downtown Los Angeles. Walk a little farther and you'll come to a dirt path bordered by a chain-link fence on the right. Follow the path a short way downhill for views of the stadium. Return to the road and continue walking north. On weekends this road gets a good deal of car traffic, but there is plenty of room for pedestrians, and it's nicely framed by palm trees. To your right, you'll get a bird's-eye view of the Los Angeles Police Academy's shooting range. At about 2 miles, you'll come to a gate and a dirt trail on the left. Follow that as it winds away from the paved road and past views of the northwestern side of Elysian Park. You'll pass a water tower on the right and views of Glendale and the Verdugo Mountains on the left. Continue on the trail as it

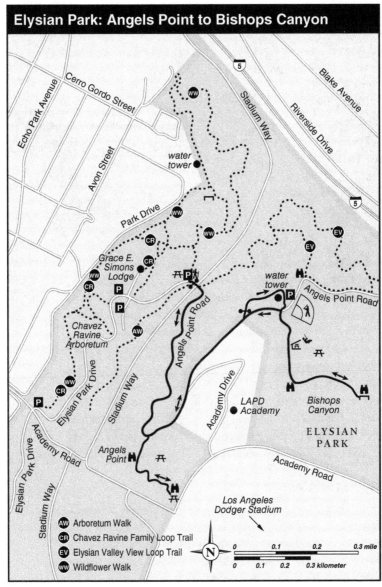

Elysian Park: Angels Point to Bishops Canyon

AW Arboretum Walk
CR Chavez Ravine Family Loop Trail
EV Elysian Valley View Loop Trail
WW Wildflower Walk

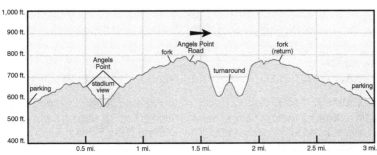

DISTANCE & CONFIGURATION: 3-mile balloon	**MAPS:** USGS *Los Angeles;* at kiosk in front of Grace E. Simons Lodge
DIFFICULTY: Moderate	**WHEELCHAIR ACCESSIBLE:** No
SCENERY: Dodger Stadium, palm trees, evergreens	**FACILITIES:** Restrooms, water, picnic tables, playgrounds
EXPOSURE: Sunny	**CONTACT:** 213-485-5054; **laparks.org**
TRAFFIC: Moderate	**/dos/parks/facility/elysianPk.htm**
TRAIL SURFACE: Paved road, packed dirt	**COMMENT:** Dogs must be leashed at all times in the park.
HIKING TIME: 1.75 hours	
ACCESS: Daily, 5 a.m.–9 p.m.; free; park in lot at Grace E. Simons Lodge	

loops back to Angels Point Road and passes a ball field. Just past this, you'll see a sign for Elysian Fields; turn left on the road, and walk by picnic pavilions, a parking area, and a large playground. All this used to be the Bishops Canyon landfill, a collection point for tons of household and construction refuse that was sealed in 1969 and turned into a recreational area by sanitation and park officials in the 1990s.

The area differs from the rest of Elysian Park in that there are few trees or shrubs here, but its bluff-top views make it worth a visit. The road ends at another cluster of picnic tables and a rocky promontory with views of the stadium and downtown L.A. This provides an even better view of the stadium (from the "Think Blue" side) than Angels Point. On weekends, this area gets very busy with ball players and groups having birthday parties and other events under the picnic pavilions, which are often reserved in advance. From here you can retrace your steps along Angels Point Road and back to the parking lot.

Nearby Activities

Take some time before or after your hike to walk through the open-air Chavez Ravine Arboretum near the parking lot for Grace E. Simons Lodge. For more information, call 213-485-5054 or visit **laparks.org/dos/horticulture/chavez.htm.**

For a bite to eat in an unusual setting, try the Academy Café, the commissary of the Los Angeles Police Academy, located within the park. After sampling a Hot Squad club sandwich, you can stroll through a circa 1950 rock garden adjacent to the academy's shooting range. The café is located at 1880 N. Academy Rd. and is open daily for breakfast and lunch.

GPS TRAILHEAD COORDINATES   N34° 5.159' W118° 14.575'

From I-5, take Exit 138 (Stadium Way), and follow signs to Dodger Stadium. In 0.8 mile, turn right at Grace E. Simons Lodge, and park along the curb or farther down the road in the parking lot adjacent to the lodge. The trailhead is just behind you to the right.

4 Elysian Park:
WILDFLOWER TRAIL

Thick patches of yellow wildflowers give this trail its name.

In Brief

Yellow wildflowers and birds dominate this easy loop trail in the spring. It's a popular jogging path year-round, but it never seems overcrowded. A small secluded garden with a bench can be found at the midway point.

Description

The 600-acre Elysian Park is the city's oldest park and second only in size to Griffith Park. No stranger to controversy, the park saw three of its communities uprooted to make room for Dodger Stadium in 1950, and later it was divided in half by the Pasadena Freeway.

Still, it's a great place for a solitary run or hike, though its lack of good trail maps can be confusing for those unfamiliar with the area. Birders also frequent the park; recent sightings include red-tailed hawks, western bluebirds, black-headed grosbeaks, and Lucy's warblers. On weekends, the park is full of picnicking families, exercise hounds,

DISTANCE & CONFIGURATION: 2.5-mile loop	**ACCESS:** Daily, 5 a.m.–9 p.m.; free
DIFFICULTY: Easy	**MAPS:** USGS *Los Angeles;* at kiosk near Grace E. Simons Lodge
SCENERY: Wildflowers; birds; groves of ficus, oak, and sycamore trees	**WHEELCHAIR ACCESSIBLE:** No
EXPOSURE: Sun and shade	**FACILITIES:** Restrooms, picnic tables, water fountains, playground
TRAFFIC: Moderate	**CONTACT:** 213-485-5054; **laparks.org /dos/parks/facility/elysianPk.htm**
TRAIL SURFACE: Packed dirt	
HIKING TIME: 1.25 hours	**COMMENTS:** No bikes are allowed on this trail, and dogs must be leashed.

and nature lovers. If there happens to be a home baseball game, the area is even livelier; try to plan your visit so it doesn't coincide with the beginning or end of a game, or you will likely find yourself caught in a massive traffic jam.

The Wildflower Trail begins just beyond a lush, grassy picnic area landscaped with palm trees and picnic tables. Look for the white fire-road gate near the sign for Grace E. Simons Lodge, a rental facility for birthday parties, weddings, and corporate gatherings. Begin walking on the dirt trail past rows of tall pine and sycamore trees. To your right is a shady ravine that serves as a buffer to Stadium Way, which runs parallel with the first leg of the trail. In the spring, you'll soon reach the thick patches of yellow wildflowers that give the trail its name. At about 0.5 mile, the path dips downward and gives way to prominent views of both sides of I-5, one of L.A.'s busiest roads. Hiking this trail during rush hour makes it all the sweeter as you look down on the gridlock below. Beyond the freeway and industrial areas that surround it, you can also see the Verdugo and San Gabriel Mountains. It's not long, however, before the path curves around to the left and heads uphill away from the freeway. Just shy of 1 mile, you'll pass a green water tower and glimpse private homes on the right, though they are well shrouded by trees and brush. As the uphill path levels, you'll reach a shady resting place with a bench, trash cans, and landscaping. This is the Marian Harlow Memorial Grove, a peaceful place to stop and rest for a moment.

For a shorter hike, take the path to the left of the garden back to the trailhead. To extend this hike, you can continue to the right for another mile or so. The trail widens a bit here and on clear days has views of the downtown L.A. skyline—first filtered through the trees, then wide-open views. You will probably see more foot traffic along this leg of the trail, as it can also be easily accessed from a small parking lot on Academy Road. At 1.2 miles, you'll pass another trail that leads back to the parking lot. I had intended to take this trail back to my car, but the cloudless day made me want to prolong the hike, so I continued on the main trail as it loomed over Grace E. Simons Lodge and the Chavez Ravine Arboretum on my left. After about 0.5 mile, I reached the Academy Road parking lot and reversed course on a paved path that led back to the parking lot.

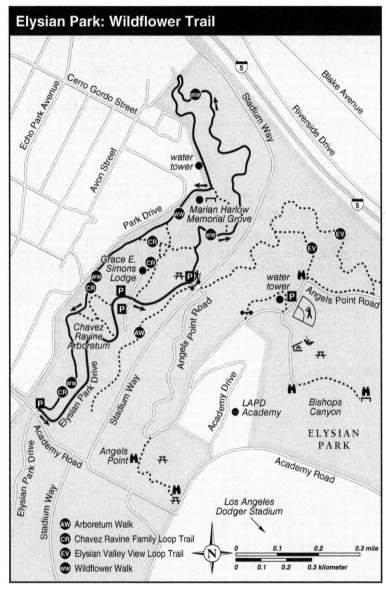

Elysian Park: Wildflower Trail

AW Arboretum Walk
CR Chavez Ravine Family Loop Trail
EV Elysian Valley View Loop Trail
WW Wildflower Walk

Los Angeles
Dodger Stadium

ELYSIAN
PARK

Bishops
Canyon

LAPD
Academy

Angels
Point

Chavez
Ravine
Arboretum

Grace E.
Simons
Lodge

Marian Harlow
Memorial Grove

water
tower

water
tower

Angels Point Road

Academy Drive

Stadium Way

Elysian Park Drive

Academy Road

Park Drive

Avon Street

Cerro Gordo Street

Echo Park Avenue

Blake Avenue

Riverside Drive

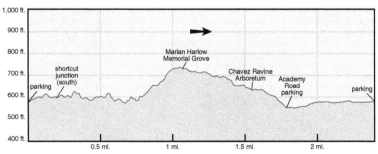

Nearby Activities

Take some time before or after your hike to walk through the open-air Chavez Ravine Arboretum, near the parking lot for Grace E. Simons Lodge. Founded in 1893 by the Los Angeles Horticultural Society, the arboretum has more than 1,000 varieties of trees from around the world, including redwoods from northern California, pines from the Rocky Mountains, and eucalyptus from Australia. For more information call 213-485-5054 or visit **laparks.org/dos/horticulture/chavez.htm.**

GPS TRAILHEAD COORDINATES

N34° 5.210' W118° 14.596'

From I-5, take Exit 138 (Stadium Way), and follow signs to Dodger Stadium. In 0.8 mile, turn right at Grace E. Simons Lodge, and park along the curb or farther down the road in the parking lot adjacent to the lodge. The trailhead is just behind you to the right.

5 Ernest E. Debs Regional Park:
CITY VIEW AND
WALNUT FOREST TRAILS

A view of Highland Park from the City View Trail

In Brief

An array of native plants, flowers, and wildlife dominates the trails on this 282-acre tranquil hillside between Chinatown and South Pasadena. At the trail's peak, rest at a bucolic pond and take in the views of downtown Los Angeles. More than 130 species of birds make their home here, and the Audubon Society runs the park's nature center.

Description

The official name is Ernest E. Debs Regional Park, but everyone calls it Debs Park. The Audubon Society opened a nature center at the Griffin Avenue entrance in 2003, offering guided hikes, nature camps, and other activities geared toward kids and families.

More than 130 species of native and visiting birds, including the red-tailed hawk, barn owl, blue-gray gnatcatcher, and lesser goldfinch live here, according to the Audubon Society. The park is also home to ringneck snakes, coyotes, pocket gophers, skunks, and

DISTANCE & CONFIGURATION: 2.6-mile balloon	**ACCESS:** Daily, sunrise–sunset; free
DIFFICULTY: Moderate	**MAPS:** USGS *Los Angeles;* at nature center and **tinyurl.com/debsparkmap**
SCENERY: Hills, city views, pond	**WHEELCHAIR ACCESSIBLE:** No
EXPOSURE: Sunny	**FACILITIES:** Restrooms, water fountains, picnic tables, benches
TRAFFIC: Light	
TRAIL SURFACE: Dirt and paved path	**CONTACT:** 323-221-2255; **laparks.org**
HIKING TIME: 1.5 hours	**/dos/parks/facility/debsEERegionalPk.htm**

dozens of types of butterflies, including the Western tiger swallowtail and the painted lady. It's worth grabbing a park trail guide from the nature center before embarking on your hike, but it's tough to get lost on any of the trails. Most visitors take Walnut Forest Trail or City View Trail to the pond at the park's peak. There is also a short, easy Butterfly Loop just behind the nature center that's great for young children.

To reach the Walnut Forest Trail, walk back toward the entrance from the parking lot to the fire-road gate. Turn right and head up the dirt path as it winds north on a gradual incline. You'll pass a couple of narrow dirt trails on the left, but continue to stay to the right on the wide path. After a brief dip downward, the Walnut Forest Trail begins to climb gradually past coastal sage scrub, toyon bushes, and eucalyptus and walnut trees. In the spring, you can also expect to see arroyo lupine, goldenbush, laurel sumac, and morning glories along this route. On the left you'll see (and hear) the Pasadena Freeway, as well as the rooftops of hillside homes in the distance. At about 0.4 mile, you'll pass stone steps on your left that lead nowhere as the path curves around to the right. You'll also pass an unmarked trail on the right at 0.6 mile. This is the City View Trail. It's a steeper, more exposed climb than the Walnut Forest Trail. I recommend sticking to the Walnut Forest Trail on the way up and taking the City View Trail, which can also be accessed from the north near the pond, on the way back (unless you have small children, in which case the wider and smoother Walnut Forest Trail is best).

After about 1 mile, the dirt path ends and you'll come to a paved road. Turn right and follow it past a gazebo with a picnic table and benches on the left. As the path climbs, pass a few more benches on the left and more toyon bushes and walnut and palm trees. On a clear day, you'll be able to see downtown L.A. straight ahead. At about 1.4 miles, come to a Y with a cluster of pine trees in the center. Continue right on the unmarked Summit Ridge Trail and follow it a few hundred yards to the entrance to the pond on your right. The pond sneaks up on you. It's not far off the trail, but it's well camouflaged by trees and shrubs. With its hillside location and views of downtown L.A. and Dodger Stadium, it reminds me of nature's version of the infinity pool, a popular L.A. swimming pool design that makes the water seem like it meets the sky. You might want to allot some time to linger here before turning around; there are benches, and the pond is stocked with large-mouth bass, bluegill, and black bullhead (fishing is permitted). It's truly a beautiful setting in an area of Los Angeles where you least expect it.

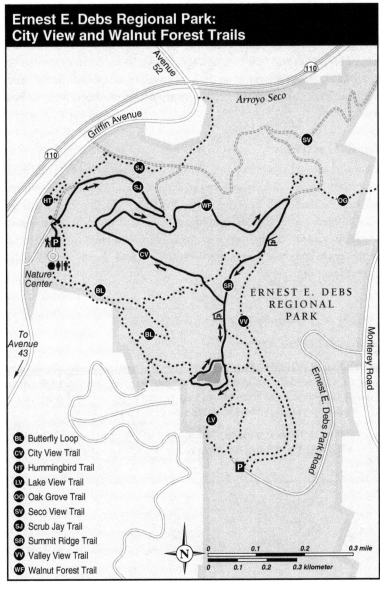

**Ernest E. Debs Regional Park:
City View and Walnut Forest Trails**

BL Butterfly Loop
CV City View Trail
HT Hummingbird Trail
LV Lake View Trail
OG Oak Grove Trail
SV Seco View Trail
SJ Scrub Jay Trail
SR Summit Ridge Trail
VV Valley View Trail
WF Walnut Forest Trail

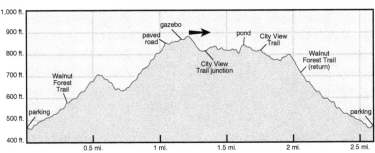

From the pond, you can retrace your steps back to the Walnut Forest Trail or return along the City View Trail (the City View Trailhead is 0.4 mile on the left as you walk back along the Summit Ridge Trail). The City View Trail is narrower and less shady, but it has better views of downtown L.A. and the Arroyo Seco, the dry riverbed that runs parallel to the Pasadena Freeway, than the other trails. You can also see the Metro Gold Line's Highland Park station and the 19th-century adobe architecture of the Southwest Museum from here.

Nearby Activities

The Audubon Center at Debs Park (open Tuesday–Saturday) is worth a stop, not only for its trail maps and free binocular rentals but also for its environmentally friendly architecture. The walls are reinforced by melted-down handguns and scrap metal; the carpeting is woven with leaves from the Mexican agave plant, and the cabinets are made with pressed sunflower seeds. Jogging strollers, binoculars, and child backpack carriers are available to borrow, and there is a children's garden out back. For more information, visit **debspark.audubon.org**.

GPS TRAILHEAD COORDINATES

N34° 6.002' W118° 12.024'

From downtown Los Angeles, take CA 110 north and exit at Avenue 43. Make a right onto Avenue 43 and then an immediate left onto Griffin Avenue. In 0.5 mile, the entrance will be on the right across from a soccer field. There is also an entrance and parking lot off Monterey Road on the north side of the park.

Alternate directions: From Pasadena, take CA 110 south to Avenue 52. Turn left and follow Avenue 52 as it turns into Griffin Avenue. In 0.4 mile, the park entrance will be on the left.

6 Griffith Park: AMIR'S GARDEN

A secluded picnic area at Amir's Garden

In Brief

A steep but manageable path leads past green hills and a large water tower to a 2-acre oasis of palm trees, ferns, succulents, and other native plants and flowers cared for by volunteers.

Description

Griffith Park, tucked into the eastern end of the Santa Monica Mountains, is the largest municipal park in the United States. Its 4,100 acres include the Los Angeles Zoo, a 1926 merry-go-round, four municipal golf courses, a world-renowned observatory, and miles of hiking trails that make you forget you're in the middle of the nation's second-largest city. A comprehensive list of trails in the park is available at the Griffith Park Visitor Center at 4730 Crystal Springs Dr.

Amir Dialameh was an Iranian immigrant who created a lush garden on a hillside in Griffith Park after a brush fire swept through the area in 1971. Dialameh cared for the garden until his death in 2003 at the age of 71. He could be found tending the terraced hillside on most days, and he once told a local newspaper that the secrets to a healthy, happy life were staying away from doctors and lawyers and "hiking, lots of hiking." A group of hikers who developed a friendship with Amir help keep up the garden. To get to the trailhead, walk to the lower end of the Mineral Wells parking lot. You will want to take the middle dirt trail up a fairly steep grade. You'll see green hills to your left and city views of Glendale and the Verdugo Mountains behind you. At about 0.3 mile, the path curves sharply around and heads toward a large green water tower. It will appear as though the path ends at the water tower, but it actually just curves around it to the left and continues upward. The ascent starts to become more gradual here. You'll be able to see the Harding

DISTANCE & CONFIGURATION: 1-mile out-and-back	**ACCESS:** Daily, 6 a.m.–sunset; free
DIFFICULTY: Moderate	**MAPS:** USGS *Burbank;* at Griffith Park Ranger Headquarters, 4730 Crystal Springs Dr.
SCENERY: Chaparral-covered hills, city views	
	WHEELCHAIR ACCESSIBLE: No
EXPOSURE: Sunny	**FACILITIES:** None
TRAFFIC: Light	**CONTACT:** 323-913-4688; **laparks.org /dos/parks/griffithpk** or **amirsgarden.org;** Twitter **@amirsgarden**
TRAIL SURFACE: Packed dirt	
HIKING TIME: 45 minutes	

Golf Course below and city sprawl giving way to the Verdugo Mountains on your left. Soon you will see the wobbly painted benches that mark the entrance to Amir's Garden. There are also trash cans and a hitching post with a sign cautioning horses to keep out of the garden. Inside the makeshift entrance are a few picnic tables; groves of Christmas berry, pepper, and pine trees; and gardens of asparagus ferns, oleander, jade, geraniums, and ice plants. Take a deep breath and revel in the garden's restorative scent. You can follow a flight of stone steps down a terraced hillside to explore the garden further. The circular path leads back to the picnic tables where you started.

One small disadvantage of this trail is that you're likely to hear traffic noise from nearby I-5 and CA 134 all the way to the garden. It doesn't fully disappear until you reach the garden entrance. On the flip side, this trail is rarely crowded. Bring a book or journal and spend the morning relaxing on a bench and soaking up Dialameh's peaceful creation.

Nearby Activities

Amir's Garden Trailhead is close to several Griffith Park attractions, including the historic merry-go-round, pony rides (**griffithparkponyride.com**), and Shane's Inspiration, a wheelchair-accessible playground. The Griffith Observatory, the park's best-known attraction, is about a 10-minute drive away at 2800 E. Observatory Rd. Its exhibits, planetarium shows, and public star parties are well worth a visit. For more information, go to **griffithobs.org.**

GPS TRAILHEAD COORDINATES   N34° 8.703' W118° 17.611'

From the Golden State Freeway (I-5), take Exit 141 (Los Feliz Boulevard). Head southwest on Los Feliz Boulevard, and make an immediate right onto Crystal Springs Drive. Go 1.5 miles, and just past the park ranger headquarters on the right, turn left at the stop sign onto Griffith Park Drive. Continue 1.2 miles, past Harding Municipal Golf Course, to the Mineral Wells Picnic Area. Park at the picnic area.

Alternate directions: From CA 134 in Burbank, exit at Forest Lawn Drive. Head south on Forest Lawn Drive, and then make an immediate left on Zoo Drive and a right onto Griffith Park Drive. Continue 1.4 miles to the Mineral Wells Picnic Area.

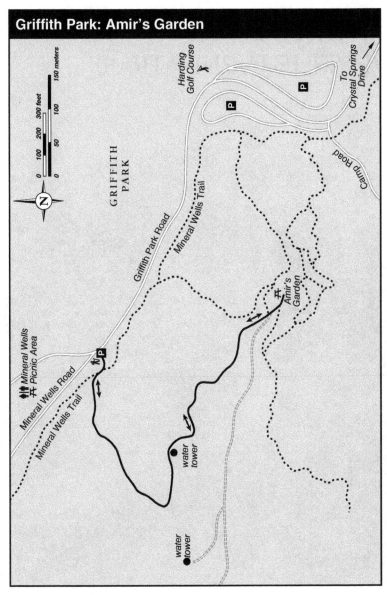

Griffith Park: Amir's Garden

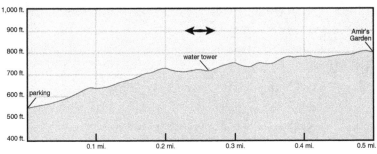

7 Griffith Park:
CHARLIE TURNER TRAIL

A view of the Griffith Observatory from Mount Hollywood (Charlie Turner Trail)

In Brief

Also known as the Mount Hollywood Trail, this popular 3-mile trek begins at the Griffith Observatory and leads to a viewpoint with unparalleled 360-degree views of the Los Angeles basin. The gradual 650-foot elevation gain and easy access attract a wide variety of hikers.

DISTANCE & CONFIGURATION: 3-mile balloon	USGS *Burbank;* at Griffith Park Visitor Center, 4730 Crystal Springs Dr.
DIFFICULTY: Moderate	**WHEELCHAIR ACCESSIBLE:** No
SCENERY: Panoramic city and mountain views	**FACILITIES:** Water fountains, picnic tables
EXPOSURE: Mostly sun	**CONTACT:** 323-913-4688; **laparks.org**
TRAFFIC: Heavy	**/dos/parks/griffithpk**
TRAIL SURFACE: Packed dirt and sand	**COMMENTS:** Expect big crowds on weekends; arrive early to secure a spot in the parking lot or you will end up parking along the road that leads to the trailhead, adding an extra 0.25–0.5 mile to the hike.
HIKING TIME: 1.5–2 hours	
ACCESS: Daily, sunrise–sunset; free	
MAPS: USGS *Hollywood* and	

Description

Griffith Park, tucked into the eastern end of the Santa Monica Mountains, is the largest municipal park in the United States. Its 4,100 acres include the Los Angeles Zoo, a 1926 merry-go-round, four municipal golf courses, a public observatory, and miles of hiking trails that make you forget you're in the middle of the nation's second-largest city.

If you like solitude with your hikes, this trail is not for you. Like Runyon Canyon and Inspiration Point at Will Rogers State Historic Park, it is hugely popular and attracts an eclectic mix of exercise hounds, dog walkers, families, and text-messaging addicts who don't always watch where they're going. On a recent hike, I overheard a young man talking about what his studio boss's 14-year-old daughter was going to wear to the Oscars, dodged a 5-year-old boy careening down the hill with his yoga pants–wearing mother, and heard at least five languages spoken. This is one of my favorite hikes in all of Los Angeles. It's like a speed tour of the best (and sometimes worst) of living in Southern California. On a clear day, you will see the Hollywood sign, the Pacific Ocean, the San Gabriel Mountains, and the entire Los Angeles basin from downtown to Century City spread before you. On a not-so-clear day, you will have a front-row seat to the brown smog that carpets the city and often gives it a bad name.

The trailhead begins at the north end of the observatory parking lot and is marked by a sign for MOUNT HOLLYWOOD/CHARLIE TURNER TRAILHEAD. Follow the dirt path north as it gradually ascends toward Mount Hollywood. Good views come into play soon after you leave the parking lot. After about 0.2 mile, you will pass a clearing with picnic tables on the left and a couple of benches facing the Hollywood sign. Soon you will pass a trail on the left that heads downhill and back to Observatory Road. Continue straight on the main path as it crosses a small bridge and then curves to the left. The next 0.5 mile or so is mostly flat until you reach a small viewpoint overlooking the Hollywood Hills. From here, the trail heads east and begins to climb more aggressively toward the top of the mountain. At 1 mile, you will come to a trail junction. The trail to the right leads to a rocky promontory with views of Griffith Observatory and downtown Los

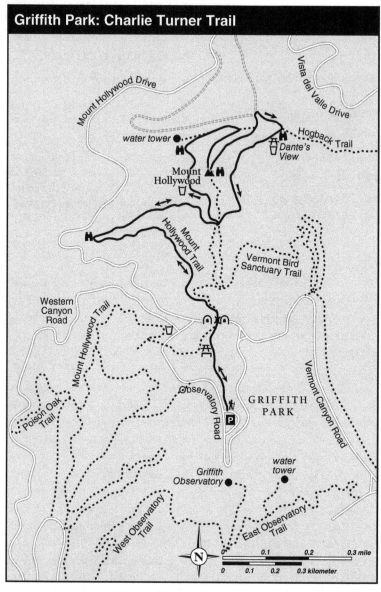

Griffith Park: Charlie Turner Trail

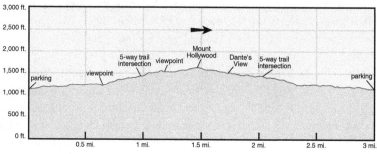

Angeles. The other three trails lead to your final destination of Mount Hollywood. The one in the middle is the steepest. I suggest following the path to the far left, which offers more views of the Hollywood Hills as well as other trails within Griffith Park.

At 1.3 miles, you will pass another small clearing that overlooks the Hollywood sign and a large water tower. Continue another 0.25 mile or so to your final destination: a large clearing surrounded by a wooden fence with picnic tables and hitching posts. Leave time to pause and drink in the stunning views that surround you—the Hollywood sign to the west, the San Gabriel Mountains to the north, downtown Los Angeles to the southeast, and Griffith Observatory, triple-domed and gorgeous, just below you to the south.

For a different perspective on the way down the mountain, follow the path to the right as you leave the clearing. It leads past another small cluster of picnic tables that face north and then winds down the east side of the mountain past Dante's View, a landscaped acre created by Griffith Park regular Dante Orgolini in the 1960s and lovingly maintained, first by another park devotee, Charlie Turner, after whom the trailhead is named, and more recently by City Councilman Tom LaBonge. Take a moment here to rest, use the water fountain, or just admire the south-facing views that inspired these men to carve out such a beautiful place.

To return to the trailhead, follow the path back to the trail junction (where you turned left on the way up) and retrace your steps down the mountain.

Nearby Activities

It's easy to combine this hike with a visit to Griffith Observatory, an astronomical and architectural landmark that has been featured in movies like *Rebel without a Cause* and *The Terminator.* Reopened after extensive renovations in 2006, the triple-domed building has a 300-seat planetarium, rooftop telescopes, and many celestial-themed exhibits that can be viewed for free. It's closed on Mondays. For more information, visit **griffithobs .org.** The observatory has a full-service café, but a quirkier eating option is The Trails Café (2333 Fern Dell Dr.; **facebook.com/thetrailscafe**), an outdoor snack shack just down the road. Order a meat pie, vegan chili, or apple pie à la mode and relax at one of the adjacent picnic tables.

GPS TRAILHEAD COORDINATES   N34° 7.154' W118° 17.969'

From the Golden State Freeway (I-5), take Exit 141 (Los Feliz Boulevard), and head west for 1.5 miles. Turn right onto Vermont Avenue, and drive up the hill through a residential neighborhood until you see a sign welcoming you to Griffith Park. In 0.8 mile you will reach the Greek Theatre, after which the road curves around to the left and then in another 0.5 mile goes through a tunnel. Drive through the tunnel, turn left at the stop sign, and continue to the observatory parking lot. On weekends cars will line either side of the road if the parking lot is full.

8 Griffith Park:
HOLLYRIDGE TRAIL

In Brief

Fantastic views of the Hollywood sign and chaparral-covered hills dominate this busy Griffith Park trail.

Description

Griffith Park, tucked into the eastern end of the Santa Monica Mountains, is the largest municipal park in the United States. Its 4,100 acres include the Los Angeles Zoo, a 1926 merry-go-round, four municipal golf courses, a world-renowned observatory, and miles of hiking trails that make you forget you're in the middle of the nation's second-largest city. A comprehensive list of trails in the park is available at the Griffith Park Visitor Center at 4730 Crystal Springs Dr. This trail, along with Bronson Caves and Amir's Garden, offers a good representation of what the park has to offer, but keep in mind that there are many other options.

You'll drive through one of L.A.'s hippest neighborhoods before reaching the base of the Hollyridge Trail. Beachwood Canyon has been home to Madonna, Humphrey Bogart, Aldous Huxley, and countless aspiring actors who fill the many apartment buildings on lower Beachwood Drive. In the 1920s, the area was part of an upscale real estate development known as Hollywoodland (look for the stone gates and guard tower as you drive toward the trail base). As an advertising gimmick, the developers erected a huge sign with the development's name atop Mount Lee, which looms above the canyon. The letters were refurbished and shortened to Hollywood (thanks to gale-force winds) in 1949. This trail is one of the easiest ways to get a close-up view of the famous sign.

From the dirt parking lot just south of the Sunset Ranch horse stables, follow the sign for Hollyridge Trail. The wide dirt trail climbs moderately for 0.25 mile past a leveled area with views of the Los Angeles basin. As you round the corner, the Hollywood sign will suddenly come into view. You may see some people snapping photos here; this path attracts as many starstruck tourists as it does residents because of its proximity to Hollywood. I did this hike on a rainy day during the first weekend of January, and it still had a decent amount of traffic. The crowds were largely made up of out-of-town sports fans who had come to L.A. for the annual Rose Bowl and parade and were determined to check out the sign before they left, bad weather or no.

Continue following the path north, and you'll pass an entrance to Sunset Ranch on the left. Don't be surprised if you also see a few horseback riders on this trail. The ranch rents horses and offers weekly dinner rides through Griffith Park that begin here. To your right, you'll be able to see green hills and the Griffith Observatory in the distance.

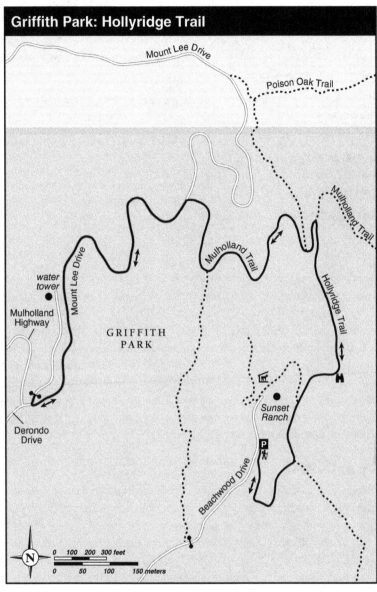

Griffith Park: Hollyridge Trail

Mount Lee Drive

Poison Oak Trail

Mulholland Trail

Mulholland Trail

Hollyridge Trail

Mount Lee Drive

water tower

Mulholland Highway

GRIFFITH PARK

Sunset Ranch

Derondo Drive

Beachwood Drive

H

P

N

0 100 200 300 feet

0 50 100 150 meters

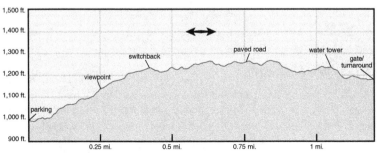

1,500 ft.

1,400 ft.

1,300 ft.

1,200 ft.

1,100 ft.

1,000 ft.

900 ft.

paved road

water tower

gate/ turnaround

switchback

viewpoint

parking

0.25 mi.   0.5 mi.   0.75 mi.   1 mi.

DISTANCE & CONFIGURATION: 2.5-mile out-and-back	**MAPS:** USGS *Burbank;* at Griffith Park Visitor Center, 4730 Crystal Springs Dr.
DIFFICULTY: Easy	**WHEELCHAIR ACCESSIBLE:** No
SCENERY: Hills, Griffith Observatory, Hollywood sign	**FACILITIES:** None
EXPOSURE: Sunny	**CONTACT:** 323-913-4688; **laparks.org /dos/parks/griffithpk**
TRAFFIC: Heavy	**COMMENTS:** Citing traffic and congestion, local residents have led a fight to restrict access to this trail in recent years. A gate now blocks cars from using the dirt parking lot, and street parking is limited. Be sure to check signs before leaving your car.
TRAIL SURFACE: Paved road and dirt path	
HIKING TIME: 1.75 hours	
ACCESS: Gate: Daily, sunrise–sunset; free	

After about 0.5 mile, you'll come to a switchback on the left that follows a dirt trail uphill. Take that to continue on Hollyridge. If you go straight, you'll wind up on Mulholland Trail, and eventually in Brush Canyon, near the Bronson Caves.

From here, the trail climbs gently to about 1,200 feet, giving way to sweeping views of the L.A. basin on a clear day. Continue another 0.25 mile until you reach a paved road, Mount Lee Drive. From here, you can either turn right and follow the steep trail to Mount Lee, which overlooks the sign from an elevation of about 1,500 feet, or turn left and walk past a water tower until the road dead-ends at a housing development and a gate that warns you to go no farther. Both options will net you great views of the sign; the Mount Lee trail is a little more strenuous than Hollyridge.

Nearby Activities

Sunset Ranch, just north of the Hollyridge Trailhead, is a sprawling horse ranch that boards horses and rents by the hour. It's worth a peek before or after hiking even if you're not interested in renting a horse. The ranch has been in operation since the 1920s; the original red barn is still the facility's main building. Its popular Friday Night Dinner Ride includes a guided sunset ride through Griffith Park, dinner at a Mexican restaurant, and a moonlit ride back to the ranch. For more information, go to **sunsetranchhollywood.com.**

GPS TRAILHEAD COORDINATES

N34° 7.720' W118° 18.916'

From US 101, exit at Gower Street and head east on Franklin Avenue. Make an immediate left onto North Beachwood Drive, and follow it about 2 miles until it dead-ends. Park on North Beachwood Drive or in a dirt lot just past the entrance gate.

9 Mount Washington:
JACK SMITH TRAIL

In Brief

Named for a beloved *Los Angeles Times* metro columnist, this trail begins with a rigorous climb up five flights of steps, and then tapers to a gradual incline through the pretty hillside neighborhood of Mount Washington, tracing the route of a former railway that carried residents to and from their homes in the early 1900s. A rapid elevation gain of 500 feet puts this urban hike on the strenuous side. It's best if combined with a visit to the peaceful grounds of the Self-Realization Fellowship complex and the historic Southwest Museum.

Description

This trail is named for Jack Smith, the beloved late *Los Angeles Times* columnist and Mount Washington resident who often wrote about the quirks and beauty of his longtime neighborhood. After Smith died in 1996, his wife, Denise (also known as Denny), and other members of the community worked to name a trail in his honor. It's more of a brisk urban walk than a wilderness hike, but it is a great way to explore the hidden hillsides and historic architecture of Mount Washington.

Located just north of downtown Los Angeles, Mount Washington is a close-knit enclave of historic houses, wide streets, and nature parks. It was used for sheep- and cattle-raising in the 19th century before a couple of developers targeted it for residential homes. A two-car railway carried residents up and down the hillside between their homes and the flatlands in the early 1900s. The Mount Washington Hotel, now the headquarters for the Self-Realization Fellowship, a worldwide spiritual organization with temples throughout Los Angeles, once attracted celebrities such as Charlie Chaplin for its city-to-ocean views and get-away-from-it-all environment.

Begin the hike by walking up Avenue 43 from Marmion Way. The paved road ends at Glenmuir Avenue, and you will see a flight of stairs in front of you. Climb the steps (about 70 of them), which are flanked by cactus plants, lilacs, and oak trees, until you reach Canyon Vista Drive. Follow Canyon Vista via the sidewalk as it continues to climb past a variety of houses, from Spanish-style to modernist, some shrouded from view by fences or shrubs, others brightly colored with open landscapes. On the left, weather permitting, you can see downtown Los Angeles. Behind you is the hillside neighborhood of Montecito Heights.

At about 0.4 mile, Canyon Vista Drive merges with Mount Washington Drive. You'll want to bear right and continue climbing uphill along a white-fenced ridge on the left side of the road. On a clear day, this portion of the hike offers uninhibited views of the downtown Los Angeles skyline. Continue following Mount Washington Drive until it dead-ends at San Rafael Avenue. Turn right on San Rafael, and you will find yourself on one of Mount Washington's finest streets, marked by stunning architecture and big landscaped yards. On the right side of the road, fronted by big iron gates, sits the former Mount Washington Hotel,

DISTANCE & CONFIGURATION: 4.25-mile out-and-back	**HIKING TIME:** 1.5 hours
DIFFICULTY: Moderate–strenuous	**ACCESS:** 24/7; free
SCENERY: City views, residential development, black walnut woodland	**MAPS:** USGS *Los Angeles*
EXPOSURE: Sun and shade	**WHEELCHAIR ACCESSIBLE:** Mostly accessible, except for stairs portions
TRAFFIC: Light	**FACILITIES:** None
TRAIL SURFACE: Paved sidewalk, steps	**CONTACT:** n/a

now the international headquarters for the Self-Realization Fellowship. An interesting architectural note: It was built by the same firm that built the famous Grauman's Chinese Theatre in Hollywood. At 0.75 mile, you will pass Mount Washington Elementary School on the left. If you time your hike for the early afternoon, as I did, don't be surprised at the noise and traffic levels here as school lets out. This is also the site of the Jack and Denny Smith Library and Community Center, another effort to honor the L.A. columnist and his wife.

For a short, worthwhile detour, hang a left on Sea View Avenue and follow it about 0.25 mile until the road turns to dirt; on a clear day, you can see as far as Catalina Island and the Palos Verdes Peninsula. The dirt path passes a wooden bench (an ideal place to rest with a book or thermos of coffee) and eventually turns back to paved road and puts you back on San Rafael Avenue. The housing gets a little denser here as San Rafael Avenue crosses Sea View Lane and curves around to the right. At Moon Avenue, stay to the right and look for a sign for Heidelberg Park on the right.

Follow Moon Avenue to the right as it skirts a small hillside park and several private homes. Moon turns into Crane Boulevard and continues down the hill, eventually meeting up with Museum Drive and the entrance to the Southwest Museum, a historic landmark that is home to the largest collection of American Indian and southwestern US artifacts. Now owned by Griffith Park's Autry Museum, it has limited hours (check **theautry.org** before you go), but its beautiful hilltop grounds are open to the public most days.

Nearby Activities

The lush grounds of the international headquarters for the Self-Realization Fellowship (3880 San Rafael Ave.), a religious organization founded by Paramahansa Yogananda, are open to the public every day but Monday. There's a big stone table near the rose garden and benches placed discreetly throughout, making this a fine mid-hike stop.

GPS TRAILHEAD COORDINATES   N34° 5.762' W118° 12.603'

From the Pasadena Freeway (CA 110), take the Avenue 43 exit. Head west to Figueroa Street, and turn right onto Figueroa. In 0.1 mile turn left onto West Avenue 45; then make another immediate left onto Marmion Way. Park along Marmion near the intersection with West Avenue 43. Walk up West Avenue 43 to the flight of stairs that ascends west.

Mount Washington: Jack Smith Trail

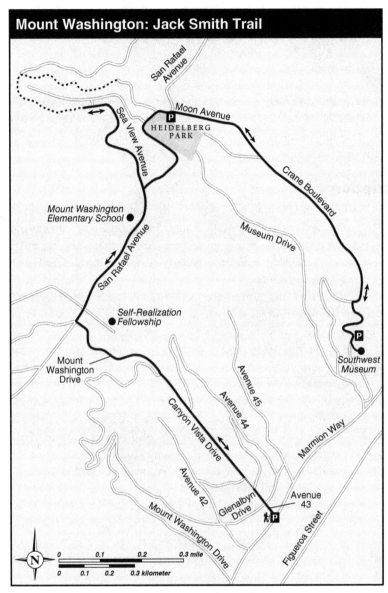

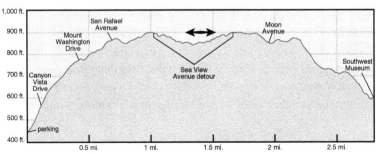

10 Runyon Canyon

In Brief

This 130-acre park two blocks north of Hollywood Boulevard offers a peaceful respite right in the middle of the city. The always-busy trail is popular with dog owners and impossibly beautiful people looking for an energetic outdoor workout that comes with spectacular views of the Los Angeles basin.

Description

Runyon Canyon has three entrances: Two are at the bottom, or south end, of the park, and one begins at the north end, off Mulholland Drive. For the best workout and views, most hikers begin at the Fuller Avenue gate on the park's southeast corner and follow it counterclockwise. Parking in the dense neighborhood around the trailhead can be challenging, especially on weekends.

Once known as No Man's Canyon, the property takes its current name from Carman Runyon, a coal magnate from the East who used the property in the 1930s as a hunting and riding retreat. The city and the Santa Monica Mountains Conservancy bought the property in 1984 and turned it into a public park. Its former life as a playground for Hollywood stars is evidenced by the dilapidated tennis courts and the remains of terraces and building foundations along the main trail loop.

From the gate, take the lower fire road as it starts to climb past a grassy children's play area on the left and several exposed picnic tables. Expect to see a good number of dogs romping around a water pump here. The park also attracts its share of celebrities and impossibly beautiful people, thanks to its proximity to Hollywood and the surrounding hills of million-dollar mansions. Bobcats, deer, raccoons, and rattlesnakes also inhabit the canyon, but daylight sightings are rare.

From the picnic tables, continue north on the fire road. After about 0.5 mile, the road curves sharply around and winds past the old tennis courts, now used as a setting for yoga classes. Soon you'll approach Inspiration Point, a level area with a long bench and views of the city stretching below and to the east and west. Here, the paved road ends and you'll begin a steep climb up steps and a sloped dirt path surrounded by brush and cactus. Watch for the occasional dog or runners making their way swiftly down the narrow path. On a clear day, you'll be able to see the Hollywood sign and the Griffith Observatory in the distance to your right. Be sure to bring lots of water and sunscreen, as there are few shady areas and the afternoon sun can be brutal.

The steep climb ends at Cloud's Rest, another stopping point with a couple of benches (usually occupied) and even better views of the city. From here the dirt path levels and continues about 0.2 mile to a fork, where you can turn left and head downhill

DISTANCE & CONFIGURATION: 3.5-mile balloon	**ACCESS:** Daily, sunrise–sunset; free
DIFFICULTY: Strenuous	**MAPS:** USGS *Hollywood;* at kiosk beyond trailhead
SCENERY: Panoramic views of the city, mountains, and distant Pacific Ocean; wild chaparral surrounds the trails	**WHEELCHAIR ACCESSIBLE:** Lower and upper portions of trail
EXPOSURE: Sunny	**FACILITIES:** None
TRAFFIC: Heavy	**CONTACT:** 323-666-5046; **laparks.org /dos/parks/facility/runyoncanyonpk.htm**
TRAIL SURFACE: Paved road and packed dirt	**COMMENTS:** This is a popular spot for dog walkers. Unleashed dogs are permitted on the loop trail.
HIKING TIME: 1.5 hours	

along a paved pathway known as Runyon Canyon Road (no cars are allowed, but you might pass a few baby strollers), which winds back to the Fuller Avenue gate.

Instead of heading back down the hill, you may opt to veer right on Runyon Canyon Road and continue north for another (slightly easier) climb to Indian Rock. To get to Indian Rock, go through the iron gate. Dogs must be leashed at this point. You'll pass several private, gated homes and a small horse ranch on the right. Just past the ranch, turn left and follow the dirt path uphill past a few unsightly antenna towers. You'll soon come to a T in the path; turn right (the left path dead-ends to a private home) and walk another 0.25 mile or so. You'll reach a narrow path almost covered in shrubs that continues climbing upward. As you approach the top, you may start to hear echoes of "wow" and "awesome" from the hikers who made it to the top before you. At nearly 1,300 feet, this observation point offers a truly stunning view of Los Angeles, especially on clear days after it rains. The entire city stretches below you, framed by the Pacific Ocean to the right and, in winter, the snow-capped San Gabriel Mountains to the left. One of the best times to take it all in is in the early evening just before sunset. This point can also be accessed easily from Mulholland Drive. There's a small parking lot, but be aware that it closes punctually at sunset.

From here, you'll retrace your steps down the hill and back to the main loop, taking a right at the fork onto Runyon Canyon Road. When you reach the bottom, turn left away from the Vista Drive gate and walk along a shady path lined with palm trees and drought-resistant evergreens until you reach the Fuller Avenue gate.

Nearby Activities

When the bustle of Runyon Canyon is too much, head a block west to Wattles Garden Park (1824 N. Curson Ave.; **laparks.org/dos/parks/facility/wattlesgardenpk.htm**). Once a private estate, it is now a peaceful place for a stroll or picnic, with a sprawling lawn framed by palm trees and views as good as the ones over at Runyon.

GPS TRAILHEAD COORDINATES

N34° 6.318' W118° 20.937'

Take US 101 to the Cahuenga Boulevard exit, and follow Cahuenga south to Franklin Avenue. Turn right onto Franklin and follow it for a mile, past the La Brea Avenue intersection. Turn right onto Fuller Avenue, and park on the street (there's a 2-hour limit in most areas). The road dead-ends at the Runyon Canyon gate.

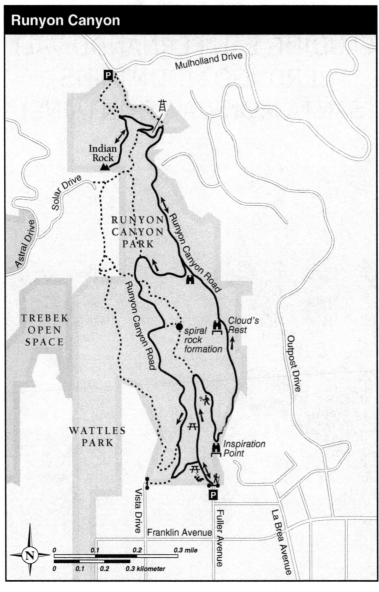

Runyon Canyon

Mulholland Drive

P

Indian Rock

Solar Drive

Astral Drive

RUNYON CANYON PARK

Runyon Canyon Road

TREBEK OPEN SPACE

spiral rock formation

Cloud's Rest

Runyon Canyon Road

Outpost Drive

WATTLES PARK

Inspiration Point

Vista Drive

Fuller Avenue

La Brea Avenue

Franklin Avenue

N

0   0.1   0.2   0.3 mile
0   0.1   0.2   0.3 kilometer

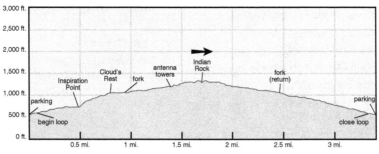

3,000 ft.
2,500 ft.
2,000 ft.
1,500 ft.
1,000 ft.
500 ft.
0 ft.

Inspiration Point
Cloud's Rest
fork
antenna towers
Indian Rock
fork (return)
parking
begin loop
parking
close loop

0.5 mi.   1 mi.   1.5 mi.   2 mi.   2.5 mi.   3 mi.

WEST

(INCLUDING SAN FERNANDO VALLEY, VERDUGO MOUNTAINS, SANTA MONICA MOUNTAINS)

A hiker enjoying the walk along Fryman Canyon (see page 63)

West (including San Fernando Valley, Verdugo Mountains, Santa Monica Mountains)

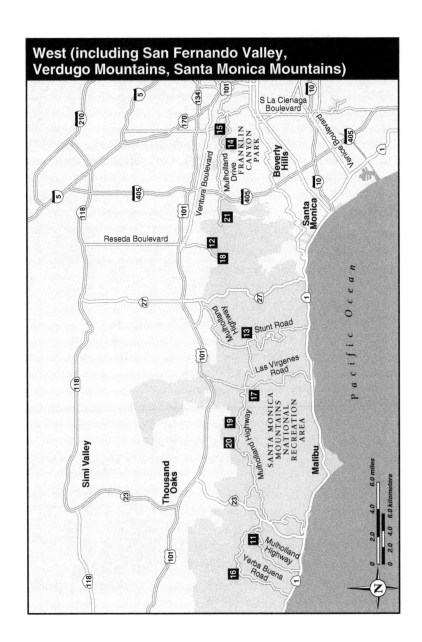

11 Arroyo Sequit Trail

In Brief

This low-profile trail off Mulholland Highway in the western Santa Monica Mountains crosses an open meadow and then weaves in and out of a gorge bursting with an impressive variety of wildflowers each spring.

Description

Arroyo Sequit, which means "dry riverbed," is a former ranch that was taken over by the Santa Monica Conservancy in the mid-1980s. Besides its role as a hiking destination, it is also used by Santa Monica College as an astronomical observation area. Naturalists estimate that the 155-acre park is home to more than 50 species of wildflowers, including Indian warrior, scarlet pitcher sage, monkeyflower, deerweed, owl's clover, bush sunflowers, and morning glory. It is best visited in the spring, when the wildflowers and views of chaparral-covered mountains dominate the trail. During other times of the year, the scenery can be a bit brown and uninspiring. Even in the spring, this path is uncrowded. My husband, sons, and I hiked this on a Saturday afternoon during the peak spring wildflower season, and we had the entire place to ourselves.

To get to the trailhead, follow the paved road about 0.2 mile to a small house. Follow the signs for the nature trail, which winds around to the left past another small house, an outhouse, and a cluster of benches used by astronomy students at Santa Monica College. We spotted what appeared to be corn and wild artichoke plants growing along this part of the trail.

The paved road ends just past the observation benches, and the trail turns to dirt and grass and passes a few large coast live oak trees and picnic tables before crossing an open meadow and giving way to nice views of Boney Mountain to the northwest. Exposure is high on this part of the trail, so be liberal with the sunscreen. After peaking at about 1,300 feet, the trail descends into the canyon via long switchbacks and has a few patches of shade. After nearly a mile, you will come to the first (and easiest) stream crossing. Look for a seasonal waterfall on the left as you cross.

At 0.7 mile, look to your right and you will see three large white satellite dishes jutting from otherwise green hills. Continue downhill and, at about the 1-mile marker, you will reach another stream crossing, this one much steeper and more difficult than the first. The heavy rains in winter 2005 apparently washed out large chunks of the stream banks and left them steep and high. It's passable, but it does require some scrambling and stone-hopping. Wear appropriate footwear and keep in mind that the hike might not be as kid-friendly as it once was.

The situation is similar at the next stream crossing, just a few hundred yards away. After the fourth stream crossing, the path begins to climb again, and you will come to a T.

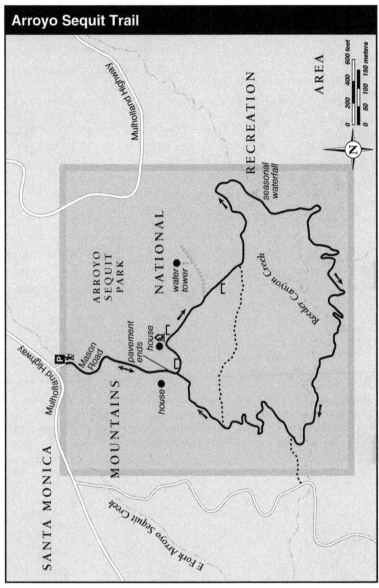

Arroyo Sequit Trail

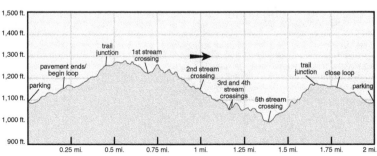

DISTANCE & CONFIGURATION: 2-mile balloon	**MAPS:** USGS *Triunfo Pass;* at kiosk near trailhead and **nps.gov/samo/planyour visit/upload/ArroyoSequit.pdf**
DIFFICULTY: Easy	
SCENERY: Wildflowers, chaparral, open meadow	**WHEELCHAIR ACCESSIBLE:** No
	FACILITIES: None
EXPOSURE: Sunny	**CONTACT:** 805-370-2300; **nps.gov/samo /planyourvisit/arroyosequit.htm**
TRAFFIC: Light	
TRAIL SURFACE: Dirt	**COMMENTS:** This rarely crowded trail is great for kids and dogs. If you hike it following rainy weather, expect to get your feet wet and muddy at the stream crossings.
HIKING TIME: 1 hour	
ACCESS: Daily, 8 a.m.–sunset; free	

Take the right path uphill, and follow the wall of the gorge back to the open meadow and picnic area. This is a good place to stop and rest or have a snack under one of the oak trees. From here, you can retrace your steps past the private homes and back to the parking area.

GPS TRAILHEAD COORDINATES
N34° 5.324' W118° 53.438'

From US 101, take the exit for CA 23/Westlake Boulevard south, and follow it south about 7 miles until it runs into Mulholland Highway. Turn right onto Mulholland, and follow it 2 winding miles to the park entrance on the right. The small sign and gate are easy to miss. The address is 34138 Mulholland Hwy., Malibu.

12 Caballero Canyon Trail

In Brief

There's not much in terms of scenery along this trail near one of L.A.'s busiest freeways, but its steady almost 600-foot elevation gain via switchbacks provides a good workout. It is also a popular link to Dirt Mulholland, a wide, no-cars path that leads to several major hiking destinations in the Santa Monica Mountains.

Don't be put off by the gated communities that line Reseda Boulevard near the trailhead. This path quickly disappears into chaparral and sage scrub and makes you feel like you're a world away from suburban sprawl.

Description

The Caballero Canyon Trail was around long before the nearby gated residential developments and landscaped Marvin Braude Mulholland Gateway Park showed up. It's a favorite Sierra Club hike in part because it leads to Dirt Mulholland, the 7-mile unpaved stretch of Mulholland Drive between Encino and Woodland Hills. From here, hikers can access the Santa Monica Mountains Backbone Trail, Temescal Canyon, and other trails leading all the way to the Pacific Ocean. Today, more hikers seem to use the shiny new gateway park (it opened in 2000) to connect with other mountain trails, but Caballero Canyon still attracts its share of hikers, mountain bikers, and others who don't want to pay the parking fee at Marvin Braude Mulholland Gateway Park.

Look for the trailhead on the east side of Reseda Boulevard just north of the entrance to Braemar Country Club. The dirt-and-gravel trail begins a gradual descent past a dusty trail kiosk that hasn't been updated in ages. I encountered more mountain bikers than hikers on this trail on a Saturday afternoon. Most of them were headed north on the trail toward Reseda Boulevard.

A couple of unmarked narrow trails veer off the main path near the beginning of this hike. Stick to the main trail as it ascends to the south.

At about 0.75 mile, you will come to a turnoff for an unmarked narrow trail on the left. This leads to a seasonal streambed, though you won't be able to see it or hear it well from the canyon trail. You want to continue straight in tandem with Reseda Boulevard. Most of the path is flanked by tall grass, a scattering of sycamore trees, and coastal sage shrub, with the crest of the Santa Monica Mountains in full view most of the time. In the spring and summer, you can also spot clumps of California dodder, a leafless parasitic weed with orange buds that resembles spun sugar.

The path makes a sharp left at the 1-mile marker, heading east toward the hills before climbing south again. There is little shade along most of the path, so bring plenty of sunscreen and insect repellent. The path continues to climb past a bench and water fountain, then reaches a fire-road gate. If you look behind you at this point, you will get nice views of the San Fernando Valley on a clear day. Walk 50 more yards uphill and you will reach

DISTANCE & CONFIGURATION: 3.1-mile out-and-back	**ACCESS:** Gates: Daily, sunrise–sunset; free
DIFFICULTY: Moderate	**MAPS:** USGS *Canoga Park*
SCENERY: Chaparral, coastal sage scrub	**WHEELCHAIR ACCESSIBLE:** No
EXPOSURE: Sunny	**FACILITIES:** None at trailhead; public restrooms available a mile up Reseda Boulevard at Marvin Braude Mulholland Gateway Park
TRAFFIC: Light	
TRAIL SURFACE: Dirt and gravel path	**CONTACT:** 805-370-2300; **nps.gov/samo**
HIKING TIME: 1 hour	**/planyourvisit/marvinbraude.htm**

Dirt Mulholland and signs for other Santa Monica Mountains paths, including Topanga State Park, Temescal Ridge, and Westward Ridge, which leads to a former missile observation post that was folded into the Santa Monica Mountains Recreation Area in 1996 and turned into a park. From here, you can retrace your steps back to the parking lot or turn right and follow Dirt Mulholland west toward Marvin Braude Mulholland Gateway Park, which empties you back on Reseda Boulevard. The downside to this loop route is that the last mile requires you to walk past the aforementioned residential developments. It's a bit jarring after the wilderness feel of Caballero Canyon, which is why I prefer to take the out-and-back option and return via the canyon.

GPS TRAILHEAD COORDINATES
N34° 8.562' W118° 32.452'

From the Ventura Freeway (US 101), take the Reseda Boulevard exit, and head south about 2 miles. Park on Reseda across from Braemar Country Club, and look for the trailhead on the left side of the road.

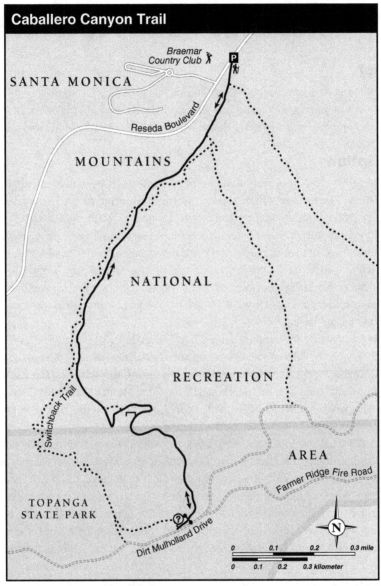

Caballero Canyon Trail

SANTA MONICA

Braemar
Country Club

Reseda Boulevard

MOUNTAINS

NATIONAL

RECREATION

Switchback Trail

AREA

Farmer Ridge Fire Road

TOPANGA
STATE PARK

Dirt Mulholland Drive

N

| 0 | 0.1 | 0.2 | 0.3 mile |

| 0 | 0.1 | 0.2 | 0.3 kilometer |

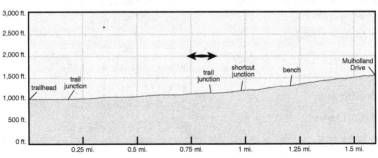

13 Calabasas Peak Motorway

In Brief

Serene hills and dramatic sandstone rock formations dominate the scenery of this uphill Santa Monica Mountains trail, which has an elevation gain of nearly 1,000 feet. During the hot summer months, hike this trail in the early evening and enjoy the sunset and cooler air.

Description

From the parking lot, cross Stunt Road to the white gate and begin walking uphill along the fire road. There is very little shade on this trail, so bring plenty of sunscreen and water. The path continues on a gradual ascent, giving way to splendid vistas of hillsides covered by rocky outcrops and toyon, laurel sumac, sagebrush, buckwheat, and ceanothus shrubs. In no time at all, you'll feel worlds away from the city bustle. This is also a good place to spot Santa Susana tarweed, a native, hard-to-find plant with yellow, bell-shaped flowers that blooms between June and August and tends to grow amid the area's sandstone rock formations. Other wildflowers found here are cliff aster, sunflowers, clarkia, and golden bush.

This trail is fairly well known among L.A. hikers, but I've never seen more than a handful of people here. Mountain bikers and horseback riders also use the trail on a regular basis. At about 0.8 mile, you'll come to a right turnoff for Red Rock Canyon Park, a former Boy Scout camp that was purchased by the Santa Monica Mountains Conservancy in 1986. The park has water fountains, a picnic area, and a pit toilet; it can also be accessed by car from Topanga Canyon Boulevard.

To reach Calabasas Peak, take the left fork on the fire road and continue on the uphill climb. The dramatic rock formations you see on the right are the result of centuries of wind and water erosion. They lend an otherworldly element to the hike, making the trail seem much farther from the suburban sprawl and traffic-choked highways than it actually is. The trail continues to steepen as it makes a switchback to the right and approaches the peak.

The trail gives way somewhat abruptly to sweeping views of the San Fernando Valley, Santa Monica Mountains, and Pacific Ocean. You can rest here and call it a day, or get

---

DISTANCE & CONFIGURATION:
3.8-mile out-and-back

DIFFICULTY: Difficult

SCENERY: Chaparral- and boulder-covered hills, suburban landscape

EXPOSURE: Sunny

TRAFFIC: Moderate

TRAIL SURFACE: Dirt fire road

HIKING TIME: 1.5 hours

ACCESS: 24/7; free

MAPS: USGS *Malibu Beach*

WHEELCHAIR ACCESSIBLE: No

FACILITIES: Water fountains, picnic area, pit toilet at Red Rock Canyon Park on trail

CONTACT: 310-589-3200; lamountains.com/parks.asp?parkid=47

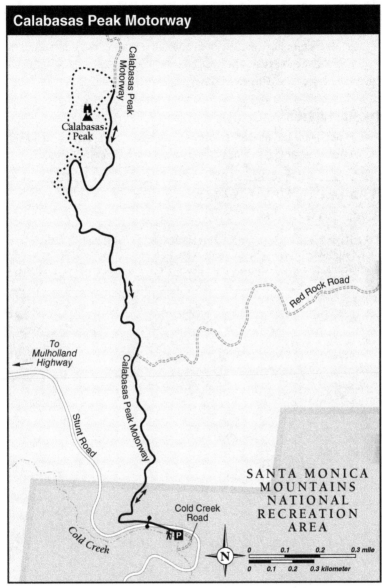

Calabasas Peak Motorway

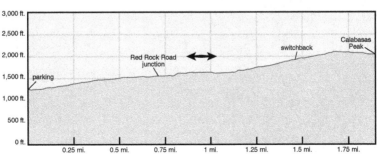

extra credit by following a left narrow trail uphill to an elevation of 2,100 feet and even better vistas. The fire road continues northeast toward Old Topanga Canyon Road from here, but most hikers turn back at this point. You can retrace your steps back to the Stunt Road lot, or if you'd like to extend the hike, consider turning off at the Red Rock Canyon path on the way back down. This tacks about 3 miles onto the hike.

Nearby Activities

If you want a cool drink and festive atmosphere after your hike, La Paz, at 4505 Las Virgenes Rd. in Calabasas, stocks 50 kinds of tequila and specializes in Yucatán cuisine.

GPS TRAILHEAD COORDINATES

N34° 5.738' W118° 38.986'

From US 101, exit at CA 27/Topanga Canyon Boulevard, and head south 1.4 miles to Mulholland Highway. Turn right and follow Mulholland 5.3 miles to Stunt Road. Make a left onto Stunt, and drive about 1 mile to a pullout parking area on the right.

14 Franklin Canyon:
RANCH AND HASTAIN TRAILS

In Brief

Beginning at a bucolic 3-acre reservoir and duck pond, this well-graded path winds through patches of oak forest before a gradual ascent leads to scenic views of Santa Monica and the Pacific Ocean. You will see pockets of development along the way, but heavy woodland and chaparral-covered slopes make this hike seem deeper in the wilderness than it actually is.

Description

Looking for a way to distribute water brought from the Owens Valley to Southern California, William Mulholland and the Department of Water and Power created a reservoir and power system in Franklin Canyon in the early 1900s. Luckily for today's hikers, this move helped prevent further development of the canyon, which today is surrounded by the densely populated neighborhoods of Coldwater Canyon and Beverly Hills. The family of oil baron Edward L. Doheny used the south end of the canyon for a retreat in the 1930s. After several attempts were made to turn the property into private housing developments, the Santa Monica Mountains Conservancy purchased it and turned over ownership to the National Park Service in 1981. Its 605 acres include an upper and lower reservoir, a nature center, an outdoor amphitheater, and the original Spanish-style home built by Doheny in 1935.

When I started hiking this trail, a padlocked chain-link fence midway up the mountain blocked access to the top and forced an abrupt turnaround. Plans for a private development had been in the works, but permit issues and protests held it up, and the trail is now open and leads to a clearing with expansive views of the San Fernando Valley, the Los Angeles Basin, and the Pacific Ocean.

From the parking lot of the Sooky Goldman Nature Center, walk south on Franklin Canyon Drive. The Upper Franklin Reservoir is on your left, though it is shrouded by thick forest. To your right is Heavenly Pond, a hidden pond with a few benches and an abundance of big-bellied frogs and ring-necked ducks. Follow the paved road to the left across the dam. Here's where you can get a good look at the reservoir, which resembles a tranquil lake and has been the site of many film and TV shoots, including *Combat!* and the opening fishing sequence of *The Andy Griffith Show*. TV shows such as *Matlock* and *Quantum Leap* and such films as *Dr. Dolittle 2* and *Nightmare on Elm Street* have also been shot here. (A complete list is available at the park's nature center.)

At the end of the dam, you can either continue on Franklin Canyon Drive or head up a narrow dirt path called Ranch Trail. The latter path is more serene, passing through patches of thick brush, poison oak, and sycamore trees (in contrast, you'll probably

DISTANCE & CONFIGURATION: 4.9-mile out-and-back	ACCESS: Daily, 7 a.m.–sunset; free
DIFFICULTY: Moderate	MAPS: USGS *Beverly Hills;* at Sooky Goldman Nature Center near the Coldwater Canyon entrance, kiosks along the trails, and **lamountains.com/maps/franklinCanyon.pdf**
SCENERY: Water views, wild chaparral, birds	
EXPOSURE: Filtered shade and full sun	WHEELCHAIR ACCESSIBLE: First mile
TRAFFIC: Moderate	FACILITIES: Public restrooms at nature center and Franklin Canyon Ranch
TRAIL SURFACE: Paved road and packed dirt	CONTACT: 310-858-7272; **lamountains.com/parks.asp?parkid=14**
HIKING TIME: 2.5 hours	

encounter some cars and bicycles along Franklin Canyon Drive). After about 0.5 mile, the dirt path starts to descend back to the paved road.

At this point, you'll reach a fork in the road where Franklin Canyon meets Lake Drive. The white stone structure in front of you is known as the apple press building, though the Doheny family allegedly used it as a horse stable. Follow Lake Drive to the left for about 0.5 mile until you reach a trail kiosk and a small gravel parking lot. Turn left and follow the sign for Hastain Trail. The wide dirt path rises steadily up a chaparral-covered slope, with huge clusters of cactus and a handful of expensive homes lining the hills to your right. Here's where you'll want to make sure you have plenty of water and sunscreen, because there is little shade.

Despite the proximity to busy Coldwater Canyon Drive, wildlife is common throughout the park. Recent sightings by Park Service rangers include red-tailed hawks, bobcats, coyotes, and plenty of gray squirrels. Continue up the dirt path 0.25 mile to a level area where you can take in the cityscape views of west Los Angeles. On a clear day, you will be able to see the Pacific Ocean from Santa Monica down to Palos Verdes Peninsula. From here, the path continues to climb another 0.25 mile past an open gate (once padlocked, due to plans to build private homes along the ridge). Continue another 0.7 mile to a clearing with terrific city-to-ocean views. A trail off to the left heads toward a residential neighborhood, but a gate blocks vehicle access and construction debris blocks pedestrian access.

From the clearing, retrace your steps back to the upper reservoir and parking lot.

Nearby Activities

Sooky Goldman Nature Center is a wonderful place to check out before or after your hike. Kids will love the interactive nature displays, and hikers can pick up trail maps, refill water bottles, and use the clean and modern restrooms. The center also regularly hosts free docent-led hikes for all ages. Themes include Nature Rambles, Franklin Canyon and the Movies, and Morning Birds. Call 310-858-7272, ext. 131, for hours and an updated schedule.

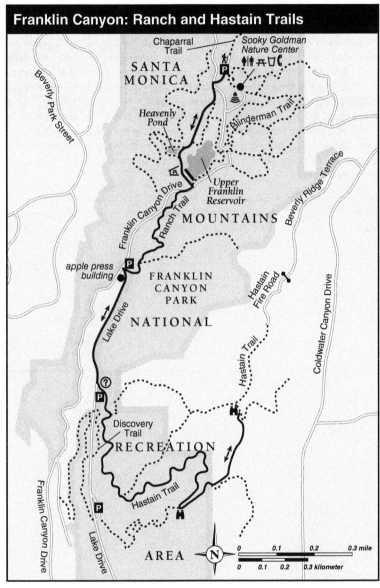

Franklin Canyon: Ranch and Hastain Trails

Chaparral Trail

Sooky Goldman Nature Center

SANTA MONICA

Heavenly Pond

Blinderman Trail

Franklin Canyon Drive

Ranch Trail

Upper Franklin Reservoir

MOUNTAINS

Beverly Park Street

Beverly Ridge Terrace

apple press building

FRANKLIN CANYON PARK

Hastain Fire Road

Coldwater Canyon Drive

Lake Drive

NATIONAL

Hastain Trail

Discovery Trail

RECREATION

Franklin Canyon Drive

Hastain Trail

Lake Drive

AREA   N

| 0 | 0.1 | 0.2 | 0.3 mile |
| 0 | 0.1 | 0.2 | 0.3 kilometer |

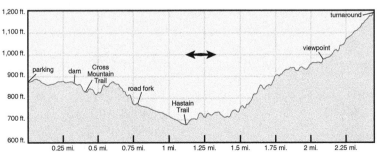

1,200 ft.   turnaround

1,100 ft.

1,000 ft.   viewpoint

900 ft.   parking   dam   Cross Mountain Trail

800 ft.   road fork

700 ft.   Hastain Trail

600 ft.
0.25 mi. 0.5 mi. 0.75 mi. 1 mi. 1.25 mi. 1.5 mi. 1.75 mi. 2 mi. 2.25 mi.

GPS TRAILHEAD COORDINATES   N34° 7.246' W118° 24.626'

From downtown L.A., take US 101 north to the exit for Coldwater Canyon Avenue, and follow it south 2.5 miles to Mulholland Drive. Turn right (west) onto Franklin Canyon Drive, and head straight on a narrow, twisting road past a sign that reads ROAD CLOSED 800 FEET (a small sign on the right reads FRANKLIN CANYON PARK). Soon you'll come to the entrance gate. Continue about 0.5 mile to a stop sign (be sure to make a full stop; ticketing is common). You can either park in the large lot on the left or continue to a smaller gravel parking lot on the left in front of Franklin Canyon Lake.

Be sure to make complete stops on the narrow roads leading into and through the park. Cameras are set up to catch cars rolling through the stop signs, and violators will be mailed a ticket.

Alternate directions: From Sunset Boulevard, follow Beverly Drive 0.3 mile north to Coldwater Canyon Drive. Veer right and continue about 1 mile to the intersection of Mulholland Drive. Turn left and head straight on Franklin Canyon Drive, and then continue as above.

15 Fryman Canyon Loop

In Brief

This moderate hike is a reliable, well-maintained exercise route that's easily accessible from Hollywood and the San Fernando Valley. It's also dog-friendly, with plenty of trash cans, plastic-bag dispensers, and water troughs. Most people take the loop that begins with an uphill climb under sycamore trees, gives way to valley views, and empties into a street of private homes and back to the parking lot.

Description

Look for the BETTY B. DEARING MOUNTAIN TRAIL sign to the right of the parking lot entrance. The trailhead begins here, and you'll probably see a jogger or two warming up by the gate and a few dogs getting their leashes strapped on by their owners. Fryman Canyon is part of the 128-acre Wilacre Park, which also includes Franklin and Coldwater Canyon Parks and is run by the Santa Monica Mountains Conservancy.

Follow the paved fire road as it curves upward past toyon (Christmas berry) bushes and sycamore trees. You'll see quite a mix of hikers, from serious runners to dog walkers and moms with kids, yet the path is wide enough that it never seems overcrowded. The traffic noise from Laurel Canyon Boulevard below you to the right can be heavy, but it will soon fade as you get farther into the canyon. Don't get too comfortable with the shade—the trail soon gives way to sky and the often-brutal valley sun. It continues to ascend somewhat sharply for about a mile, until it reaches a rusty barbed-wire fence on the left and the remains of a driveway that leads nowhere. At 0.3 mile, the path turns to packed dirt, and the ascent becomes more gradual and open. This path gets slick and muddy after it rains, but it usually dries up quickly.

Through the trees to the right, you'll see a scattering of hillside homes (some look more like villas) in the distance and the entire sprawling San Fernando Valley beyond that. At 0.6 mile, an inviting wooden bench appears on the right (courtesy of a Santa Monica Mountains Conservancy donor); it's a good place to rest, guzzle some water, and take in the valley views. From here, the dirt path curves sharply south and winds upward again. Rattlesnake warning signs dot this area, but I've never spotted one; occasional coyote sightings are also possible. At about 1.3 miles, you'll come to a wide clearing covered with loose wood chips. The path to the right leads to Coldwater Canyon Boulevard and the entrance to the headquarters of TreePeople, a nonprofit group that promotes energy and water conservation and holds summer concerts and other events in its outdoor amphitheater. It's worth a detour to check out the yurt offices, environmental exhibits, and reflection garden that make up the TreePeople complex. For more information, visit **treepeople.org.**

To the left are a couple of benches, water fountains for dogs and people, and more views of shrouded hills and the valley. Continue straight (south) on the path until you

DISTANCE & CONFIGURATION: 2.6-mile loop	ACCESS: Daily, 8 a.m.–sunset; parking lot fee; free street parking, but be aware of the no-parking zones
DIFFICULTY: Moderate	
SCENERY: Native plants and trees, hill and valley views	MAPS: USGS *Van Nuys;* **lamountains.com /maps/wilacre.pdf**
EXPOSURE: Mostly sun, some shade	WHEELCHAIR ACCESSIBLE: No
TRAFFIC: Heavy, especially on weekends	FACILITIES: Public restrooms at parking lot
TRAIL SURFACE: Paved road and packed dirt	
HIKING TIME: 1.5 hours	CONTACT: 818-766-8445; **lamountains.com/parks.asp?parkid=66**

reach a dirt path on the right with a wooden guardrail. Follow it upward for a quick detour to check out a small display (courtesy of TreePeople) of native rock formations and the trees of Fryman Canyon, including valley oaks, the only deciduous oak in the Santa Monica Mountains, and black walnut trees.

Back on the dirt path, continue south about 0.25 mile until you reach a yellow gate that marks the perimeter of the state-owned park. You can either turn back here and retrace your steps to the parking lot or continue straight down Iredell Lane, a low-traffic street that will instantly let you know you're back in Los Angeles proper, with its security gates, buzz of Weedwackers, and Mercedes-filled driveways. The road empties into Fryman Road and takes you back to the trailhead.

Nearby Activities

TreePeople, a conservation group whose headquarters are located directly across Cold-water Canyon Boulevard from the eastern end of Franklin Canyon Drive, regularly holds tree-care workshops and full-moon hikes. During the summer, the group hosts concerts, plays, children's shows, and staged readings at its outdoor amphitheater. For more information, visit **treepeople.org.**

GPS TRAILHEAD COORDINATES
N34° 7.996' W118° 23.509'

From US 101, take Laurel Canyon Boulevard south about 1.5 miles to Fryman Road. Turn right onto Fryman, and make an immediate right into a gravel parking lot. There is also free street parking along Fryman Road.

Alternate directions: From Hollywood, head north on Laurel Canyon Boulevard until you reach Fryman Road. Turn left at the light and right into the parking lot.

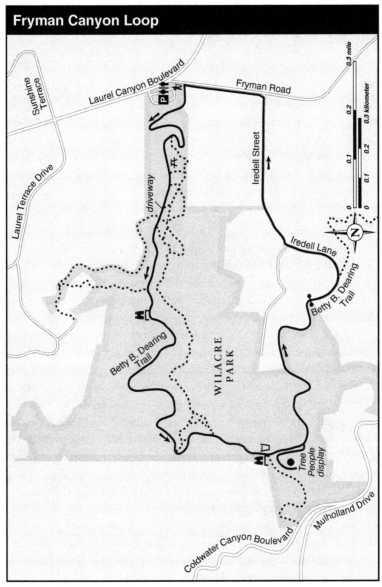

Fryman Canyon Loop

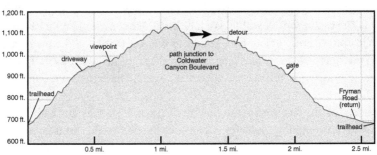

16 Grotto Trail

In Brief

Located on the grounds of a former Boy Scout camp about 5 miles north of Pacific Coast Highway, this trail offers a nice sampling of the scenery that characterizes Santa Monica Mountains hiking: open fields, shady streambed, live oak forest, and volcanic-rock walls. It ends at a cool and somewhat gloomy grotto where you can splash around before making the arduous uphill trek back to the car. A difficult scramble over boulders for the last 200 yards puts this hike in the strenuous category.

Description

The Circle X Ranch was a working ranch until 1948, when a service organization called Circle X bought the property and donated it to the Boy Scouts for a wilderness retreat. Tucked away in one of the more remote areas of the western Santa Monica Mountains, it is home to Sandstone Peak, the highest point in the mountain range at 3,100 feet, and a rare Mediterranean ecosystem that includes coastal sage scrub and red shank chaparral, a treelike shrub with reddish-brown bark, threadlike leaves, and small bunches of seasonal white flowers. From the 101, it's a teeth-clenching drive along a mountain ridge off Mulholland Drive to the ranch, but that's part of the adventure and prepares you for the interesting hike to come. It's tough not to be impressed by the views of the Conejo and San Fernando Valleys, especially if you're a passenger in the car and do not have to concentrate on the hairpin turns. Other trails that can be accessed from Circle X are Sandstone Peak, which leads to the highest peak in the Santa Monica Mountains, and Canyon View, an easy 2-mile hike that spurs off the Grotto Trail. Also nearby but not accessible from the main parking lot is the Mishe Mokwa Trail, a challenging 6-mile loop known for its dramatic cliffs, rock formations, and valley and ocean views. The trailhead for that is next to a dirt pullout about a mile north of the main entrance.

The original Circle X Ranch is now a ranger office. It is located at the upper parking lot and is a good place to stop for maps and information on the history of the property. Old photos from the ranch's heyday decorate the walls. A shaded bench, water fountain, and unisex bathroom are just outside the office.

From the parking lot, take the paved road south toward the picnic area and Grotto Trailhead. The road winds downhill past another office complex and a basketball court to the shady picnic area. The Grotto Trailhead is at the far end of the picnic area. You can also leave your car here, but keep in mind that the small lot fills up quickly with picnickers on weekends. If there are no spaces, you will have to turn around and drive back to the upper lot.

After leaving the picnic area, the trail turns into a singletrack dirt path and reaches the turnoff for Canyon View Trail after 0.4 mile. Continue straight and cross a dry streambed, and then follow the trail uphill briefly before it levels and winds through a

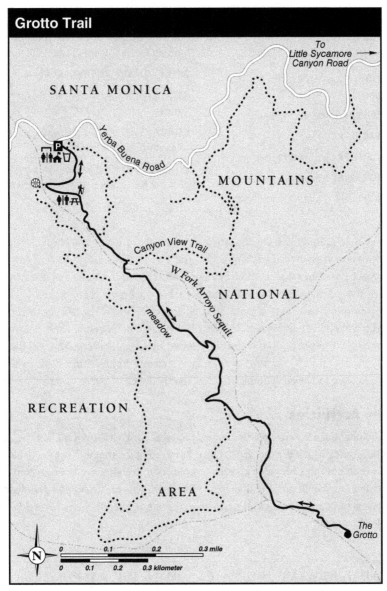

Grotto Trail

SANTA MONICA

MOUNTAINS

To
Little Sycamore
Canyon Road

Yerba Buena Road

Canyon View Trail

W Fork Arroyo Sequit

NATIONAL

meadow

RECREATION

AREA

The
Grotto

N

| 0 | 0.1 | 0.2 | 0.3 mile |
| 0 | 0.1 | 0.2 | 0.3 kilometer |

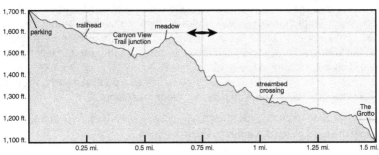

DISTANCE & CONFIGURATION: 3-mile out-and-back	MAPS: USGS *Triunfo Pass;* at ranger station and **nps.gov/samo/planyourvisit /upload/CircleX_1_fin-2.pdf**
DIFFICULTY: Moderate	
SCENERY: Boney Mountain, oak forest, grassland	WHEELCHAIR ACCESSIBLE: No
EXPOSURE: Sun and shade	FACILITIES: Restrooms, water, picnic tables
TRAFFIC: Moderate	CONTACT: 805-370-2300; **nps.gov/samo /planyourvisit/circlexranch.htm**
TRAIL SURFACE: Dirt fire road	
HIKING TIME: 1.5 hours	COMMENTS: No bikes are allowed past the picnic area, and dogs must be leashed.
ACCESS: Daily, 8 a.m.–sunset; free	

wide-open field. Behind you are distant views of the rugged cliffs and pinnacles of Boney Mountain. Soon after crossing the meadow, the trail begins a steep descent toward the bottom of the gorge and shady oak forest. Turn left at the stream and head downstream to a pond. At this point, it seems as if the trail ends, but the best is yet to come.

Keep in mind that dogs are not allowed from this point on. To get to the upper grotto, you will scale a narrow rock ledge and a few large boulders for about 0.2 mile, and then climb down to the pool of water surrounded by a small cavern. You will likely find other hikers cooling off, aware that they face a steady uphill climb back to the park entrance. Be sure to conserve some water for the trek back.

Nearby Activities

A new National Park Service visitor center opened at King Gillette Ranch in the heart of the Santa Monica Mountains in 2012. Once home to razor mogul King C. Gillette, the solar-powered complex includes a 1920s-era mansion designed by Wallace Neff and an information center with maps and history of the area, plus meadows and grasslands that draw birders and naturalists. It's also known as the site where TV's *The Biggest Loser* was filmed. Parking is $7.

GPS TRAILHEAD COORDINATES   N34° 6.518' W118° 56.213'

From US 101, take the CA 23/Westlake Boulevard exit, and head south 7.2 miles until it merges with Mulholland Highway. Make a slight right onto Mulholland, and in 0.4 mile, turn right onto Little Sycamore Canyon Road (it will become Yerba Buena Road at the Ventura County line), and follow it about 5.6 miles to Circle X Ranch. The entrance is on the left side of the road.

The drive is a bit of a roller-coaster ride full of sharp curves and hairpin turns. Allow for extra drive time and watch out for mountain bikers.

Alternate directions: Take CA 1/Pacific Coast Highway to Yerba Buena Road. Turn right and follow the road about 5.5 miles to Circle X Ranch.

17 Malibu Creek State Park:
M*A*S*H TRAIL

In Brief

This no-dogs-allowed trail starts off flat and easy as it passes through shady valleys of live oaks and wildflowers, then turns rugged with boulders and brush before arriving at the now-desolate site of the old *M*A*S*H* TV series. Worthwhile detours include a rock pool and climbing wall and a man-made lake that fans of the 4077th might also recognize.

Description

The 20th Century Fox studio purchased this 4,000-acre property from a group of home-owners in the late 1940s. Besides *M*A*S*H*, movies and TV shows filmed here include *Butch Cassidy and the Sundance Kid, Dr. Dolittle,* and *Fantasy Island,* though few remnants of the sets remain. Fox sold the property to the state of California in 1974, and it opened to the public in 1976.

The M*A*S*H Trail begins at the bottom of a flight of steps in front of the restrooms at the southwestern corner of the parking lot. Follow it down across a small bridge, past signs marked BACKCOUNTRY TRAILS and NO DOGS ALLOWED. After about 0.3 mile, you'll see another bridge in front of you (during rainy season, it's usually flooded and impassable). This leads to the Rock Pool, a swimmable stretch of water framed by volcanic cliffs that has served as a backdrop for *The Swiss Family Robinson,* the Tarzan movies, *Planet of the Apes,* and many other films.

To get to the *M*A*S*H* site, continue straight on the fire road past an open grassy area dotted with newly planted trees. On weekends, this area is usually swarming with families who have come to the park to picnic, ride bikes, and splash around in the creek. This trail is often billed as an easy walk because it's mostly flat, but it's not for kids. The latter half of the hike isn't well marked and requires quite a bit of scrambling around boulders and heavy brush, especially in the winter when the creek floods parts of the trail. I recommend bringing lots of water and a walking stick. Also, despite the proximity to the Pacific Ocean, this area gets very hot in the summer; bring plenty of sunscreen and insect repellent.

After you pass a left turnoff for the visitor center and campground at 0.9 mile, it gets a little more tranquil. Live oaks shade the road, and a few picnic tables are tucked discreetly out of the way. The path will begin to narrow and climb gradually upward past pleasant views of hills covered with boulders and chaparral. As you continue to climb, you'll pass a turnoff on the left that leads to a building foundation, perhaps one of the original adobe homes that sat on the property before it was sold to Fox. Soon you'll also pass turnoffs for Lookout Trail (to the right), which leads uphill to a ridge overlooking the valley, and Century Lake (to the left). The lake—a bucolic marshland setting that is home to ducks, coots, herons, and redwing blackbirds—is worth a detour if you have

DISTANCE & CONFIGURATION: 5-mile out-and-back	**MAPS:** USGS *Malibu Beach;* **malibucreek statepark.org/MASH.html**
DIFFICULTY: Moderate	**WHEELCHAIR ACCESSIBLE:** No
SCENERY: Oak forest, creek, abandoned TV show sets	**FACILITIES:** Restrooms, water, picnic areas, campsites, visitor center open weekends only
EXPOSURE: Sun and shade	
TRAFFIC: Moderate	**CONTACT:** 818-880-0367; **malibucreek statepark.org**
TRAIL SURFACE: Dirt path, dry creek bed	
HIKING TIME: 2.5 hours	**COMMENTS:** Weekends draw lots of families with small children to this area.
ACCESS: Daily, 7 a.m.–sunset; $12 per car day-use fee	

time, but keep in mind that it's another 2 miles to the *M*A*S*H* site. Stay on Crags Road as it follows Malibu Creek on your left. At about 2.5 miles, you'll come to a bridge; bear right after crossing it, and follow a dry streambed. Again, in winter, this area can flood, so you might have to turn right before you cross the bridge and hike through brush and debris to get back on the trail. You might start to feel like you're lost and in the middle of nowhere, but it probably won't last long. Just keep following Crags Road and the dry creek bed for another 0.5 mile until you reach the *M*A*S*H* site. Chances are that you'll run into other hikers at the site because it can also be accessed from Kanan Road on the western end of the park. You'll also know you've made it when you come to two rusted-out vehicles—a jeep and an ambulance once used as props on the show—and a lone picnic table. Nearby a small hill leads to a clearing that served as a helicopter landing pad. This is all that's left of the outdoor set of one of TV's most popular shows.

From here, you can continue following the Crags Road to Reagan Ranch and Malibu Lake, or retrace your steps back to the main parking lot.

Nearby Activities

Take time to stop at the park visitor center, about a mile's walk from the main parking lot via the lower or higher roads and open only on weekends. Besides maps and restrooms, it has black-and-white photos of Hot Lips, Hawkeye, Radar, and the rest of the *M*A*S*H* cast, plus native plant and wildlife exhibits.

GPS TRAILHEAD COORDINATES

N34° 5.789' W118° 43.034'

From the Ventura Freeway (US 101), exit at Las Virgenes Road, and head south 4 miles to Malibu Creek State Park. The entrance is on your right. Follow the entrance road to the far western corner of the lot, near the restrooms.

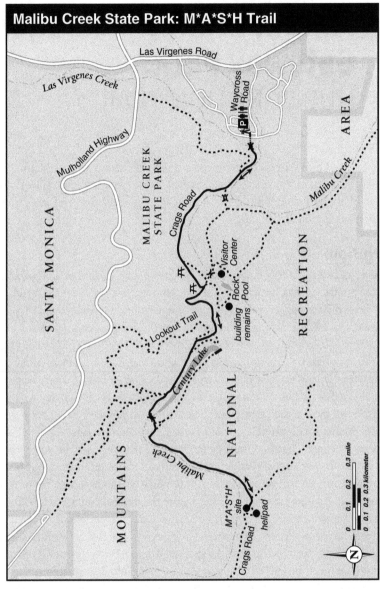

Malibu Creek State Park: M*A*S*H Trail

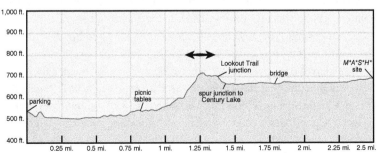

18 Marvin Braude Mulholland Gateway Park:
HUB JUNCTION TRAIL

In Brief

This popular trail offers an excellent introduction to the Santa Monica Mountains trail system. After a steep ascent, it eases to a gradual incline on a well-maintained dirt path flanked by chaparral and seasonal wildflowers. It also connects to several other trails with varying degrees of difficulty.

Description

Named after a Los Angeles city councilman who championed the preservation of the Santa Monica Mountains, Marvin Braude Mulholland Gateway Park opened in 2000 and encompasses 17 acres of once-rugged land above the unpaved portion of Mulholland Drive known as Dirt Mulholland. Environmental groups protested that the landscaped park and its irrigation system would have a negative effect on the hillsides of nearby Caballero Canyon. Despite the opposition, the park opened as a slightly scaled-down version of the original plan. Local families and exercise hounds pack the place on weekends. Don't be put off by the upscale gated communities you see on the way up Reseda Boulevard to the park. Once you pass through the fire-road gate, you will feel as though you're a world away from urban sprawl. The farther south you walk, the more serene and natural it gets.

To get to the main trailhead, walk up the fire road that begins at the north end of the parking lot. To the left are two pathways that lead to a short landscaped loop with rock benches and mountain and valley views. This is a nice spot to have a picnic or rest after your hike. There is also a grassy hillside just before the trailhead on the left, with a bench and plenty of room for sprawling.

Walk up the wide, dirt fire road about 0.2 mile until you reach a Y and a sign marking the entrance to Topanga State Park, an 11,000-acre park known for its 36 miles of hiking trails, views of the Pacific Ocean, and variety of geologic formations.

To the left is Dirt Mulholland and turnoffs for Caballero Canyon and Encino Hills Drive. Follow Dirt Mulholland west toward Temescal Fire Road 30 and Topanga Canyon Boulevard. After 0.3 mile, you will come to another Y. Take the left path south, following the brown sign for Temescal Ridge Road and Hub Junction. From here, it's a gentle uphill 2-mile hike past open grassland, chaparral slopes, and coast live oaks to Hub Junction, a four-way junction that links up with the Backbone Trail, Will Rogers State Historic Park, and Eagle Spring, a loop trail known for its series of boulder outcrops. Hub Junction also has good views of a cluster of red sandstone rocks known as the Sespe

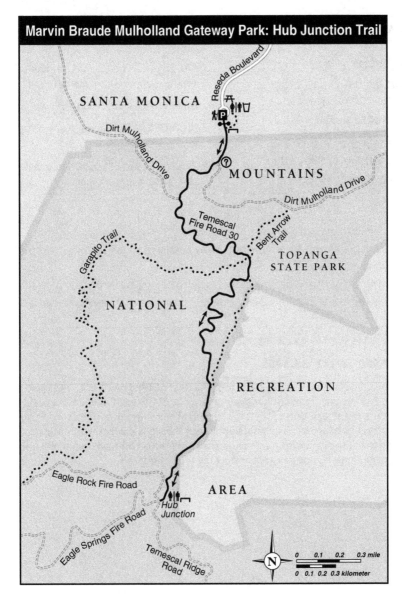

Marvin Braude Mulholland Gateway Park: Hub Junction Trail

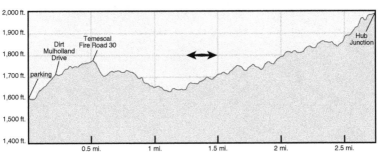

DISTANCE & CONFIGURATION: 5.5-mile out-and-back	ACCESS: Daily, sunrise–sunset; $5 fee at self-pay station or street parking
DIFFICULTY: Moderate	MAPS: USGS *Canoga Park;* **lamountains .com/maps/marvinBraude.pdf**
SCENERY: Chaparral-covered hills, San Fernando Valley views	
EXPOSURE: Sunny	WHEELCHAIR ACCESSIBLE: No
TRAFFIC: Moderate–heavy	FACILITIES: Restrooms, water, picnic area
TRAIL SURFACE: Packed dirt	CONTACT: 310-589-3200; **lamountains .com/parks.asp?parkid=34**
HIKING TIME: 2.25 hours	

Formation, a nonmarine layer of rock that accumulated as the sea filled with sediment about 50 million years ago.

From here, you can retrace your steps back to the parking lot or extend the hike a few more miles and head deeper into the mountains on any of the aforementioned trails.

GPS TRAILHEAD COORDINATES

N34° 7.908' W118° 33.191'

From the Ventura Freeway (US 101), take the Reseda Boulevard exit, and head south about 3.4 miles past residential developments until the road ends at the park. Parking is along the street. Don't forget to check in at the self-pay parking station, or park on the street outside the gate before you reach the signs marked FEE PARKING.

Heed the stop signs within this park; they are photo-enforced, and many unhappy hikers complain of getting tickets in the mail after their visit.

19 Paramount Ranch:
HACIENDA TRAIL TO BACKDROP TRAIL

In Brief

Ideal for families and fans of Hollywood Westerns, this sun-scorched trail meanders through grassy meadows to the former site of TV's *Dr. Quinn, Medicine Woman* and other movies and TV shows with Western themes. Its links to other unmarked trails within the ranch property encourage wandering, but the relatively small size of the property (400 acres) and the visibility of major roads from the paths make it tough to get lost.

Towering over the area from the south is Sugarloaf Peak, the highest point in the Santa Monica Mountains at 1,515 feet.

Description

In 1927 Paramount Pictures bought rural property in the Santa Monica Mountains and for 20 years used it as a setting for dozens of Westerns, including *The Virginian, Wells Fargo,* and *Gunsmoke.* The ranch has also been the setting for Western-themed TV shows such as *The Cisco Kid* and *Bat Masterson.* It was used as a racetrack in the 1950s before the National Park Service bought part of the property in 1980 and revitalized the old movie ranch and added hiking trails. The area is still used as a working movie ranch. From 1992 to 1997, it served as the early Colorado setting of *Dr. Quinn, Medicine Woman.* It's quite popular with tourists and families, but the trails never seem crowded because most visitors show up to gawk at the cluster of faux Western buildings at the ranch entrance without venturing to the trails beyond them.

Paramount Ranch's handful of trails are named for the ranch's celluloid past, though few props remain beyond the façades of Western Town. Medicine Woman Trail leads past the site where *Dr. Quinn* was shot. The Bwana Trail takes you through the grasslands of Africa as featured in the 1952 movie *Bwana Devil.* And the Backdrop Trail is a nod to the area of the ranch that can be used for any type of shot because it has no telephone poles or other distinctive features, according to a brochure available at the entrance.

None of the trails are marked with signposts, but they are all well maintained and easy to navigate. To get to the Hacienda Trail, walk past the dusty streets and storefront façades of Western Town and turn right on the wide gravel path located behind the barbershop. You will pass a large picnic pavilion on the right; to the left is the train depot that was used in *Dr. Quinn.* At 0.3 mile, the gravel trail narrows and comes to a T. Turn left and follow the trail up a gradual incline past brush and seasonal golden currant flowers. You'll see chaparral-covered hills in the distance. The bulk of this hike is shadeless, so bring plenty of sunscreen and water.

DISTANCE & CONFIGURATION: 3.6-mile out-and-back	MAPS: USGS *Point Dume;* at kiosk at entrance to Western Town and **nps.gov /samo/planyourvisit/upload/Paramount _Ranch_fin.pdf**
DIFFICULTY: Easy–moderate	
SCENERY: Rolling hills, meadows, woodland	
EXPOSURE: Sunny	WHEELCHAIR ACCESSIBLE: Portions near trailhead
TRAFFIC: Moderate	
TRAIL SURFACE: Dirt and gravel	FACILITIES: Restrooms in parking lot, water fountains, picnic tables
HIKING TIME: 2 hours	
ACCESS: Daily, sunrise–sunset; free	CONTACT: 805-370-2300; **nps.gov/samo /planyourvisit/paramountranch.htm**

Just after crossing a small seasonal stream, you'll come to a Y in the trail. The left path leads past Witches' Wood, a narrow dirt trail on a gradual incline shaded partially by oak trees. This area got its name from the fortune-tellers who set up booths here for the Renaissance Pleasure Faire during the 1970s and 1980s, according to a park brochure.

I made a quick detour up this path, and then reversed course back to the Y and headed right. After crossing another small drainage area, the trail turns narrow and flat with heavy sun exposure. It is flanked by tall grassy meadow on both sides.

I wasn't a regular watcher of *Dr. Quinn,* but it was easy to picture Jane Seymour (also known as Dr. Mike) tending to rattlesnake bites and other 19th-century maladies amid this pristine landscape. I was also reminded of the opening scene in *Little House on the Prairie,* when Laura, Mary, and Carrie Ingalls run tumbling down a grassy meadow.

At about 1.3 miles, the path descends gradually, and then climbs again and brings you back to the 21st century as the Spanish-tile rooftops of Calabasas and Cornell Road come into view. It turns a little more secluded before reaching another Y. The left path leads to the unmaintained Paramount Ridge Trail (and eventually private homes), whereas a right turn will take you downhill past a horse stable before the trail hits Medea Creek and, beyond that, private property. From here, you may retrace your steps back along the Backdrop Trail or hook up with the Bwana Trail, which runs parallel to the Backdrop Trail and Medea Creek and leads back to Western Town and the parking lot.

Nearby Activities

Western Town is worth a stop on your way to or from your hike. It is still used regularly as a site for filming movies and TV shows and remains open to the public during shooting. The National Park Service visitor center at King Gillette Ranch is also nearby. Once home to razor mogul King C. Gillette, the solar-powered complex is surrounded by meadows and grasslands and includes a 1920s-era mansion designed by Wallace Neff and an information center with maps and history of the area. It's also known as the site where TV's *The Biggest Loser* was filmed. Parking is $7.

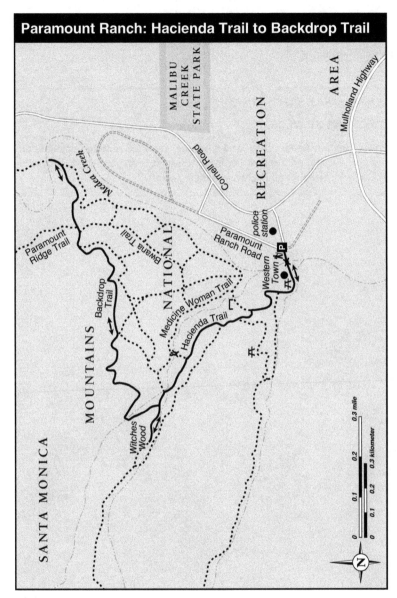

Paramount Ranch: Hacienda Trail to Backdrop Trail

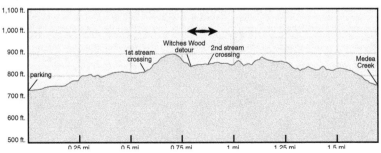

Every May, the ranch hosts the annual Topanga Banjo-Fiddle Contest, a one-day festival of live music, dancing, food, and cowboy storytelling. For more information, visit **topangabanjofiddle.org.**

GPS TRAILHEAD COORDINATES

N34° 7.003' W118° 45.462'

From US 101, exit at Kanan Road, and continue south 0.5 mile to Cornell Road. Bear left onto Cornell, and go 2 miles. Paramount Ranch is on your right, just before the intersection with Mulholland Highway. Park in the lot.

20 Peter Strauss Trail

In Brief

This low-traffic trail switchbacks up a hillside and through an oak- and sycamore-shaded glen. The vast lawn in front of the ranch house is perfect for a picnic accompanied by a serenade from the resident peacocks.

Description

This 40-acre property in the Santa Monica Mountains operated as a resort known as Lake Enchanto from the mid-1930s to the 1960s. The swimming pool, now closed to the public, was once the largest pool on the West Coast, holding 650,000 gallons of water and accommodating 3,000 people at a time. Actor Peter Strauss bought it in 1976 after falling in love with the area while shooting the *Rich Man, Poor Man* TV series at nearby Malibu Lake. He restored the house and grounds, and then six years later sold it to the Santa Monica Mountains Conservancy for $1.2 million, a reported $1 million more than he had paid for it. One of the alleged conditions of the sale was that the ranch and trail be named after him, according to a local newspaper report.

This is easily the least-traveled path that I have experienced in the Santa Monica Mountains. I did this hike on a perfect-for-hiking sunny Saturday afternoon and didn't encounter a soul, unless you count the peacock that lives on the property. It's also an excellent hike when summer temperatures reach the triple digits in the San Fernando Valley because the hot sun rarely penetrates the thick groves of oak and sycamore trees that shade most of the trail.

The biggest challenge is parking, because the ranch parking lot tends to be closed more often than it's open. I parked on Waring Drive, a residential street on the north side of Mulholland, after checking to make sure there were no restricted-parking signs, and then walked across the street to the ranch gate.

Look for the stone tower and a sign that reads PETER STRAUSS RANCH, LAKE ENCHANTO, and pass through the gate between them. The original ranch house is on the right just beyond a lush green lawn with a couple of picnic tables. To the left is Triunfo Canyon Creek and the remains of a dam built in the 1940s by the owners of Lake Enchanto.

Follow the driveway past the circular cactus garden and look for a sign that says AMPHITHEATRE to the left of the house. Don't be surprised if you are greeted by the honking of the ranch's peacock. Other birds spotted here include the canyon wren, great blue heron, and black-headed grosbeak.

Follow the dirt path past the amphitheater and a grove of eucalyptus trees as it switchbacks up a hillside. The path is a little rugged here with drainage ruts, but it soon gets smooth and well maintained. When you reach the horse stables, follow the path uphill and to the left. It will start to get shady with a few patches of sun. The trail levels for 0.25 mile or so and gets sunny, and you will be able to see million-dollar homes peeking

DISTANCE & CONFIGURATION: 1.5-mile balloon	**ACCESS:** Daily, 8 a.m.–sunset; free
DIFFICULTY: Easy	**MAPS:** USGS *Point Dume;* **nps.gov/samo /planyourvisit/upload/Peter-Strauss -Ranch_v3.pdf**
SCENERY: Chaparral, oak, eucalyptus, and sycamore trees	
EXPOSURE: Mostly shady	**WHEELCHAIR ACCESSIBLE:** Portions
TRAFFIC: Light	**FACILITIES:** Restrooms
TRAIL SURFACE: Dirt path	**CONTACT:** 805-370-2300; **nps.gov/samo /planyourvisit/straussranch.htm**
HIKING TIME: 45 minutes	

out amid the trees on the left. It then descends wooden steps into an oak- and sycamore-shaded glen. You can hear some car and motorcycle noise from nearby Mulholland Highway, but the cool tunnel of shade that surrounds you helps muffle it and makes it seem like you're a million miles away from civilization. In the spring, wildflowers blooming here include milkmaids, wild sweet pea, crimson pitcher sage, Angel's gilia, and purple nightshade. I also spotted chickweed, mountain mahogany, spring vetch, and wild cucumber plants during my trek.

At about 0.75 mile, the trail descends to a T. The path to the right extends the hike by about 0.25 mile and dead-ends at a chain-link fence that separates the ranch from private property. Retrace your steps back to the T and follow the path straight. Soon you'll reach a playground and the driveway that leads back to the trailhead.

Nearby Activities

On Sunday afternoons in summer, the ranch opens its doors to bands who perform free outdoor concerts under the oak trees at the amphitheater. For more information, go to **nps.gov/samo.**

Troutdale Inc., at the corner of Kanan and Troutdale Roads, is a man-made pond and recreation area. On weekends, it fills up with families who picnic under the oak trees with their freshly caught fish (barbecue pits and cleaning facilities are available). Admission is $7 per person and includes equipment and fishing license; plus there's a fee charged for each fish caught. For more information, call 818-889-9993.

Another nearby destination is The Old Place (**oldplacecornell.com**), a unique 1970s-era restaurant that describes itself as "the size of a shoebox." Once a hangout for Steve McQueen, Bob Dylan, and other celebrities who lived in nearby Malibu, it now serves "honest food cooked over fire" Thursday–Sunday, plus brunch on weekends. Reservations are a must.

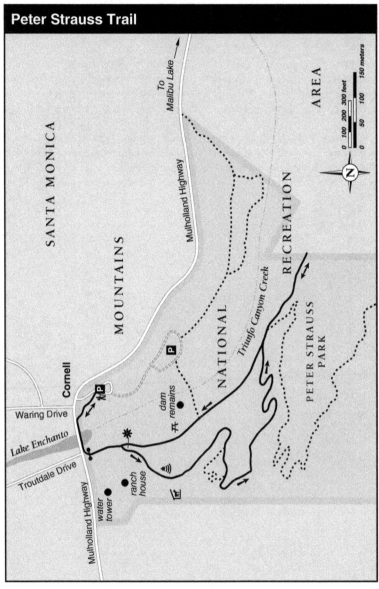

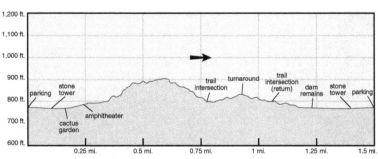

GPS TRAILHEAD COORDINATES

N34° 6.857' W118° 46.781'

From downtown L.A. and the San Fernando Valley, take US 101 to the Kanan Road exit, and follow it south 3 miles to Troutdale Drive. Turn left onto Troutdale, and continue 0.4 mile to Mulholland Highway. The pedestrian entrance to the ranch will be right in front of you. Turn left onto Mulholland, and follow signs to the parking lot on the right.

   The parking lot for the ranch is often closed in the weeks following heavy rains, but the property itself usually opens to hikers after a couple of days. Street parking is available across Mulholland Highway along Waring Drive.

21 San Vicente Mountain:
OLD NIKE MISSILE SITE

In Brief

This easy Santa Monica Mountains hike begins at the east end of the dirt road extension of Mulholland Drive and maintains a steady ascent past sweeping views of the San Fernando Valley to a former Nike missile control site that has been turned into a mountaintop park.

Description

This trail certainly isn't the most picturesque or serene of all the hikes in the Santa Monica Mountains, but it offers a unique peek at Cold War–era Los Angeles amid the multimillion-dollar mansions and mountain-bike culture that now mark the area, and it reminds the young that Nike wasn't always another word for sneaker. Between 1954 and 1968, this park was one of 16 missile control sites established to guard the skies of Los Angeles from a nuclear attack by Soviet planes. Situated on a mountaintop 1,950 feet above sea level with sweeping views of downtown L.A., the Pacific Ocean, and the San Fernando Valley, the area was considered an ideal site for detecting planes up to 100 miles away. It closed in 1968, but the radar tower, guard shack, and barbed-wire fence remain. The Santa Monica Mountains Conservancy, which acquired the site in 1995, planted oak trees, added picnic tables, and turned the officers' barracks into restrooms. It's a strange place for a picnic, with the disassembled radar tower and barbed-wire fence looming above, and it seems to attract more mountain bikers looking for a pit stop than hikers. But it's quieter than most other Santa Monica Mountains trails, and the panoramic views are tough to match.

From the dirt parking lot, walk around the fire-road gate and follow the wide dirt path up a gradual incline. The path is flanked by yellow wildflowers in the spring. To the right are wide-open views of the San Fernando Valley. The next mile is completely exposed, so come prepared with a hat and plenty of sunscreen, especially during the hot summer months. There aren't many landmarks or items of interest until you reach a dilapidated guard shack and chain-link fence after about a mile or so. Look for the sign LA96C (the name bestowed by the U.S. Army on the military site), and head left up the dirt path. Soon you will come to a T. A small parking lot (for authorized vehicles only) and public restrooms are on the right; on the left are picnic tables, the radar tower, and a couple of interpretive signs that explain the site's former role.

One sign explains the reason for the site's closure. In the 1960s, the United States and the Soviets had developed intercontinental ballistic missiles that traveled so fast and so high that they rendered the Nike missiles obsolete. Another sign details the site's use of a bulky computer system that "recorded, plotted and coordinated every event to locate, intercept and destroy an enemy target." The work these computers, which occupied an entire building, did in 1961 can be done by handheld computer today. Also, according to

DISTANCE & CONFIGURATION: 3-mile out-and-back	**HIKING TIME:** 1 hour
DIFFICULTY: Easy	**ACCESS:** Gate: Daily, sunrise–sunset; free
SCENERY: Wildflowers, valley, canyon views	**MAPS:** USGS *Canoga Park*
	WHEELCHAIR ACCESSIBLE: Yes
EXPOSURE: Sunny	**FACILITIES:** Picnic tables, benches, restrooms
TRAFFIC: Light	**CONTACT:** 805-370-2300; lamountains.com/parks.asp?parkid=54
TRAIL SURFACE: Packed dirt	

a *Los Angeles Times* story about the park's grand opening, soldiers kept a garden with cacti and other plants to pass the time and "as a sign of hope."

From the T, turn left and walk up to the former helicopter platform (now the site of picnic tables and clusters of young oak trees), and then climb the steps to the slate-gray tower platform. From here, it is 15 miles to downtown Los Angeles and 10 miles to Venice Beach. If it's a clear day, you can check out the city-to-ocean views, though with decidedly less intensity than the Army officers who staffed the site once did. The place still has an ominous Cold War–era feel to it and doesn't exactly encourage lingering. I was here on a stifling hot day in May, though, and that may have added to the unwelcoming feel.

On returning to the guard station, you can either head back to the parking lot or turn left on Dirt Mulholland to extend the hike by another mile or more. The path is flat and the scenery is similar to the first mile of the hike: wildflowers, coastal sage scrub, and views of the valley to the north and chaparral-draped mountains to the south. The dirt road continues another 8 miles or so past Marvin Braude Mulholland Gateway Park and links to other Santa Monica Mountains trails, including Caballero Canyon, Temescal Ridge, and Hub Junction.

Nearby Activities

Jerry's Famous Deli (**jerrysfamousdeli.com**), about 3 miles away near the intersection of Ventura Boulevard and Havenhurst Avenue, churns out pastrami sandwiches, bagels and lox, and other hearty deli fare from morning to night. For a bit of history about the San Fernando Valley before the shopping malls and celebrities showed up, stop by Los Encinos State Historic Park, an early California rancho with a guitar-shaped lake fed by a natural spring.

GPS TRAILHEAD COORDINATES   N34° 7.744' W118° 30.809'

From I-405, take Exit 61 (Skirball Center Drive toward Mulholland Drive), and follow Skirball Center Drive north less than 0.5 mile to Mulholland. Turn left onto Mulholland Drive, and follow it 2 miles until it intersects with Encino Hills Drive. At the intersection of Encino Hills Drive, turn left onto Dirt Mulholland, an unpaved section of the road, and continue about a mile to a nondescript cluster of small buildings. Park by the chain-link fence and look for the fire-road gate. Keep in mind that the gate to Dirt Mulholland closes at sunset, and the road is often closed following heavy rains.

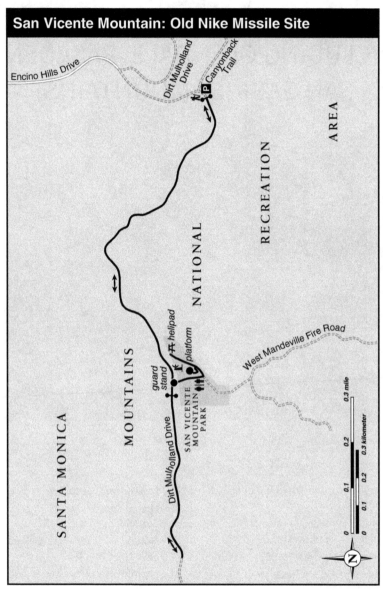

San Vicente Mountain: Old Nike Missile Site

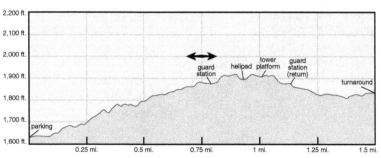

EAST

(INCLUDING GLENDALE, PASADENA, SAN GABRIEL MOUNTAINS)

Stough Canyon Nature Center Trail (see page 143)

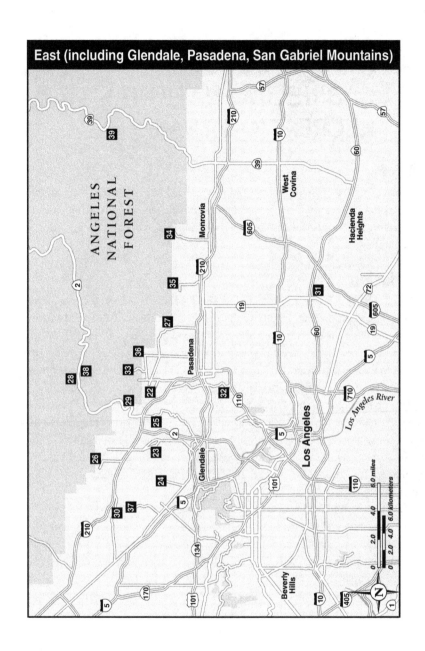

22 **Arroyo Seco:**
GABRIELINO NATIONAL RECREATION TRAIL

In Brief

This mostly flat hike begins along a paved service road with industrial views of the NASA Jet Propulsion Laboratory (JPL), and then becomes increasingly bucolic as it follows a wide gurgling stream past several picnic areas, thick groves of oak and sycamore, and big-leaf maple trees.

Description

The Gabrielino Trail is one of several in the Angeles National Forest designated as a multi-use national recreation trail. It follows the route of an original 1920s road that ran from Pasadena north up the canyon past wilderness resorts and old rustic cabins. The road lost its appeal after the Angeles Crest Highway was built, but today it has reinvented itself as a multiuse trail for hikers, horseback riders, mountain bikers, and birders. Everyone seems to coexist peacefully, but this path is not for you if you prefer solitude on the trails.

This hike, known as the Arroyo Seco stretch, covers the well-maintained lower end of the Gabrielino National Recreation Trail and features the part of the Arroyo Seco that doesn't live up to its Spanish name of "dry riverbed." Much of the hike follows a sparkling, gurgling stream past thick groves of live oak, sycamore, Douglas-fir, and big-leaf maple trees. Except for the first 0.5 mile, the path is almost entirely in the shade, making it a great year-round hike.

To get to the trailhead from the parking lot, walk across Ventura Street to the yellow fire-road gate and a sign for the Gabrielino National Recreation Trail, and follow the paved road as it heads north into the canyon. (The paved road to the left of the trailhead leads to a back entrance of the JPL, NASA's high-security spacecraft research hub.)

The left side of the road is lined with shrubs and large arroyo rocks; on the right you will pass the backyards of private homes. Soon you will pass a clearing on the left, and the sprawling JPL complex will come into view, as will Devil's Gate Reservoir, one of Los Angeles County's oldest reservoirs. Its dam was deemed seismically unsafe in the 1970s, and heavy rains have left it looking more like a no-man's-land full of silt and debris than a water basin.

The first 0.5 mile of the hike has little shade and isn't very attractive. You will pass a water treatment plant on the right and might hear generator-type roars coming from the JPL. Just past the water treatment plant, you will come to a fork in the trail. The left path leads to the back side of JPL. Continue straight on the paved road.

Things start to get a little more natural here—hillsides sprouting chaparral, sage scrub, and seasonal wildflowers come into better view on either side of the trail. Soon

DISTANCE & CONFIGURATION: 5-mile out-and-back	**FACILITIES:** Picnic areas at several points along trail
DIFFICULTY: Easy–moderate	**CONTACT:** 626-574-1613; **www.fs.usda**
SCENERY: Arroyo rocks, oak forest	**.gov/main/angeles**
EXPOSURE: Shady	**COMMENTS:** Wildfires and rainstorms
TRAFFIC: Heavy	swept through the Angeles National For-
TRAIL SURFACE: Packed and loose dirt, boulders	est in 2009 and 2010 and significantly altered trails in the San Gabriel mountain
HIKING TIME: 2.5 hours	range, including the Gabrielino. The trail
ACCESS: Gate: Daily, sunrise–sunset; free	to Gould Mesa has since reopened, but
MAPS: USGS *Pasadena*	parts of it look significantly different, with
WHEELCHAIR ACCESSIBLE: Yes, until last 0.5 mile	less vegetation and some creek access points blocked.

you'll come to a concrete-and-stone bridge, the first of several you'll encounter on your walk. Now the stream is on the right and the path turns shady and pleasant.

After about a mile, you will pass another water treatment plant on the right and cross an old wooden bridge. Just after the bridge, a sign tells you that you have officially entered the Angeles National Forest. Continue walking alongside the stream past groves of sycamore, oak, and maple trees.

Soon you'll pass a signed turnoff for Brown Mountain Trail on the right and a primitive NO SHOOTING sign. Continue straight on the Gabrielino National Recreation Trail.

At about 1.2 miles, a couple of small private homes pop up on the right, as well as a water trough made of arroyo rocks. The trail then passes through the gate of a chain-link fence and curves around to the right (north). You are now walking on loose dirt and have a good view of the stream on the left. This area of the trail has changed the most in recent years. A chain-link fence bars access to parts of the stream, and debris and fallen branches remain all around.

At 1.5 miles, the trail crosses over another bridge. On the left just after the bridge is a picnic area known as Teddy's Outpost. This is a fine spot for a picnic, but if you can hold out for another mile or so, the picnic areas to the north of Gould Mesa Campground, such as Paul Little or Niño Canyon, are much nicer. The trail continues north and passes more bridges and an occasional bench where you can rest and watch the creek gurgle.

Your first of several wide stream crossings comes at 2 miles. The crossings aren't difficult (especially during the summer and fall, when the stream all but dries up), but this is often a turnaround point for parents with infants or small children. From here the creek is on the right and the path turns into gravel for a while. At 2.1 miles, you will come to a Y. Take the lower trail to the right and keep hugging the stream. It is briefly exposed here but quickly descends back into the shady forest. This is one of the coolest and loveliest sections of the trail. Groves of oaks and alders line the stream, and green ivy covers either side of the trail in abundance. After some more boulder-hopping, the dirt path widens

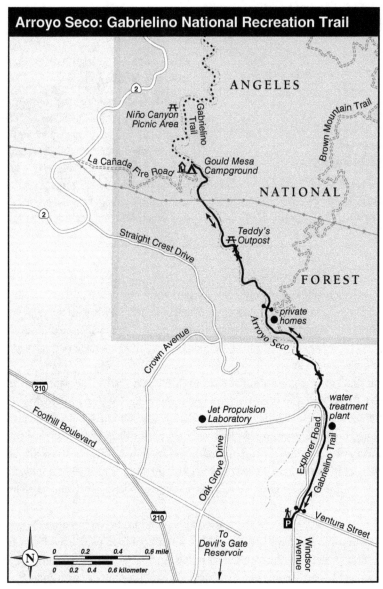

Arroyo Seco: Gabrielino National Recreation Trail

ANGELES

Niño Canyon Picnic Area

Gabrielino Trail

2

Brown Mountain Trail

La Cañada Fire Road

Gould Mesa Campground

NATIONAL

2

Straight Crest Drive

Teddy's Outpost

FOREST

private homes

Arroyo Seco

Crown Avenue

210

Foothill Boulevard

Jet Propulsion Laboratory

water treatment plant

Explorer Road

Gabrielino Trail

Oak Grove Drive

210

Ventura Street

To Devil's Gate Reservoir

Windsor Avenue

N

| 0 | 0.2 | 0.4 | 0.6 mile |
| 0 | 0.2 | 0.4 | 0.6 kilometer |

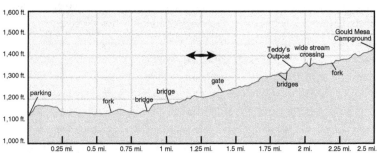

1,600 ft.											Gould Mesa Campground
1,500 ft.											
1,400 ft.								Teddy's Outpost	wide stream crossing		
1,300 ft.						gate			bridges	fork	
1,200 ft.	parking		fork	bridge	bridge						
1,100 ft.											
1,000 ft.											

0.25 mi.   0.5 mi.   0.75 mi.   1 mi.   1.25 mi.   1.5 mi.   1.75 mi.   2 mi.   2.25 mi.   2.5 mi.

and you will pass a bench under an old oak tree. Soon Gould Mesa Campground will come into view. There is a primitive toilet and large clearing bordering the stream. Camping is allowed on a first-come, first-serve basis. Birders also testify to this area's tendency to attract all kinds of warblers, such as the Western tanager, owls, and even an occasional American dipper. According to the Pasadena Audubon Society, more than 180 species of birds have been spotted along the Arroyo Seco.

You can turn around here and trek the 2.5 miles back to the JPL trailhead. This trail used to extend all the way to Switzer Falls, but natural disasters have left it challenging to navigate north of Paul Little Picnic Area. The U.S. Forest Service has closed Oakwilde Campground just north of that indefinitely.

Nearby Activities

The JPL hosts a popular two-day open house once a year, usually in October. For more information, visit **jpl.nasa.gov/events/open-house.php.** Several good eateries can be found a few blocks east on Lincoln Avenue: Lincoln (1992 Lincoln Ave.), a bakery and café, sells gourmet sandwiches, soups, pastries, and sea-salt caramels in an inviting space. Ponci Burrito Express (2291 N. Lincoln Ave.; closed Sunday) is a grab-and-go stop for inexpensive burritos and tortas (Mexican sandwiches). Across the street, El Patron Express is a sit-down café serving burritos, fajitas, and other typical Mexican eats, plus margaritas.

GPS TRAILHEAD COORDINATES

N34° 11.654' W118° 10.072'

From the Foothill Freeway (I-210) in Pasadena, take Exit 22B (Arroyo Boulevard/ Windsor Avenue). Drive 0.75 mile north on Windsor, and turn left into the small parking lot just before the stop sign at Ventura Street. Look for the fire road across the street from the parking lot.

23 Beaudry Loop

A view of downtown Los Angeles from the top of Beaudry Loop

In Brief

This nearly 6-mile hike begins in a residential Glendale neighborhood and meanders across the easternmost side of the Verdugo Mountains. An elevation gain of 1,500 feet combines a good workout with striking panoramic views of Los Angeles, Glendale, and the San Gabriel Mountains to the north.

Parts of this final leg of the hike are quite steep; be sure to wear sturdy hiking or walking shoes.

Description

Residents of Glendale, La Crescenta, and La Cañada–Flintridge use this picturesque trail on a regular basis, but any hiker will find it worth the drive. It is completely exposed and best hiked on a cool, overcast day. On clear days, expect excellent views of downtown Los Angeles, the San Fernando Valley, and the San Gabriel Mountains.

Park on Beaudry Terrace (there are no restrictions) and follow the trail west as it parallels the flood channel. Walk past a fire-road gate, and then follow the trail as it winds

DISTANCE & CONFIGURATION: 5.8-mile loop	**HIKING TIME:** 2.5–3 hours
DIFFICULTY: Moderate–strenuous	**ACCESS:** Daily, sunrise–sunset; street parking
SCENERY: Chaparral, panoramic city and mountain views	**MAPS:** USGS *Burbank* and USGS *Pasadena;* **ci.glendale.ca.us/parks/pdf/COG_TrailsAndFireRoadsBrochure.pdf**
EXPOSURE: High	
TRAFFIC: Light	**WHEELCHAIR ACCESSIBLE:** No
TRAIL SURFACE: Packed dirt, pavement	**FACILITIES:** None
	CONTACT: 818-880-0363

around to the left and up a moderate hill. At 0.4 mile, you will come to a signed junction. Either way loops back around, but I usually take the right branch (Beaudry North) on the way up and then follow the somewhat steeper south branch back down. After about another 0.5 mile of gradual ascent, you will pass an old water tank on the left; then the path hugs a sheer rock wall for a few hundred feet with views of Glendale and La Crescenta to your right. The spectacular views that mark this hike start to come into play now and pretty much stay with you for the rest of the hike.

At 2.4 miles, you will reach another trail junction. To the right is a sign for Verdugo Motorway, a fire road that links to other trails in the Verdugo Mountains. To complete the Beaudry Loop, take the branch to the left and head south toward a large set of transmitters. From here, it's another 0.5 mile to the trail's peak elevation point of 2,630 feet—on clear days you will be treated to some stellar views of the downtown Los Angeles skyline.

Continue another 0.5 mile to a three-way trail junction. The middle path dead-ends at the transmitters. If you have time and want to rest before heading back, you can follow that path and take a rest (as well as soak up the views) on the trail's sole bench near the fenced transmitters. Then return to the junction and take the leftmost path as it winds back down the mountain to your starting point. Parts of this final leg of the hike are quite steep; be sure to tread carefully.

From the trail junction near the transmitters, it's another 2 miles back to the flood channel and the trailhead.

Nearby Activities

Montrose, about 5 minutes from the trailhead, is a Glendale neighborhood known for its Mayberry-esque main street and wide variety of restaurants and mom-and-pop boutiques. From Beaudry Boulevard, head back to Country Club Drive and head north on La Cañada Boulevard. Make a left on La Crescenta Avenue, then a right on Verdugo Road and continue north to Honolulu Avenue. Turn left and you will be in the heart of Montrose. There is free parking behind the shops.

Beaudry Loop

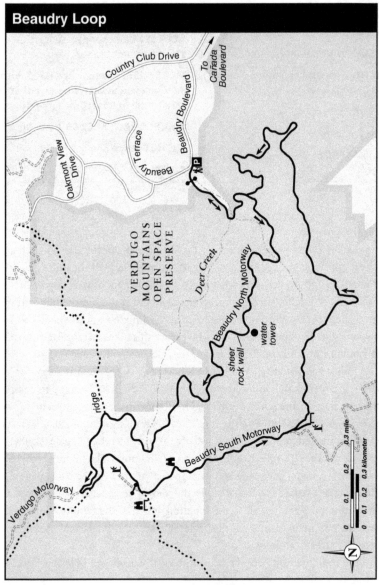

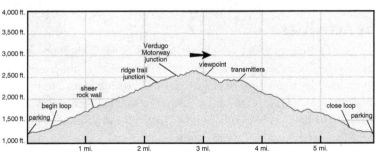

GPS TRAILHEAD COORDINATES

N34° 11.504' W118° 14.369'

From CA 134 in Glendale, exit at Glendale Avenue, and head north past Glendale Community College. After crossing Mountain Street, you will come to a fork in the road at 1 mile; veer left on La Cañada Boulevard, and follow it about 1.5 miles to Country Club Road. Turn left; then in 0.3 mile make a right at the road's end (Oakmont Country Club will be on the right). In 0.2 mile turn left onto Beaudry Boulevard, and follow it past one stop sign until you see a concrete flood channel on the left (where Beaudry Boulevard meets Beaudry Terrace). Park on the street and look for the trailhead that parallels the flood channel.

An elevation gain of 1,500 feet and panoramic views mark the Beaudry Loop.

24 Brand Fire Road Trail

In Brief

This hike follows a wide fire road that climbs 800 feet from the base of Brand Park in Glendale to the ridge of the Verdugo Mountains. Your reward is a lookout with sweeping views of the Los Angeles Basin and the San Fernando Valley. In the winter and spring, a detour along a stream to the base of a waterfall adds another easy 0.5 mile to the hike.

The best time of year to do this nearly shadeless hike is late winter or early spring, when the stream is gushing at full force and the wildflowers are in bloom. If you do hike this during the summer, bring plenty of water and sunscreen, and plan your visit for the morning or late afternoon.

Description

Brand Park, at the base of the Verdugo Mountains in Glendale, is on the grounds of an estate known as El Miradero. Today, it's a meticulously kept neighborhood park, with a baseball field, basketball courts, picnic areas, a library, and a Japanese tea garden. It gets crowded on weekends with families, Little League teams, and exercise hounds, but I have never had a problem finding a parking space in the lot.

To get to the Brand Fire Road Trail, leave your car near the Doctor's House at the park's northwest corner and follow the paved path to the right. The path winds uphill behind the house to a white gate. You'll see a large, unsightly debris basin on the right. This part of the trail is completely exposed, and there is little vegetation. Don't be discouraged by the lack of scenery, though; the longer you walk, the better it gets.

At about 0.4 mile, you'll come to a fork in the path and see a set of stone steps that lead nowhere (the remains of the El Miradero estate, most likely). The Brand Fire Road curves uphill to the right of the steps. You may also take a brief detour from the fire-road trail by following the rocky dirt path to the left. This borders a seasonal stream and leads to a pretty waterfall. It is the shadiest part of the hike. It's a good idea to have hiking boots if you take this path. It requires fording the stream at several points, stomping through dense vegetation, and climbing over a few fallen trees that partially block the path. Just before the waterfall, you'll see a couple of primitive chairs that someone has formed out of large stones next to the stream. When I did this hike midday on a Saturday in March, the sun was beating down hard, so I didn't linger.

Back on the fire road, the trail continues to steadily ascend past chaparral-covered hills, coastal sage scrub, palm trees, and seasonal yellow wildflowers. You'll begin to see views of Glendale and the San Fernando Valley as you walk. Expect to see lots of hikers and mountain bikers here on weekends; the trail also attracts many hiking groups. (I passed four on my Saturday afternoon hike.) The fire road is wide enough, however, that it's easy to overtake them if you're motivated. At about 1 mile from the trailhead, the fire

Brand Fire Road Trail

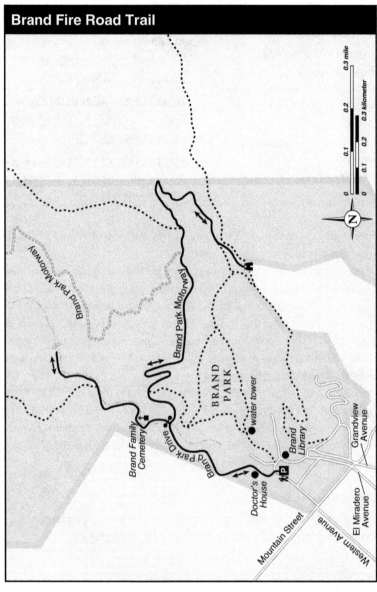

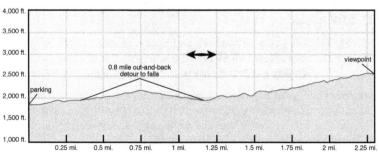

DISTANCE & CONFIGURATION: 4.5-mile out-and-back	**HIKING TIME:** 2 hours
DIFFICULTY: Moderate–difficult	**ACCESS:** Gate: Daily, sunrise–sunset. Park: Daily, 7 a.m.–10 p.m.; free
SCENERY: Chaparral-covered hills, seasonal waterfall, panoramic valley and city views	**MAPS:** USGS *Burbank*
	WHEELCHAIR ACCESSIBLE: Lower portion
EXPOSURE: Sunny	
TRAFFIC: Heavy on weekends, moderate on weekdays	**FACILITIES:** Restrooms, water
TRAIL SURFACE: Paved; loose dirt and gravel	**CONTACT:** 818-548-2184; **tinyurl.com /brandpark** or **lamountains.com/parks .asp?parkid=638**

road curves around to the left and you'll see a narrow dirt path to the right. (The dirt path is a shortcut that meets up with the fire road.)

At about 1.2 miles, the road narrows into a packed dirt-and-gravel path here and winds around to the right, then levels briefly at an elevation of 1,150 feet before it starts to climb again. If you look down and to the left, you'll also be able to spot the seasonal waterfall that sits at the end of the detour. This stretch of the trail requires more boulder-hopping, as well as scaling a couple of big drainage pipes; then it gets smooth again as you approach the mountain ridge. At about 2 miles, you will come to a dirt clearing with an elevation gain of 1,600 feet. The sweeping views of the San Fernando Valley, Glendale, and the Los Angeles Basin are tough to match; you can even see the Pacific Ocean on a clear day. There are no benches or picnic tables, but it's worth a pause. From here, you can retrace your steps to the parking lot or continue climbing another 0.25 mile to the ridge of the Verdugo Mountains for access to other trails within the Verdugo range, including Stough Canyon and La Tuna Canyon.

Nearby Activities

The 31-acre Brand Park, where the trail begins, has picnic areas, a playground, a traditional Japanese teahouse and friendship garden, and a terrific library.

GPS TRAILHEAD COORDINATES

N34° 11.010' W118° 16.634'

From I-5, take Exit 145 (Western Avenue), and head northeast on Western Avenue. In 1.5 miles turn right onto Mountain Street. At the intersection of Mountain and Grandview Avenue, turn left into the Brand Park parking lot (on Brand Park Drive).

Alternate directions: Take the Pacific Avenue exit off CA 134 in Glendale and head north; in about a mile turn left onto Kenneth Road. In 0.8 mile turn right onto Grandview Avenue. The park entrance is at the corner of Grandview and Mountain Street. Look for the ornate archway that says MIRADERO.

25 Cherry Canyon Park

The author's son hikes the Owl Trail.

In Brief

Tucked in an upscale residential community behind Descanso Gardens in La Cañada–Flintridge, this winding, peaceful hike takes you all over the chaparral-covered San Rafael Hills. Rarely crowded, it is one of the area's best-kept secrets.

Description

Cherry Canyon Park can be found in the hills just behind Descanso Gardens, a popular destination known for its abundant displays of camellias, roses, and other flowers (see "Nearby Activities" on page 102). The park was preserved in the mid-1980s with the help of the Santa Monica Mountains Conservancy and the city of La Cañada–Flintridge. It has a handful of named, well-maintained trails that spread like wandering veins across its 130 acres. Wildlife sightings include hawks, coyotes, owls, and deer.

DISTANCE & CONFIGURATION: 3.5-mile figure eight	**MAPS:** USGS *Pasadena;* **lamountains .com/maps/cherryCanyon.pdf**
DIFFICULTY: Moderate	**WHEELCHAIR ACCESSIBLE:** Portions
SCENERY: Chaparral, city views	**FACILITIES:** None
EXPOSURE: Mostly sun	**CONTACT:** 818-790-8880; **lamountains**
TRAFFIC: Light	**.com/parks.asp?parkid=629**
TRAIL SURFACE: Packed dirt	**COMMENTS:** The trail begins in a
HIKING TIME: 1.5 hours	residential area; please heed the parking
ACCESS: Daily, sunrise–sunset; free	signs and keep noise levels to a minimum.

This 3.5-mile hike combines several trails, including Owl Trail, Liz's Loop, and Descanso Motorway, to give you a moderate workout and lovely city and mountain views. However, don't be afraid to wander off the main path and explore any unmarked trails that catch your eye. The park isn't that big, and most trails tend to loop around and reconnect with the main fire road after a mile or two. I love to hike Cherry Canyon on cool, overcast mornings (sometimes known as June gloom) since there is little shade, and the fog rolling across the green hills makes them even more serene and scenic. By the time the sun finds its way out from behind the clouds, I'm heading back to my starting point and have mostly downhill trekking ahead of me.

Begin the hike by following Owl Trail (look for a sign near the parking pullout) down into a dense forest of huge oak and sycamore trees. The narrow dirt path parallels a seasonal stream for about 0.25 mile, past a wooden bench perfect for a picnic for two and a turnoff for Cerro Negro Trail (which in recent years has suffered from erosion), and then brings you out to an exposed fire road. Turn left here, and look for a sign for Liz's Loop on your right. Take this trail as it winds gently uphill, soon giving way to 180-degree views of the city of La Cañada–Flintridge framed beautifully by the San Gabriel Mountains. After about 0.5 mile, with city and mountain views still on your right, the trail bends slightly to the south and comes to a large, rusty water tank and a huge electrical tower. There's also a bench nearby (one of the few you'll find in the park), where you can take in views of the residential hills to the south. Continue another 0.3 mile to fire road gate, make a sharp right, and follow the signs toward the Descanso Motorway gate and Verdugo Hills Overlook.

From here, it's a gradual 0.8-mile descent along Descanso Motorway, high above the Glendale Freeway to the west, to a locked gate that once let hikers access Descanso Gardens. Turn around and retrace your steps 0.8 mile, but instead of turning left and hiking Liz's Loop again, stay on the wider fire road, following it south and then east as it leads you back to the parking pullout.

Cherry Canyon is also favored by trail runners, dog walkers, and equestrians, though I have rarely seen more than a handful of people during my visits here. Young children will have no problem walking the short Owl Trail (they can collect rocks and sticks along the way), though it quickly turns muddy after heavy rains.

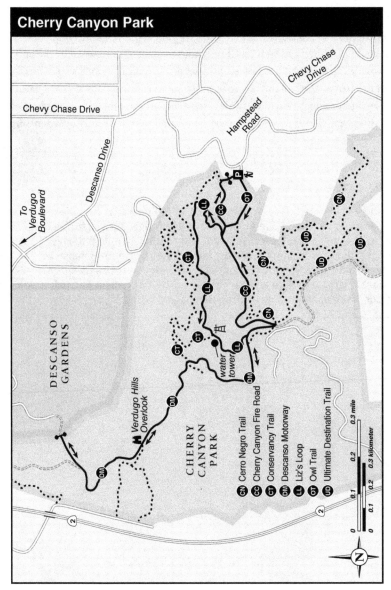

Cherry Canyon Park

CHERRY CANYON PARK

GN Cerro Negro Trail
CC Cherry Canyon Fire Road
CT Conservancy Trail
DM Descanso Motorway
LL Liz's Loop
OT Owl Trail
UD Ultimate Destination Trail

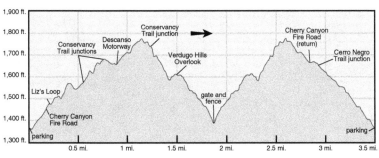

Nearby Activities

Descanso Gardens (1418 Descanso Dr.) is an exceptional public garden that offers horticulture classes, craft shows, and concerts throughout the year. Once owned by the publisher of the *Los Angeles Daily News,* it is home to the largest display of camellias in North America (the best time to see them in full bloom is January and February), as well as a Japanese garden and an international rosarium. There's also a small restaurant with an outdoor patio. It's open daily (except December 25). For more information, visit **descansogardens.org.**

GPS TRAILHEAD COORDINATES

N34° 11.647' W118° 12.227'

From the Golden State (I-5) or Ventura (CA 134) Freeways, take Glendale Freeway (CA 2) north to Verdugo Road in La Cañada–Flintridge. Turn right; then in 0.3 mile make another right onto Descanso Road, and continue 1 mile to Chevy Chase Drive. Turn right; then make another, almost immediate right onto Hampstead Road. Follow Hampstead up a winding residential road until you see signs for Cherry Canyon Park on the right. Turn right and park along a small dirt pullout on the left side of the street, or (if the pullout is full) back on Hampstead Road.

---

26 Deukmejian Wilderness Park Trails

The La Crescenta Valley from Deukmejian Wilderness Park

In Brief

This meticulously maintained park in the northernmost section of Glendale is one of the city's best-kept secrets. The hike described here ascends 700 feet to a shady streambed, then loops around to terrific views of the Verdugo Mountains and the foothill communities of La Crescenta and Tujunga.

Description

This 729-acre park operated as a vineyard and winery in the early 1900s. One of the trails is named for the former owner, a French emigrant and Los Angeles businessman named George Le Mesnager. The city of Glendale purchased the site in 1988 and named it after former California governor George Deukmejian, who grew up in the area. Its trail system opened in 1995, and the park underwent an extensive renovation in 2004 that added restrooms, a paved parking lot, and an amphitheater. A stone barn from the property's winemaking days sits near the trailhead.

DISTANCE & CONFIGURATION: 2.6-mile loop with spurs; 6.5-mile out-and-back for Crescenta View Trail to Mount Lukens	**WHEELCHAIR ACCESSIBLE:** First 0.5 mile
DIFFICULTY: Moderate	**FACILITIES:** Restrooms, water, picnic tables
SCENERY: Chaparral, sage scrub, streamside woodlands, Verdugo Mountains	**CONTACT:** 818-548-2000; **tinyurl.com /deukwilderness** or **lamountains.com /parks.asp?parkid=102**
EXPOSURE: Sunny	**COMMENTS:** The 2009 Station Fire caused major damage to the trails, vegetation, and hillsides of this northern Glendale park. Blackened tree carcasses still dot the hillsides, but it reopened in 2010 after city officials and hundreds of volunteers led an effort to rebuild the trails. You can extend your hike into the Angeles National Forest by taking the Crescenta View Trail all the way to Mount Lukens.
TRAFFIC: Light	
TRAIL SURFACE: Dirt path	
HIKING TIME: 2 hours	
ACCESS: Daily, sunrise–sunset; free	
MAPS: USGS *Sunland* and USGS *Burbank;* at trail kiosk next to barn and **lamountains .com/maps/deukmejian_map.jpg**	

The park is also used to access Mount Lukens, the highest peak within Los Angeles city limits, via the Crescenta View or Rim of the Valley Trail. It is bordered on the north, west, and east sides by the Angeles National Forest.

To get to the Dunsmore Canyon Trail, follow the paved fire road north of the parking lot. This is also the way to access Crescenta View Trail, as well as two new trails that were opened following the Station Fire: Mummy Rock and Vineyard Trails. In the spring, the path is flanked by California poppies. A plaque commemorating the property's previous use as a winery is on your left. It's also purported to be one of the hideouts of Tiburcio Vásquez, the notorious Mexican-born outlaw who committed a series of robberies and murders, then hid in the Southern California foothills until he was captured and hanged in 1875.

When the paved path ends, turn left and follow the dirt path uphill. Before heading uphill, you can walk a few hundred feet behind you (toward the stone barn) to a kiosk that includes a map of the park and information on trail conditions and the park's wildlife, which includes rattlesnakes, squirrels, rabbits, and coyotes.

The trail parallels a debris basin and the seasonal Dunsmore Canyon stream on the right as it begins its steep climb upward. There is no shade whatsoever, so be sure to bring a hat and plenty of sunscreen. Expect it to be uncomfortably hot in the summer months. The views include chaparral-covered slopes and seasonal fields of lupine and golden currant. Behind you are I-210 and the foothill communities of La Crescenta and Tujunga, all of which get increasingly distant as you continue your climb.

At about 0.75 mile, you come to a water drainage area, and the path curves around to the right and continues uphill. Soon you'll come to a wooden gate on the right. You're at an elevation of about 2,900 feet here and facing spectacular views of the foothill communities and the Verdugo Mountains. Follow the narrow gravel path past the gate as it descends to a shady oasis that overlooks the stream. There are no benches, but the

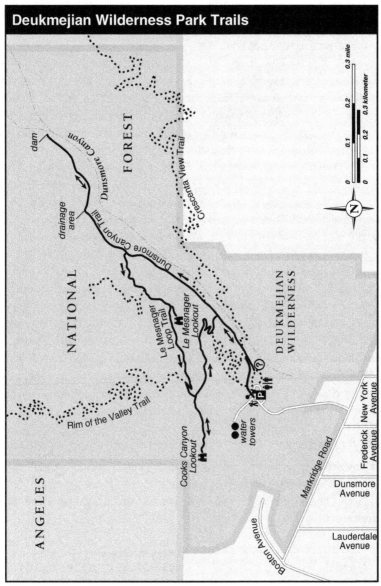

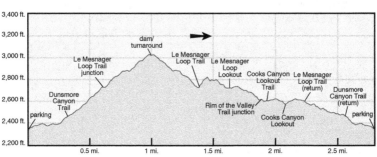

concrete dam provides plenty of comfortable (sort of) places to rest and have a drink or snack. If it's hot, be sure to dip your feet in the crystal-clear water.

From here, retrace your steps downhill to the signed turnoff for Le Mesnager Loop Trail on the right. The path winds upward immediately and is prettily framed by brush and sage scrub. It is narrower and slightly steeper than the Dunsmore Canyon Trail. At about 1.3 miles, you'll come to a signed turnoff for Le Mesnager Lookout Trail. Follow the path to the left up a steep incline to two small wooden benches and panoramic views of La Crescenta Valley and the Verdugo Mountains. If it's a cool day, this is another great spot to stop and rest, though there's not much room for more than a couple of people. I did this hike on a cool Saturday morning and saw only a handful of people anyway, mostly locals walking their dogs or hikers looking to access Mount Lukens via the park's Rim of the Valley Trail.

To continue the hike, turn around and hop back on Le Mesnager Loop Trail as it heads west on a gradual decline. There's a little shade along this portion of the hike from low-lying trees, and the Verdugos come in and out of view as the path continues downward.

At 1.5 miles, you will reach the signed turnoff for the Rim of the Valley Trail, a rigorous 3.2-mile hike that climbs 2,500 feet in elevation to the Mount Lukens summit.

For this hike, continue straight on Le Mesnager Loop Trail past rows of tall grass, wildflowers, and a grove of eucalyptus trees until you reach another signed turnoff. Take the narrow path right to another lookout area marked by a couple of large sandstone rocks (no benches this time). From here you can see the main entrance to the park below you, as well as the now-ubiquitous Verdugo Mountains. Retrace your steps downhill and back to Le Mesnager Loop Trail. The path descends steeply here, and the main park entrance is in clear view. The path then links back up with Dunsmore Canyon Trail, which you follow to the right and back to the parking lot.

Nearby Activities

The park hosts regular nature activities like guided hikes and volunteer trail restoration days. There's also a beautiful clearing near the old barn with picnic tables and views of La Crescenta Valley that are almost as good as you get while hiking. Visit **glendaleca.gov** for more information.

GPS TRAILHEAD COORDINATES   N34° 14.981' W118° 15.228'

From downtown Los Angeles, take the Glendale Freeway (CA 2) north to I-210 (Foothill Freeway) west, and take Exit 17A (Pennsylvania Avenue). Turn right onto Pennsylvania, and go 0.4 mile. Then make a left onto Foothill Boulevard, and in 0.6 mile take a right onto Dunsmore Avenue. Follow Dunsmore north until it ends in 0.8 mile. Turn right onto Markridge Road, and make an immediate left into a landscaped driveway that ends at the parking lot.

27 Eaton Canyon Falls and Henninger Flats

A stream crossing on the Eaton Canyon Falls trail

In Brief

This very popular trail parallels a seasonal stream and leads to the foot of a 30-foot water-fall and swimming hole. The last 0.5 mile requires some scrambling over boulders. Those looking for more solitude can opt for the more strenuous 7-mile round-trip trail to Henninger Flats or tackle both trails for an all-day adventure.

DISTANCE & CONFIGURATION:
3.6- to 7.4-mile out-and-back

DIFFICULTY: Moderate–strenuous

SCENERY: Stream, waterfalls, chaparral

EXPOSURE: Mostly sun

TRAFFIC: Heavy on weekends

TRAIL SURFACE: Packed dirt, rocks

HIKING TIME: 1.5–3.5 hours

ACCESS: Daily, sunrise–sunset; free

MAPS: USGS *Mount Wilson;* at nature center and **ecnca.org/hiking_trails/EC _Trail_Map.pdf**

WHEELCHAIR ACCESSIBLE: No

FACILITIES: Restrooms, water, picnic area

CONTACT: 626-398-5420; **ecnca.org /hiking_trails/henninger_flats.html**

COMMENTS: Park officials closed the Upper Falls area of Eaton Canyon in 2014 after several hikers were injured or died trying to navigate the steep terrain. Use extreme caution and stay on the trail at all times.

Description

Before setting out, stop at the nature center for a trail map and a guide to the canyon's native plants, which include honeysuckle, laurel sumac, toyon, yucca, prickly pear cactus, and matilija poppy.

From the far northern end of the parking lot, walk around a fire-road gate and head north toward a landscaped picnic area. You'll glimpse some private homes on your left. At the end of the picnic area, the path turns to dirt and is attractively framed in the spring by buckwheat, sage, and golden currant. After about 0.3 mile, the stream will come into view, as will the looming San Gabriel Mountains, which provide a nice backdrop for most of the hike. Follow the gravel-strewn path down and to the right, and cross the stream (it's usually easy to boulder-hop across without getting wet).

On a pleasant Saturday or Sunday you will see lots of families picnicking and sunbathing around the creek. After crossing the creek, turn left and follow the trail as it ducks under a handful of oak and sycamore trees. The next 0.5 mile is mostly exposed, with views of the mountains to your right. At 0.6 mile you will pass a sign for Henninger Flats and see a narrow trail heading uphill to the right. This connects to the Mount Wilson Toll Road. If you opt for this route, allow yourself enough time to get back down the mountain before sunset, when the park gates are promptly locked.

Continue hiking the main trail as it follows the stream north. There are several turnoffs along the way that you can follow to the stream and rest or rehydrate on large rocks before continuing on to the waterfall. At about 1.2 miles, you will come to a sign that reads EATON CANYON FALLS 1/2 MILE. Follow the path downhill as it passes under a bridge and zigzags back and forth across the streambed. This is where the boulder-hopping part of the hike begins; if you're not comfortable with this, or if the stream is too high due to heavy rains, you can continue straight at the sign and walk another 0.25 mile to the bridge overlooking the stream before turning back.

Eaton Canyon Falls and Henninger Flats

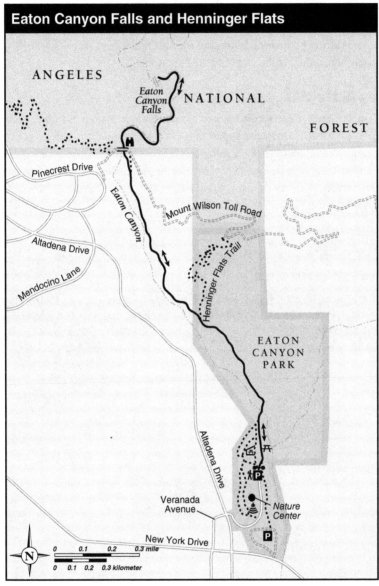

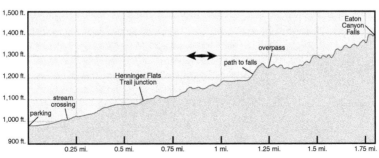

On the path to the waterfall, you'll find some shade from oaks and alders, but it's mostly exposed. Just before you reach the falls, the rocky path turns sharply to the right, and then ends at the pool at the bottom of the falls. On a busy weekend, expect to find many people here enjoying the view and the cool water.

Nearby Activities

Eaton Canyon Nature Center holds moonlight walks every Friday and other events such as rattlesnake festivals, plant sales, and birding hikes throughout the year. Visit **ecnca.org** for more info. Café Culture (1359 N. Altadena Dr.; 626-398-8654), about a mile south of Eaton Canyon Park, is a jack-of-all-trades kind of place. Besides strong coffee and an assortment of teas, it serves salads, sandwiches, stuffed grape leaves, and smoothies and sells everything from lip gloss to used books.

GPS TRAILHEAD COORDINATES

N34° 10.611' W118° 5.809'

From I-210 (Pasadena Freeway), take Exit 28 (Altadena Drive), and follow Altadena north for 1.7 miles. The park entrance is on the right, just past the intersection of Altadena and New York Drives.

---

28 Josephine Peak

Josephine Peak begins on a well-maintained fire road.

In Brief

This secluded out-and-back hike follows an abandoned dirt road on a gradual ascent to a summit of 5,560 feet. It may not be as challenging or interesting as other hikes in the area, but your reward is a 360-degree view of the San Gabriel mountain range and the unbeatable feeling that you're on top of the world.

Description

It's nearly impossible to get lost on this straightforward out-and-back trail that starts at the intersection of the Angeles Crest and Angeles Forest Highways. There are no confusing trail splits, nor are there any obvious stopping points or especially challenging stretches as there are on many other San Gabriel hikes. The road to Josephine Peak is essentially a steady climb on a wide dirt road flanked by gorgeous views of the mountains unblocked by transmission towers and other signs of urban life. Located about 9 miles north of La Cañada–Flintridge, the trailhead is easily accessible, and there's usually plenty of parking (plus bathroom facilities) near the trailhead at Clear Creek Ranger Station. Mountain bikers use this trail too, but I only saw two heading uphill during my visit here on a perfect Southern California winter day.

Make sure to display a day or annual Adventure Pass in your car's windshield before setting out. The trailhead is across the street from Clear Creek Ranger Station. Look for

DISTANCE & CONFIGURATION: 8.2-mile out-and-back	**MAPS:** USGS *Pasadena*
	WHEELCHAIR ACCESSIBLE: No
DIFFICULTY: Strenuous	**FACILITIES:** Restrooms at Clear Creek Ranger Station on Angeles Crest Highway
SCENERY: Mountain views, chaparral	
EXPOSURE: Mostly sun	**CONTACT:** 626-574-1613; **www.fs.usda .gov/main/angeles**
TRAFFIC: Light	**COMMENTS:** Leashed dogs are allowed. This trail was closed for more than three years due to damage sustained from the 2009 Station Fire. It reopened in 2013, but you can still see some charred trees and other evidence of the fire's impact, especially along the first half of the trail.
TRAIL SURFACE: Packed-dirt fire road	
HIKING TIME: 3.5 hours	
ACCESS: Daily, sunrise–sunset; Adventure Pass required to park	

the fire-road gate and sign for Josephine Road. Dogs are allowed on this trail but should be leashed, and keep in mind that there are no water provisions at any point. The road begins ascending immediately, and within 0.5 mile you'll reach a small clearing with a view of the parking area and the foothill communities to the south. Another mile of gentle climbing brings you to a rusty water tank and even better views of the clouds and surrounding mountain peaks. Strawberry Peak, another hikeable summit in the San Gabriels, is also accessible from this trail. Now it's starting to feel like you've really left the city behind. If you time it right, you might see a blanket of clouds hovering below you over the city. It reminded me of the view you might get from an airplane window seat.

After about 2.5 miles, the trail reaches the north side of the San Gabriel mountain range at Josephine Saddle and curves around to the left (west). Now you'll take in a wide-open view of the back range of the San Gabriels, whose cedar- and rock-studded hills provide a striking contrast to the green chaparral canyons that typically make up the south range. Lined with oak and spruce trees, this is by far the shadiest stretch of trail as you head into the final stretch up to the peak.

At 3.6 miles, look up for a view of the summit; you might even hear echoes of hikers who made it to the top before you. It's less than 0.5 mile to the top from here.

You'll reach a clearing with a primitive helicopter pad; then it's a short climb up a singletrack trail to the top, where there's a small clearing framed by rocks and a satellite tower. Claim a rock and settle in to enjoy the panoramic views before heading back down the mountain to civilization. If ever there was an opportunity to channel John Muir and his quiet awe at viewing the "rare loveliness" of the San Gabriels for the first time, this is it.

GPS TRAILHEAD COORDINATES   N34° 16.279' W118° 9.133'

Take Exit 20 (Angeles Crest Highway/CA 2) from I-210 toward La Cañada–Flintridge. Head north on CA 2 9.3 miles to the intersection of Angeles Crest and Angeles Forest Highways. Turn left and park in the Clear Creek Ranger Station lot across from the trailhead.

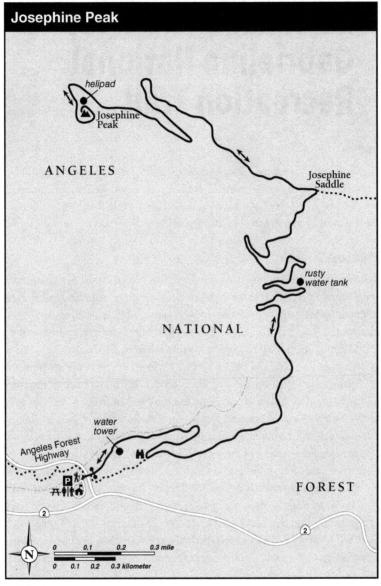

Josephine Peak

helipad

Josephine Peak

ANGELES

Josephine Saddle

rusty water tank

NATIONAL

water tower

Angeles Forest Highway

FOREST

| 0 | 0.1 | 0.2 | 0.3 mile |

| 0 | 0.1 | 0.2 | 0.3 kilometer |

N

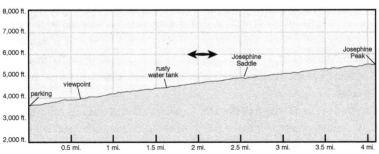

29 La Cañada Fire Road to Gabrielino National Recreation Trail

In Brief

This is a quieter and more exposed way of reaching the Arroyo Seco stream that hugs the popular Gabrielino National Recreation Trail. It takes you behind an upscale hillside neighborhood and an electricity substation, and then quickly disappears into nature as it switchbacks downhill to a streamside campground.

Description

The Gabrielino Trail is one of several in the Angeles National Forest designated as a multiuse national recreation trail. It follows the route of an original 1920s road that ran from Pasadena north up the canyon past wilderness resorts and old rustic cabins. The road lost its appeal after the Angeles Crest Highway was built, but today it has reinvented itself as a multiuse trail for hikers, horseback riders, mountain bikers, and birders.

This hike gains you access to the Gabrielino National Recreation Trail from the Angeles Crest Highway via a well-maintained fire road that skirts the back of the town of La Cañada–Flintridge. Most hikers access it via the trailhead near the NASA Jet Propulsion Laboratory. This trail is a quieter alternative to that and allows you to skip the first couple of miles of the Gabrielino National Recreation Trail, which are often crowded, and head straight for the bucolic segment of the trek. This path also allows you to access the forest 24/7, unlike most other forest trailheads, which are closed between sunset and sunrise.

From the parking pullout area, look for the sign for the Gabrielino National Recreation Trail. Walk around the fire-road gate at the north end and follow the paved road east. You will pass a sign marked 2N69 and a couple of large private homes on the left. Landscaped wildflowers and succulents flank the path here, helping mitigate the ugliness of the transmission towers that are also part of the scenery. After 100 yards or so you will pass a huge electricity substation on the right. It's loud, unsightly, and impossible to ignore, but once you're past it, the path turns greener and quieter.

At about 0.4 mile, the trail turns to dirt and starts to descend via wide switchbacks into the forest. You may hear a seasonal stream gurgling on your left, and you will start to get some nice views of chaparral-covered mountains straight ahead. To the right are the rooftops of some of La Cañada's more expensive hillside homes, but they quickly disappear from view.

For the next 0.5 mile the trail hugs the canyon wall and remains exposed to the hot sun as it continues to descend into the forest. At about 0.75 mile the path winds around to the left and briefly turns shady before passing by a clearing with a couple of pieces of

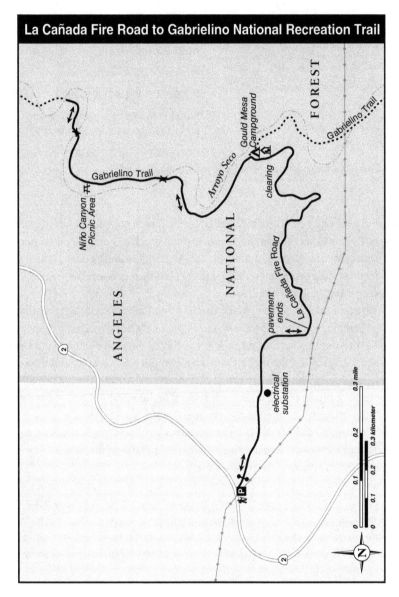

La Cañada Fire Road to Gabrielino National Recreation Trail

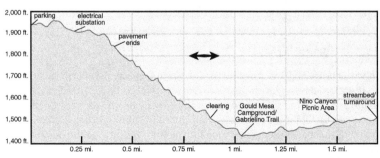

DISTANCE & CONFIGURATION: 3.4-mile out-and-back	**HIKING TIME:** 1 hour, 10 minutes
DIFFICULTY: Moderate	**ACCESS:** 24/7; free
SCENERY: Mountains, Arroyo Seco stream	**MAPS:** USGS *Pasadena*
	WHEELCHAIR ACCESSIBLE: First mile
EXPOSURE: Sunny	**FACILITIES:** Water, restrooms at Gould Mesa Campground, picnic areas
TRAFFIC: Light	**CONTACT:** 626-574-1613; **www.fs.usda**
TRAIL SURFACE: Paved and packed dirt	**.gov/main/angeles**

rusted-out machinery, a couple of dilapidated picnic tables, and piles of cut logs. Don't be discouraged by this view; things soon turn shady and much more scenic. Just after 1 mile, you will pass a sign marking the border to the Angeles National Forest. Continue on a gradual decline as the path reaches the final stretch before it connects with the Gabrielino National Recreation Trail at 1.1 miles.

You will come to a T and a sign for Gould Mesa Campground. Beyond that is the Arroyo Seco stream, which will be a welcome sight if it's a hot day. To the right are bathrooms and a water fountain. Hang a left here and follow the path north toward Oakwilde Campground. At 1.3 miles, the trail crosses over a wooden footbridge, and then winds a bit closer to the stream and passes the Niño Canyon Picnic Area on the left. This is a great place to stop for a snack, read a book, or just hang out under the shade of oak and alder forest with the background of a gurgling stream. I only saw a handful of people on this stretch of the trail (Gould Mesa to Niño Canyon) when I was here on a Saturday afternoon, in contrast to the dozens of recreation seekers I passed on the busier southern portion of the Gabrielino National Recreation Trail.

At 1.6 miles the trail crosses another wooden footbridge and soon reaches a stream crossing. This is another good place to stop and rest on one of the many big boulders that frame the stream. From here, you can cross the stream and add another 1.5 miles to the hike by continuing to Paul Little Picnic Area. Or you can turn around and retrace your steps back to the fire road and La Cañada–Flintridge. Just be sure to reserve some water for the uphill trek back.

GPS TRAILHEAD COORDINATES
N34° 13.363' W118° 11.407'

From downtown Los Angeles, take the Golden State Freeway (I-5) north to the Glendale Freeway (CA 2), and head north for 7.8 miles. Merge onto I-210. Take Exit 20 (Angeles Crest Highway). Turn left and continue about 2 miles on the Angeles Crest Highway (you'll pass the La Cañada Country Club on the right) until you see a pullout parking area on the right. Park in the lot and look for the fire-road gate at the north corner.

30 La Tuna Canyon

A view of the San Gabriel Mountains from La Tuna Canyon trail

In Brief

This moderate hike takes you deep into an oak-shaded canyon, up the north slope of the Verdugo Mountains, and then to a fire road that runs across the entire Verdugo range. The approximate 1,000-foot elevation gain is gradual, with the steepest parts coming during the last mile.

Description

La Tuna Canyon is a small community between the towns of Sun Valley and La Crescenta. *La Tuna* is the Spanish word for "prickly pear cactus," which can be found across Southern California's landscape.

Park in the pullout on the south side of La Tuna Canyon Road and look for the SANTA MONICA CONSERVANCY sign at the eastern edge of the pullout (another sign and trailhead at the west side of the pullout marks a shorter trail). Take the single-track dirt trail south as it heads away from the road. At 0.25 mile, you will come to a fallen

DISTANCE & CONFIGURATION: 4.4-mile out-and-back	**MAPS:** USGS *Burbank;* **lamountains.com /maps/laTuna.pdf**
DIFFICULTY: Moderate	**WHEELCHAIR ACCESSIBLE:** No
SCENERY: Chaparral, panoramic city and mountain views	**FACILITIES:** Picnic tables
EXPOSURE: Shade and sun	**CONTACT:** 818-880-0363; **lamountains .com/parks.asp?parkid=26**
TRAFFIC: Moderate	**COMMENTS:** This hike can be shortened to 3.5 miles by looping back via a steeper alternative trail or lengthened by continuing east to Verdugo Peak from the main fire road.
TRAIL SURFACE: Packed dirt	
HIKING TIME: 2 hours	
ACCESS: Daily, sunrise–sunset; free	

oak tree blocking the trail; climb over it and continue on the path as it veers right. Soon La Tuna Canyon Road will be visible again as the trail winds north and then zigzags to the southeast. After about 1 mile of easy walking, you will come to a trail junction. The path to the right is a steep shortcut to the top of the mountain range. The mainstream trail continues left and descends gradually into a shaded canyon dotted with oak and sycamore trees and a seasonal creek. It may seem like this trail takes you away from your final destination at the top of the mountain, but it just meanders a bit before ascending and connecting to the fire road.

At 1.5 miles, you will pass an abandoned old truck just off the trail. From here, the trail begins its final ascent to the mountain ridge that links to other trails within the Verdugo range. At just under 2 miles, you will come to a T. Stop and admire the sweeping views of the San Fernando Valley, and then turn left to continue another 0.2 mile to the main fire road, which offers even better vistas and links to other trails within the Verdugo range. Back at the T, the path to the right offers a shorter (though significantly steeper) alternative route back to the trailhead. If you choose this shortcut, the hike will total 3.5 miles instead of the 4.4 miles listed for the out-and-back hike. Just make sure to wear sturdy footwear and use caution on the way down.

I prefer to retrace my steps back through the shaded canyon to the trailhead. Though there is some shade on this hike, it is best done in the cooler winter and spring months. The trail is prone to mudslides during heavy rains and should be avoided.

GPS TRAILHEAD COORDINATES
N34° 13.989' W118° 18.606'

From downtown Los Angeles, take the Glendale Freeway (CA 2) north to I-210 West, and in 3.7 miles take Exit 14 (La Tuna Canyon Road). Turn left and go under the freeway; follow the road about 1.5 miles to the third parking pullout on the left. Look for the Santa Monica Conservancy signs that mark the two trails that begin here, and take the one to the far left.

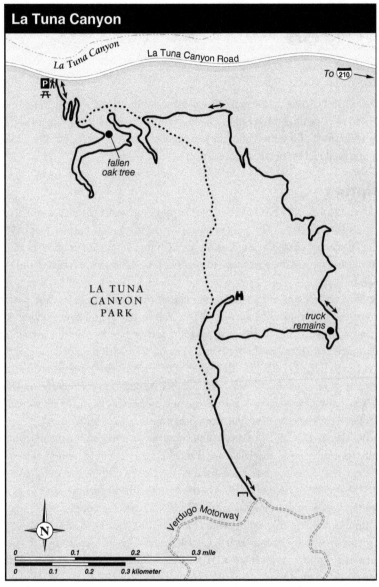

La Tuna Canyon

La Tuna Canyon
La Tuna Canyon Road
To 210

fallen
oak tree

LA TUNA
CANYON
PARK

truck
remains

Verdugo Motorway

N

| 0 | 0.1 | 0.2 | 0.3 mile |
| 0 | 0.1 | 0.2 | 0.3 kilometer |

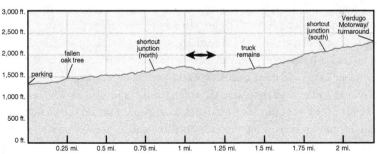

31 Legg Lake Loop Trail

In Brief

Ducks, geese, and two attractive recreational lakes dominate the scenery of this easy loop trail in a nature park near the western edge of the San Gabriel River. Legg Lake's picnic tables and lakeshores fill up with families and anglers on weekends, but the hiking trails are wide and well maintained and never seem overcrowded.

Description

Legg Lake and North Legg Lake are two of four bodies of water within the 400-acre Whittier Narrows Natural Area. The park was run by the Audubon Society from 1939 until 1970, when it was purchased by the Los Angeles County Department of Parks and Recreation. Spring and fall are the best times to visit because the weather is nicest and the trees are in bloom.

The loop trail begins at the northern edge of the Santa Anita Avenue parking lot. You'll immediately see (and hear) the lake's resident ducks and geese trying to cadge some crumbs from picnickers gathered at tables and on blankets on the lawn in front of you. Follow the gravel trail to the right as it runs parallel with the north side of the lake. Known as North Legg Lake, this is the bigger of the two lakes within the recreation area; on weekends it is often filled with paddleboats, though no swimming or wading is allowed. You'll also hear traffic noise from the nearby freeway as you begin walking, but a parking lot and the cackling of seagulls and other birds tend to buffer it.

Besides ring-necked ducks, Canada and snow geese, and California gulls, other birds commonly spotted around the lakes are mourning doves, coots, hummingbirds, swallows, killdeer, and double-crested cormorants. Cottontail rabbits, raccoons, and California ground squirrels are also abundant. On the human side, expect to see a mix of joggers, bicyclists, families with kids, lone power walkers, and strolling couples.

Continue following the trail west as it winds past restrooms and heads south at a parking lot along Rosemead Boulevard/CA 19. At the edge of the parking lot, veer to the left slightly at a sign that says BIKE ROUTE; then continue straight between the recycling bins on the right and two electric transmission towers on the left. If you make a sharp left, you'll find yourself on a shorter trail leading back to the Santa Anita Avenue parking lot. At about 1.1 miles you'll come to a palm tree and another turnoff for a path that leads to a large playground and eventually back to the parking lot. Continue straight on the loop trail as it becomes nicely shaded by palms and drought-resistant pines. You'll soon spot Legg Lake (and more quacking ducks and geese) on your left. There are more restrooms here and a concrete platform for launching model boats. The trail runs very close to the lake at this point; it's a nice spot to stop and soak up the view. This area of the park tends to be less crowded than the northern end, especially on weekdays. As the trail curves east around the lake, you'll spot a refinery on your right. In the foreground

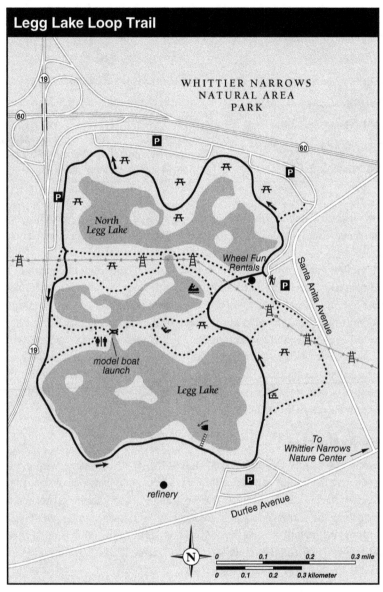

Legg Lake Loop Trail

WHITTIER NARROWS
NATURAL AREA
PARK

North
Legg Lake

Wheel Fun
Rentals

Santa Anita Avenue

model boat
launch

Legg Lake

To
Whittier Narrows
Nature Center

refinery

Durfee Avenue

N

| 0 | 0.1 | 0.2 | 0.3 mile |
| 0 | 0.1 | 0.2 | 0.3 kilometer |

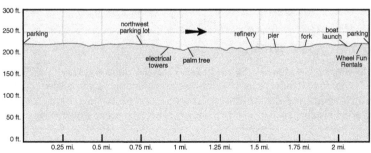

DISTANCE & CONFIGURATION: 2.2-mile loop	**ACCESS:** Daily, sunrise–sunset; $6 parking fee on weekends and holidays
DIFFICULTY: Easy	**MAPS:** USGS *El Monte*
SCENERY: Native plants, birds	**WHEELCHAIR ACCESSIBLE:** Yes
EXPOSURE: Mostly sun, some shade	**FACILITIES:** Restrooms, water, picnic tables, boat rentals
TRAFFIC: Heavy on weekends	
TRAIL SURFACE: Gravel path	**CONTACT:** 626-575-5526; **parks.lacounty .gov/wps/portal/dpr/Parks/Whittier _Narrows_Recreation_Area**
HIKING TIME: 1 hour	

are a few makeshift stables and their equine residents munching grass just beyond a chain-link fence. From here, you can access the bike path of the upper San Gabriel River to the south.

At 1.8 miles, you'll come to a Y in the path with a picnic pavilion directly in front of you. The right trail is the most direct route back to the parking lot, but I recommend opting for the left one because it is more scenic. Among the things you'll see on this route: some modest fitness equipment, a pretty green bridge that overlooks North Legg Lake, and a few kid-friendly climbing structures. You'll also pass more picnic tables and another path on the left that leads to the playground in the middle of the park. Continue to the right past a grove of palm trees and a long boat ramp, then more picnic tables, and soon you'll see the parking lot in the distance. Just before the end of the loop is a kiosk that rents bikes and boats on weekends.

Nearby Activities

Whittier Narrows Nature Center, at 1100 Durfee Rd., is a rustic cabin with interpretive displays of native plants and wildlife, a library of history and nature books, and a tiny live zoo of Western toads, lizards, a great blue heron, and even an untethered horned owl. Off the parking lot is the entrance to a mile-long nature trail that's popular with families and school groups. It's open 8 a.m.–5 p.m. From the Santa Anita Avenue parking lot, turn right and follow Santa Anita Avenue 0.4 mile to Durfee Road. Turn left on Durfee and drive 0.5 mile to the nature center on the right.

GPS TRAILHEAD COORDINATES

N34° 2.209' W118° 3.386'

From downtown L.A., take I-5 South to Exit 134B (Pomona Freeway/CA 60), and head east on CA 60 for 9.7 miles. Exit at Santa Anita Avenue, turn right, and follow the signs to South El Monte and the Whittier Narrows Natural Area. The parking lot is on your right. Parking is also available in two large lots off Rosemead Boulevard.

32 Lower Arroyo Seco Trail

View of the historic Colorado Street Bridge from the trail

In Brief

This historic Pasadena hike parallels the Arroyo Seco flood-control channel for its first mile, then winds under a grand old bridge before reaching a natural stream and turning bucolic and shady. It ends near Brookside Park, home to an aquatics center, a kids museum, and the Rose Bowl stadium. Its loose dirt path and flat surface make it a popular spot for early-evening joggers and dog walkers from the surrounding Pasadena neighborhoods.

Description

The trail begins at a sign marked HORSEBACK RIDING AND HIKING TRAIL. Follow the loose dirt trail as it winds along the east side of the concrete flood-control channel. The west side of the flood channel is also a trail, but it tends to be muddier than its eastern counterpart; the two trails eventually merge into one after they cross under the

DISTANCE & CONFIGURATION: 4-mile out-and-back	**ACCESS:** Daily, sunrise–sunset; free
DIFFICULTY: Easy	**MAPS:** USGS *Pasadena;* **ci.pasadena .ca.us/PublicWorks/Arroyo_Trails**
SCENERY: Historic bridges, flood-control channel, shady streambed	**WHEELCHAIR ACCESSIBLE:** Yes
EXPOSURE: Sunny	**FACILITIES:** None
TRAFFIC: Moderate	**CONTACT:** 626-744-7311; **ci.pasadena .ca.us/PublicWorks/Arroyo_Trails**
TRAIL SURFACE: Dirt and gravel	**COMMENTS:** No bikes are allowed, and all dogs must be on a leash. Horseback riders also frequent the trail.
HIKING TIME: 2 hours	

Ventura Freeway bridge. Expect to see a number of joggers, attracted by the loose dirt and flatness, on this part of the path. I also encountered many dog walkers here during the early spring evening that I hiked this trail.

The path is flanked by some native trees, such as oak and sycamore, but the dominant scenery during the first half of the hike is the concrete flood-control channel that was built in the 1940s by the U.S. Army Corps of Engineers after a major flood devastated the area in 1938. Canyon walls loom on each side of the channel, and if you look up and to the left, you will see some of Pasadena's finer homes peeking out from behind them. The neighborhood to the west is the exclusive San Rafael area of Pasadena; the homes here are more reminiscent of Beverly Hills estates than the Craftsman bungalow structures for which the city is known. At about 0.6 mile you will pass on the right another testament to the path's use as an equestrian trail: a large horse statue fashioned out of sticks. Continue walking straight along the channel. This is arguably the least attractive part of the hike—a chain-link fence borders either side of the channel, and the plant life is limited to random shrub clusters and an occasional oak or sycamore tree.

Look up and to the east and you will see the top of a castlelike building jutting out from the trees. This is the former Vista del Arroyo Hotel, a posh Spanish Colonial Revival resort that thrived in the 1930s. It was used as a military hospital during World War II, was restored by the government in the 1980s, and is now a U.S. Court of Appeals and federal building.

At about 1.3 miles, you will pass another small bridge on the left that crosses the flood channel; to the right is a path that leads to the park's upper parking lot. Continue straight on the trail as it heads beneath a series of bridges. The first one is the most interesting, both architecturally and anecdotally. Listed on the National Register of Historic Places, the 150-foot Colorado Street Bridge was built in 1913 to make it easier for horse-drawn wagons to cross the Arroyo Seco, and it has served as a scenic gateway to central Pasadena ever since. As the legend goes, a construction worker helping build the bridge tumbled over the side and into a vat of wet concrete below. Assuming it was futile to try to save him, his coworkers left his body in the quick-drying material. Some claim you can still hear his desperate cries and attribute them to the bridge's reputation as a popular

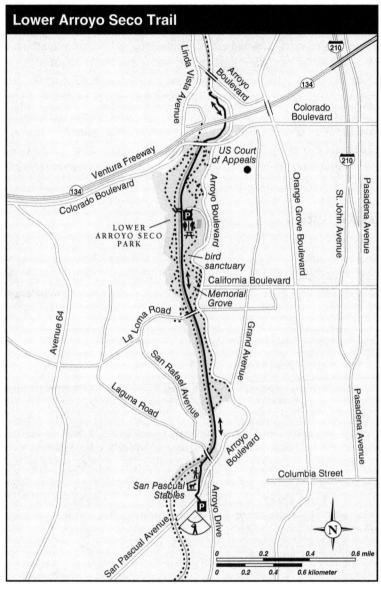

Lower Arroyo Seco Trail

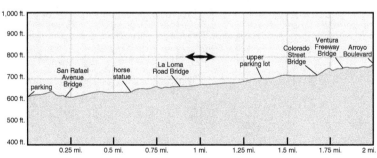

suicide spot. Between 1919 and 1937, close to 100 people reportedly jumped to their deaths from the bridge.

After passing below the Colorado Street Bridge, the path winds under the utilitarian Ventura Freeway bridge and heads uphill briefly before dropping into a shady glen with a small stream on the left. The final 0.3 mile of the hike is serene and bucolic, despite its proximity to a major commuting thoroughfare. After passing a private home on the right, the dirt path ends at a white picket fence, and you find yourself facing Arroyo Boulevard. Look north and you will see the parking lot for Brookside Park, Pasadena's largest park. It is about a 0.5-mile walk along the side of the boulevard to the park's picnic area from here. Another 0.25 mile leads to the Rose Bowl stadium. Or you can turn around and follow the flood-control channel back to the main parking lot.

Nearby Activities

At the north end of the trail is Brookside Park, home to an aquatic center, the wheelchair-accessible Reese's Retreat playground, and Kidspace Children's Museum. To the south is Arroyo Seco Golf Course, a public course with a driving range, putting green, café, and mini-golf. It's open daily, sunrise–10 p.m.; for more information, visit **arroyosecogolf.com.**

GPS TRAILHEAD COORDINATES

N34° 7.462' W118° 9.974'

From downtown Los Angeles, take the Pasadena Freeway (CA 110) north to Marmion Way/Avenue 64. Bear left and continue to York Boulevard. Turn right on York; then make a left onto San Pascual Avenue and drive about 1 mile to Lower Arroyo Seco Park. Park on the street or in the dirt lot next to the baseball field (or across from the field if all the spaces are taken), and walk north past San Pascual Stables to the trailhead. There is also a parking lot near the trailhead, but it's for stable patrons only.

Alternate directions: Take I-210 East to its end. Turn right onto California Boulevard. In 0.2 mile turn left onto Orange Grove Boulevard; then in 0.6 mile turn right onto Madeline Drive, which becomes Arroyo Boulevard. Bear right onto San Pascual Avenue to the park entrance.

33 Millard Canyon:
SUNSET RIDGE TRAIL

A steep section of the Sunset Ridge Trail

In Brief

Bordered by fern-draped rock walls, this tranquil Angeles National Forest trail begins at the bottom of a cool and shady canyon and ascends quickly via switchbacks to terrific views of the San Gabriel Valley and Los Angeles.

Description

The Sunset Ridge Trail officially begins at an elevation of 2,000 feet near the intersection of Mount Lowe Fire Road and Chaney Trail, but this hike tacks on an extra mile by beginning at the bottom of the canyon near Millard Campground. Millard Falls was once a popular and easy hike for families and locals looking to cool off in the boulder-strewn

DISTANCE & CONFIGURATION: 5-mile out-and-back or balloon	**ACCESS:** Daily, 6 a.m.–8 p.m.; free
	MAPS: USGS *Pasadena*
DIFFICULTY: Strenuous	**WHEELCHAIR ACCESSIBLE:** Portions (fire road)
SCENERY: Seasonal waterfalls, forested canyon, views of San Gabriel Valley and Los Angeles basin	**FACILITIES:** None
EXPOSURE: Shade and sun	**CONTACT:** 626-574-1613; **www.fs.usda .gov/main/angeles**
TRAFFIC: Light	**COMMENT:** The 2009 Station Fire severely damaged parts of this trail and altered the scenery. However, much of the trail has been restored, and it reopened in 2011.
TRAIL SURFACE: Dirt path, paved fire road	
HIKING TIME: 3 hours	

creek on a hot day. But drought conditions, wildfires, and bear activity have kept visitors away in recent years. When I last hiked this trail, the campground was closed, but the trail to the falls was still as shady and peaceful as I remembered it.

From the parking area, you'll walk past a fire-road gate and past a couple of rustic cabins. Continue toward the campground and look for the dark-wood sign marking the Sunset Ridge Trail on the right. It's a singletrack trail that immediately begins ascending the mountain. There's no relief from the elevation gain for nearly a mile, when you reach Mount Lowe Fire Road, but the canyon views and serenity you soak up along the way should help propel you along.

At the fire road, you'll see a trail register and a watering trough made out of local arroyo rocks. There is also an interpretive sign with a hand-drawn map and information on Mount Lowe Railway, a top tourist attraction in Southern California from 1896 to 1936. Millions of visitors rode the cable incline railway to a luxury resort complex that sat atop Echo Mountain and looked out over the then-bucolic Los Angeles basin. The resort burned in the early 1900s; a century later, the area surrounding it is a popular trail system that leads to the remains of the old resort, among other destinations throughout the Angeles National Forest.

After admiring the views and marveling at how green the town of Altadena looks from above, pick up the fire road as it heads northeast. This is the shadeless portion of the trail, but it also has impressive wide-open views of Altadena and the Los Angeles basin. At about 0.4 mile, bear left on a dirt path marked SUNSET RIDGE TRAIL. The path quickly turns shady and secluded as it begins a gentle descent north, then east along Millard Canyon's southern wall. In the spring, gorgeous yellow wildflowers cover the rocky hills that border the right side of the path. This trail is also popular with mountain bikers, so stay alert for "to your left" or other shouted warnings. This is a good hike if you're looking for a brief escape from everyday stress. The green mountains have a calming effect and make you feel like you're far deeper into the wilderness than you actually are.

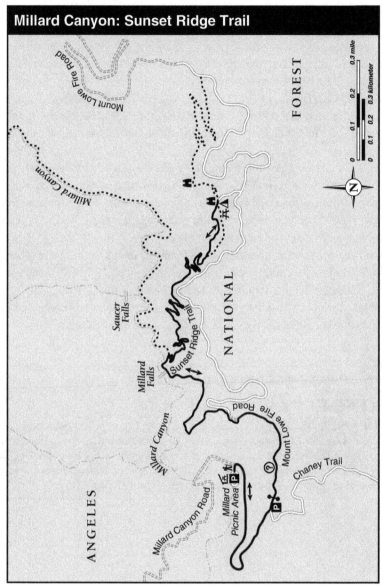

Millard Canyon: Sunset Ridge Trail

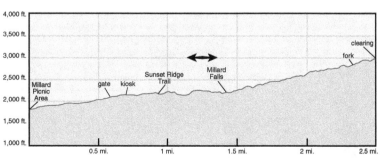

At about 0.9 mile, the Sunset Ridge Trail veers right and ascends into dense woodland. Continue on the trail as it climbs in long and short switchbacks up the fern-draped canyon wall. The path turns steep, narrow, and pleasantly shady with occasional patches of sunlight. Not long ago, sounds of the canyon stream serenaded hikers along this stretch, but years of drought have decreased that likelihood. After about 0.5 mile of climbing, two more seasonal waterfalls may come into view through the trees. Known as Punchbowl and Saucer Falls, these cascades are located on the other side of the canyon and tough to access up close. Better views await as you continue climbing the switchbacks to an elevation of 2,800 feet.

At about 1.9 miles, you will come to a level dirt clearing with good views of the San Gabriel Valley and Los Angeles basin. Resist the temptation to stop, and continue a few more steps to a turnoff for a trail that leads uphill to a couple of big-cone pine trees and even better views. There are no benches, but it's a good place to rest and mark the almost halfway point of this quiet and contemplative hike.

From here, continue another 0.5 mile to a clearing and rustic campsite. There's also a historic Works Progress Administration marker and a picnic table with sweeping views. Continue briefly on the dirt trail until it rejoins Mount Lowe Fire Road. You can turn right and take the fire road back to the trail register, or retrace your steps back down the canyon. The shadier out-and-back option is a wiser choice in summer.

GPS TRAILHEAD COORDINATES
N34° 12.972' W118° 8.775'

From the Foothill Freeway (I-210), take Exit 26 (Lake Avenue), and head north to the end, about 3.6 miles. Turn left onto Loma Alta Drive, and in 1 mile turn right onto Chaney Trail. Drive north about 2 miles to the end. Park in the large parking lot. A California Adventure Pass is required to park here, as well as near the fire-road gate at the top of the canyon. (To purchase, see page xii for details.)

34 **Monrovia Canyon Park:**
BILL CULL AND FALLS TRAILS

Monrovia Canyon Falls

In Brief

Canopies of coast live oak, big-leaf maple, and sycamore trees line this pleasant trail, which is named after a volunteer and follows a stream and man-made dams to a 50-foot waterfall that runs year-round.

Description

Located on the southern fringe of the Angeles National Forest, 80-acre Monrovia Canyon Park is run by the city of Monrovia and was the site of a resort lodge used by city dwellers

DISTANCE & CONFIGURATION: 2.6-mile out-and-back	**WHEELCHAIR ACCESSIBLE:** No
DIFFICULTY: Moderate	**FACILITIES:** Restrooms, water fountains, picnic areas
SCENERY: Dense woodland, waterfall	**CONTACT:** 626-256-8246; **cityofmonrovia**
EXPOSURE: Shady	**.org/publicworks/page/parks**
TRAFFIC: Moderate	**COMMENTS:** Dogs are allowed in the park, but they must be kept on leashes.
TRAIL SURFACE: Dirt path	For a longer hike, try 7-mile Ben Overturff
HIKING TIME: 1.5 hours	Trail, named for the Monrovia contractor who built a resort here in the early 1900s.
ACCESS: Gate: Wednesday–Monday, 8 a.m.–5 p.m.; $5 parking fee	Look for the trailhead on the right side of the road after you pass the entrance sta-
MAPS: USGS *Azusa;* at entrance gate and nature center	tion. The Ben Overturff Trail is closed on Tuesdays and Wednesdays.

as a weekend getaway between 1911 and 1945. In addition to hiking trails, it has several shady picnic areas and a nature center that hosts education programs and guided hikes. The Falls Trail, either via the Bill Cull Trail or the nature center parking lot, gains 600 feet in elevation and is shorter and more crowded than the Ben Overturff Trail. The Falls Trail seems to attract a good number of solo hikers, though families and large groups tend to dominate the area on weekends.

The Falls Trail can be accessed via the nature center or from the Bill Cull Trail. The Bill Cull Trail begins just beyond the park's entrance station on the left. The trail is fairly easy to follow on its own, but small signs posted along the way direct you toward the waterfall. Follow the narrow dirt path as it winds uphill along a sunny slope and parallels a stream below. In the late winter and spring, you can also expect to see an abundance of yellow and purple wildflowers. Watch for poison oak, which is plentiful here. At 0.2 mile, the path curves around to the right (the relatively new Cunningham Overlook Trail goes straight) and continues on a gradual incline through dense groves of white alder, maple, sycamore, and coast live oak trees. I've spotted the occasional opossum and lots of gray squirrels and salamanders here; the park is also home to mountain lions, Southern Pacific rattlesnakes, deer, coyotes, and gray foxes. At about 0.5 mile, you'll pass the first of several man-made dams along the trail on your right. A little farther along, the trail crosses the stream (it's narrow and big rocks make crossing easy) and you come to a short flight of stone steps. Follow these straight, and then head left to continue toward the waterfall. If you turn right, you'll find yourself at a picnic area and parking lot in the middle of the park.

From here, the path continues to the left of the stream and descends into a shady clearing strewn with large rocks. Continue walking as the path weaves back and forth on both sides of the stream. At about 1.3 miles, you'll reach the waterfall, which is usually gushing at full force. The boulders flanking the waterfall make for a good place to stop

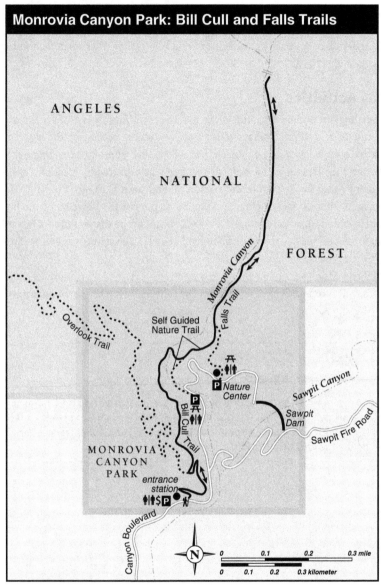

Monrovia Canyon Park: Bill Cull and Falls Trails

ANGELES

NATIONAL

FOREST

Monrovia Canyon

Overlook Trail

Falls Trail

Self Guided
Nature Trail

Sawpit Canyon

P Nature
Center

Bill Cull Trail

Sawpit
Dam

Sawpit Fire Road

MONROVIA
CANYON
PARK

entrance
station

Canyon Boulevard

N

0   0.1   0.2   0.3 mile
0   0.1   0.2   0.3 kilometer

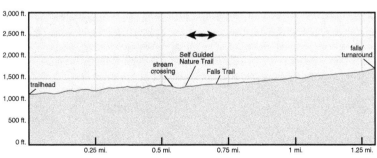

3,000 ft.

2,500 ft.

2,000 ft.
falls/
turnaround

Self Guided
Nature Trail

1,500 ft.
stream
crossing
Falls Trail

trailhead
1,000 ft.

500 ft.

0 ft.

0.25 mi.   0.5 mi.   0.75 mi.   1 mi.   1.25 mi.

and enjoy a sack lunch. Or take a few moments for reflection before retracing your steps back to the parking lot.

The trails are occasionally closed due to rain or other weather-related conditions; it's always a good idea to call ahead to check: 626-256-8282.

Nearby Activities

Before heading out of the park, stop at the nature center for displays of flora and wildlife native to the park, and pay homage to the redwood statue of Samson the Hot Tub Bear. As the story goes, Samson, an old black bear, spent several months hanging out in a hot tub in the area until he ingested a plastic bag and was captured by local officials. He got used to being cared for by people and couldn't be released back into the wild. Monrovia residents made him a cause célèbre, and donations poured in to save him from being put to sleep. He ended up at the Orange County Zoo (in a cage that featured a hot tub) and lived out the rest of his days there until he died in 2001. The statue was erected in 2003 as a paean to all animals that have died needlessly.

Old Town Monrovia's main street, Myrtle Avenue, is lined with antiques shops, sidewalk cafés, and mom-and-pop restaurants. On Fridays, 4–8 p.m., there's a farmer's market along Myrtle Avenue.

GPS TRAILHEAD COORDINATES

N34° 10.394' W117° 59.455'

Take I-210 to Monrovia, and take Exit 34 (Myrtle Avenue); drive north 1.2 miles through Old Town Monrovia to Foothill Boulevard. Turn right; then in 0.2 mile make a left onto Canyon Boulevard and follow it for about 1.7 miles to the park entrance. Park in the lot just below the entrance station.

---

35 Mount Wilson Trail to Orchard Camp

First Water is a shady stop along the Mount Wilson Trail.

In Brief

This popular and historic hike begins near a former speakeasy on Mira Monte Avenue and weaves tough uphill climbing with scenic city views and quiet streamside stopping points. It can be easily turned into an all-day adventure by continuing another 3.5 miles to the Mount Wilson Observatory. With its relatively easy street parking, this trail tends to be somewhat less congested than other nearby trails in Chantry Flats and Eaton Canyon, especially on weekends.

Description

The Mount Wilson Trail was created in 1864 by Benjamin "Don Benito" Wilson as a way to bring timber down to his ranch (the city of Pasadena had yet to be founded). In the late 1880s, pack burros carried telescopes and other materials up the trail to the Mount Wilson Observatory, the preeminent 1904 research facility that yielded discoveries by Edwin

DISTANCE & CONFIGURATION: 7-mile out-and-back	**MAPS:** USGS *Pasadena* and USGS *Mount Wilson*
DIFFICULTY: Strenuous	**WHEELCHAIR ACCESSIBLE:** No
SCENERY: City and mountain views, chaparral hillsides	**FACILITIES:** Restrooms at Mount Wilson Park
EXPOSURE: Mostly sunny	**CONTACT:** 626-574-1613; **www.fs.usda**
TRAFFIC: Heavy on weekends	**.gov/main/angeles**
TRAIL SURFACE: Packed dirt	**COMMENTS:** Parts of this trail are narrow and hug the side of the canyon, with no protective barriers from steep drops. It's wise to stay on the trails and use caution at all times.
HIKING TIME: 3 hours	
ACCESS: Daily, sunrise–sunset; free parking on Mira Monte Avenue	

Hubble and Harlow Shapley that transformed the field of astronomy. Orchard Camp was the halfway point for travelers to camp and refuel, and later became a popular trail resort. The foundations of some of the buildings remain, and today the camp remains a shady and peaceful rest spot or turnaround point for San Gabriel hikers.

Begin your hike on Mira Monte Avenue at Mount Wilson Trail Drive in Sierra Madre. A public bathroom is on the other side of Lizzie's Trail Inn next to the playground. Free street parking is available along North Mountain Trail. To get to the trailhead, follow the paved Mount Wilson Trail Drive north to the dirt road and keep left after you've walked past several residences. You'll gain a total of 2,100 feet in elevation on this hike, much of it in the first mile and a half. Soon you'll have scenic views of the San Gabriel Valley and a comforting sense that you've left the freeways and shopping malls far behind for a few hours. After about 1.6 miles of mostly uphill trekking via long switchbacks, you'll come to a trail sign and split. The trail to the right takes you down to First Water, a shady streamside area framed by large rocks and seasonal waterfalls; this makes a great stop for thirsty dogs and kids.

From here, it's a moderate 2 miles to Orchard Camp. Take the trail to the left as it levels off and brings you farther into the mountains. This part of the hike is a pleasant mix of shade and long, level stretches, though you still have a few moderate ascents ahead of you. At 3.5 miles, you'll come to a sign noting that Manzanita Ridge is another 1.9 miles and Mount Wilson itself is 3.5 miles farther up the mountain. To the right is a small clearing shaded by an antiquarian oak and anchored by the arroyo rock foundations left from Orchard Camp's days as a rustic resort. From here, you can turn around and retrace your steps back to Sierra Madre, or refuel before ascending another 2,000 feet to the top of the mountain for a 14-mile round-trip hike. (Hikers who make it to the top like to reward themselves with sandwiches or sundaes at the observatory's Cosmic Cafe, open on weekends April–November.)

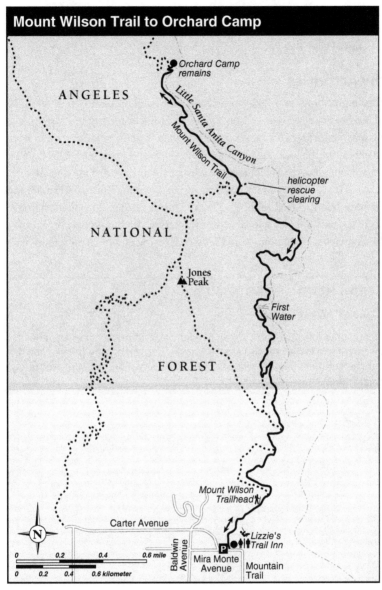

Mount Wilson Trail to Orchard Camp

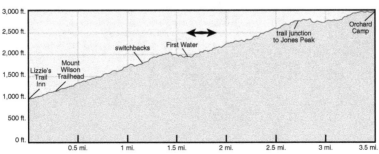

On the way back down, enjoy the views of Santa Anita racetrack and the surrounding area framed by the upside-down V of the mountains converging. It's an unusual vista of the San Gabriel Valley that you won't find on other trails.

Nearby Activities

Gambling, moonshine, and 20¢ sandwiches were once a feature of Lizzie's Trail Inn, perched just below the Mount Wilson Trailhead. Now the former speakeasy is a museum and only open Saturday, 10 a.m.–noon. If you plan it right, you can stop in before your hike and check out the local history books, old signs, and jovial vibe. Last time I stopped by, there was a huge cake to celebrate the 93rd birthday of one of the docents.

If Lizzie's is closed, try Mary's Market at 561 Woodland Dr. (**sierramadrenews.net /marysmarket.htm**), closed Mondays. Tucked into a residential neighborhood a couple of blocks to the east, it's also a local institution serving up home-style breakfasts and hot and cold sandwiches. A hamburger is $2.60 and nothing on the menu is more than $6.

GPS TRAILHEAD COORDINATES

N34° 10.328' W118° 2.812'

From I-210, take Exit 31 (North Baldwin Avenue), and drive north 1.3 miles through the town of Sierra Madre to Mira Monte Avenue. Turn right, and in less than 0.5 mile, look for the trailhead/Mount Wilson sign on the left. Park on Mira Monte or North Mountain Trail Avenue.

---

36 Sam Merrill Trail to Echo Mountain

Stone pillars mark the entrance to the Sam Merrill Trail.

In Brief

This path dips briefly into a shaded canyon and past a dry riverbed, then begins to climb via long switchbacks up Echo Mountain to an altitude of 1,400 feet. The reward is the ruins of a turn-of-the-20th-century mountain resort with sweeping views of downtown Los Angeles and the San Gabriel Valley.

DISTANCE & CONFIGURATION: 5.9-mile out-and-back	**HIKING TIME:** 3.5 hours
	ACCESS: Daily, sunrise–sunset; free
DIFFICULTY: Strenuous	**MAPS:** USGS *Pasadena* and USGS *Mount Wilson;* at kiosk beyond trailhead
SCENERY: Native plants and trees, panoramic views	
	WHEELCHAIR ACCESSIBLE: First 0.5 mile
EXPOSURE: Mostly sunny	
	FACILITIES: None
TRAFFIC: Heavy on weekends	**CONTACT:** 626-574-1613; **www.fs.usda**
TRAIL SURFACE: Packed dirt	**.gov/main/angeles**

Description

Stone pillars and an old iron gate mark the entrance to this former estate in Altadena, a laid-back community just north of Pasadena. The grounds are now a part of the Angeles National Forest, and a plaque at the entrance dedicates the property as "a quiet refuge for people and wild life forever." This is one of my favorite trails in Los Angeles County—the hikers are friendly and polite, the views are spectacular, and it offers a history lesson to boot. The looping switchbacks make the hike seem longer than it actually is. Save for a few red-tailed hawks, I have never seen much wildlife here, but the Pasadena Audubon Society considers the area a bird-rich refuge. It's a prime spot for the group's annual Christmas bird count; among the species members have spotted and logged in recent years are fox sparrows, great horned owls, and European starlings.

From the gate at Lake Avenue and Loma Alta Drive, follow the rutted driveway east about 200 yards until it begins to curve north. (If you stay on the driveway, you'll wind up at a rusted old water tank—this is not a bad walk, but it's nothing compared to the stunning views offered by the Merrill Trail.) Turn off the driveway onto a dirt trail and walk a few yards to a kiosk with a hand-drawn map and some old photos and information on the history of the area. Here you can also sign a guest book, which lets park rangers know who is on the trail.

Mount Lowe Railway, designed by professor, inventor, and Civil War balloonist Thaddeus S. C. Lowe, was a top tourist attraction in Southern California from 1896 to 1936. Millions of visitors rode the cable incline railway to a luxury resort complex that sat atop Echo Mountain and looked out over the then-bucolic Los Angeles basin. The resort burned in the early 1900s; 30 years later, Altadena residents built a trail along the same route the railway had followed. During the next decade, a retired Altadena resident named Samuel Merrill overhauled and maintained the path. After he died in 1948, the trail was named after him.

From the kiosk, follow the Lower Sam Merrill Trail, which dips north into Las Flores Canyon by way of a narrow dirt path lined with cactus, brush, and boulders. After about 0.5 mile, reach a dry riverbed and concrete debris dam (you may see a few picnickers or sunbathers camped out here). Once on the other side of the canyon, the trail winds south and turns into long switchbacks that begin the 2-mile climb up Echo

Sam Merrill Trail to Echo Mountain

ANGELES

NATIONAL

FOREST

Mount Lowe Railway Trail

Sam Merrill Trail

To Inspiration Point

Mount Lowe Railway Trail

Sam Merrill Trail

Echo Mountain House ruins

Echo Mountain

Las Flores Canyon

THE COBB ESTATE

Loma Alta Drive

Sam Merrill Trailhead

Lake Avenue

Alta Pine Drive

N

0   0.1   0.2   0.3 mile
0   0.1   0.2   0.3 kilometer

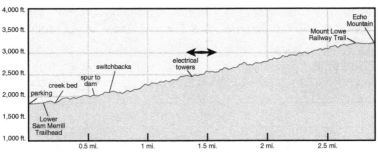

4,000 ft.
3,500 ft.
3,000 ft.
2,500 ft.
2,000 ft.
1,500 ft.
1,000 ft.

Echo Mountain

Mount Lowe Railway Trail

electrical towers

switchbacks

spur to dam

creek bed

parking

Lower Sam Merrill Trailhead

0.5 mi.   1 mi.   1.5 mi.   2 mi.   2.5 mi.

Mountain. The trail is shaded at first by forest, but it won't be long before you glimpse Altadena rooftops and the Los Angeles basin beyond. It's tempting to linger, but the views only get better as you ascend.

You're halfway to the top when you reach a flat area with three electrical transmission towers and panoramic valley-to-ocean views. To the left and below is the rusted water tower that the old driveway leads to (you may be tempted to smirk at the hikers who chose this path over Merrill Trail; go ahead—they can't see you).

Some people turn back here, satisfied with the vistas and the mile-plus uphill workout. If you want to continue to the top of the mountain, keep following the switchbacks for another 0.5 mile until you reach a junction with wooden markers. Bear right on the Echo Mountain Trail and continue to follow the old roadbed to the ruins of the resort. You'll pass a huge wheel cog on the left that once hauled the cable cars up the incline, as well as several signs with photos and text explaining the construction of the railway and resort. There is also an original megaphone from the resort's heyday, encouraging visitors to use it and see how Echo Mountain got its name. The final stop is a wide, flat area covered with a maze of stone ruins of the old hotel. There are few trees up here, but it's a nice spot to rest for a while on a cool day and enjoy the view.

From here, most hikers turn back and retrace their steps along the switchbacks to the Sam Merrill Trail. Hardier souls can hike another steep 0.5 mile to Inspiration Point, where there are more great views and an enclosed pavilion.

If you do this hike in the summer, you'll want to get an early start, before the sun rises from behind the northern ridge of the San Gabriels. There is very little shade, and water and sunscreen are a must. If you're hiking in the winter or spring, it's pleasant to time it so you're descending as the sun begins to set; just make sure to give yourself enough time to get back to Lake Avenue before dark.

Nearby Activities

Lake Avenue, between I-210 and the trailhead, is home to several venerable Southern California eateries. The Hat (491 N. Lake), established in 1951, serves legendary pastrami dip sandwiches; just up the road, the old-school Roma Deli (918 N. Lake) is known for its Italian cold cut sandwiches, made with love by the proud and elderly Rosario. For a sit-down meal, Roscoe's Chicken 'n' Waffles (830 N. Lake) serves tasty fried chicken and has a devoted following.

GPS TRAILHEAD COORDINATES   N34° 12.248' W118° 7.834'

From the Foothill Freeway (I-210), take Exit 26 (Lake Avenue), and head north to the end, about 3.6 miles, to Loma Alta Drive. Park on Lake or Loma Alta. The trail begins at the intersection of Lake and Loma Alta at the iron gate marked COBB ESTATE.

37 Stough Canyon Nature Center Trail

The steep beginning of Stough Canyon Nature Center Trail

In Brief

This peaceful, sunbaked trail in the Verdugo Mountains follows a gradual incline along a well-maintained fire road to an elevation of 1,000 feet. Benches donated by local community groups dot the trail, so hikers can take some time to soak up the prime viewpoints.

Description

This uphill trail in the Verdugo Mountains above Burbank is popular with residents of the surrounding neighborhoods but (undeservedly) doesn't get much recognition beyond the east San Fernando Valley. The Verdugos are a geologically detached part of the San Gabriel Mountains encompassing 9,000 acres; they are run by the Angeles District of the state park system and are home to chaparral, coastal sage brush, coast live oak trees, and toyon and lemonade berry bushes.

The modern nature center is a hub for maps, wildlife updates, and organized children's activities. It also hosts weekly group hikes for all ages and fitness levels; call 818-238-5440 for details. The center is closed on Mondays and most holidays, but you can always access the restrooms or view a detailed color map of the area before beginning your hike.

The Stough trailhead begins beyond a gate to the west of the nature center, climbing steadily uphill along a wide gravel path. Soon the parking lot and all signs of civilization will

DISTANCE & CONFIGURATION: 2.4-mile out-and-back	11 a.m.–5 p.m.; Saturday–Sunday, 9 a.m.–5 p.m.; free
DIFFICULTY: Moderate	**MAPS:** USGS *Burbank;* at Stough Canyon
SCENERY: Hills, valley views	Nature Center (next to trailhead) and
EXPOSURE: Full sun	**burbankca.gov/home/show**
TRAFFIC: Light	**document?id=3425**
TRAIL SURFACE: Dirt fire road	**WHEELCHAIR ACCESSIBLE:** No
HIKING TIME: 1.75 hours	**FACILITIES:** Restrooms, water fountains
ACCESS: Daily, sunrise–sunset. Stough Canyon Nature Center: Tuesday–Friday,	**CONTACT:** 818-238-5440; **tinyurl.com /stoughcanyonnc**

start to vanish, and you'll find yourself surrounded by chaparral- and scrub-covered hillsides. Don't be surprised if you pass a few random mountain bikers on their way downhill; this trail extends to La Tuna Canyon Road on the north side of the mountains and is a popular riding path. At about 0.25 mile, you'll come to the first of several benches donated by the Burbank Rotary Club. Continue following the trail uphill until it reaches another bench. Here, you'll come to a Y; the right side is a continuation of the fire trail. The left side is the beginning of a narrower, more strenuous uphill path. Both end up at the same point.

As you continue to gain altitude along the fire trail, you'll come to another bench with sweeping views of the San Fernando Valley. At 0.9 mile, the trail comes to a T. This east–west road is known as the Saddle and extends from one end of the Verdugos to the other. The right path eventually connects with Wildwood Canyon Park and the Brand Park Fire Road to the east, whereas the left one leads to the neighborhoods of Sunland and Tujunga. This is another good place to stop and drink in 360-degree views of mountains and cityscape before heading west and continuing to climb. Keep in mind that this trail gets very hot in the summer; bring plenty of water and sunscreen even on cooler winter days. As you near the intersection with the Old Youth Campground Trail, you'll be able to see traffic from I-210 in the distance and, beyond that, Mount Baldy. From here, you can retrace your steps back to the parking lot.

Nearby Activities

Stough Canyon Nature Center hosts a variety of year-round activities, from fitness and full-moon hikes to woodcarving workshops. Call 818-238-5440 for more information.

GPS TRAILHEAD COORDINATES   N34° 12.805' W118° 18.421'

From I-5, take Exit 146 (Olive Avenue); head northeast on Olive for 1.1 miles to Sunset Canyon Drive. Turn left onto Sunset Canyon and continue 1 mile to Walnut Avenue. Make a right onto Walnut, and follow it 1.1 miles, past the Starlight amphitheater and DeBell municipal golf course, until you reach the nature center's parking lot. The trailhead is to the left of the building.

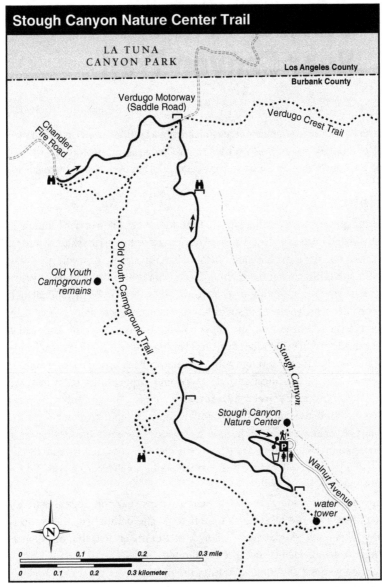

Stough Canyon Nature Center Trail

LA TUNA
CANYON PARK

Los Angeles County
Burbank County

Verdugo Motorway
(Saddle Road)

Verdugo Crest Trail

Chandler
Fire Road

Old Youth
Campground
remains

Old Youth Campground Trail

Stough Canyon

Stough Canyon
Nature Center

Walnut Avenue

water
tower

N

| 0 | 0.1 | 0.2 | 0.3 mile |

| 0 | 0.1 | 0.2 | 0.3 kilometer |

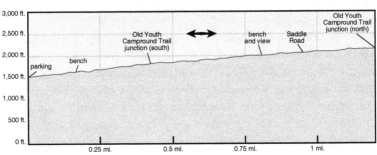

38 Switzer Falls via Bear Canyon Trail

In Brief

The first half of this hike is a pleasant meander along a boulder-strewn creek to the remains of a turn-of-the-20th-century resort; then the trail edges upward along a rock wall before dropping back down into the canyon near a small pool fed by a 15-foot waterfall.

Description

The falls and picnic area are named for Commodore Perry Switzer, who founded a resort here in the 1880s and used to lead visitors from Pasadena to the campsite via burro. Today, the logistics required to get here are much easier. You simply drive up the breathtaking Angeles Crest Highway from the town of La Cañada–Flintridge and leave your car in a pullout just above the campground. The area is well known in hiking and picnicking circles, so don't expect a whole lot of solitude, especially on weekends.

To get to the trailhead from the upper parking lot, walk past the fire-road gate and down the paved road. It's a 300-foot drop in elevation from the lot to the trailhead—not so bad going down, but it can be rough going on the way back up after a long hike. The road ends at the Switzer Falls picnic area. If it's a weekend, expect to see many people hanging out here. If it's a hot summer weekend, expect even more. The bottom of the canyon is an oasis of cool, with dense oak forest surrounding the gurgling Arroyo Seco creek. The fire road drops you at the west end of the parking lot. Look for the signed trail marker for the Gabrielino National Recreation Trail/Switzer Falls, and cross the narrow footbridge to get to the dirt path. On your right is the stream and a small clearing with a dozen or so picnic tables and barbecue grills.

Continue walking alongside the stream into a dense oak and alder forest. Beware the poison oak that lines the hillsides along this trail. The path is wide here and typically crowded with families, dogs, and frolicking kids, but the crowds thin out soon after you pass another restroom facility on the left at about 0.4 mile.

Once you've gone about 0.5 mile from the picnic area, expect easy back-and-forth boulder-hopping across the stream. The path is also paved for a short distance—expect a few minor potholes caused by winter rainstorms.

Just shy of a mile from the picnic area, you will begin to see the remains of Switzer's resort in the form of stone walls and cabin foundations. The resort was a top attraction for solace-seeking Southern Californians in the early 1900s; it suffered damage from flooding in the 1930s and finally was demolished in the 1950s. Soon you will come to a fork in the path and another GABRIELINO NATIONAL RECREATION TRAIL sign. Follow the trail to the right and cross the stream to get to Bear Canyon and a bird's-eye view of the falls. If you head straight on the narrower trail, you will soon run into a sign warning

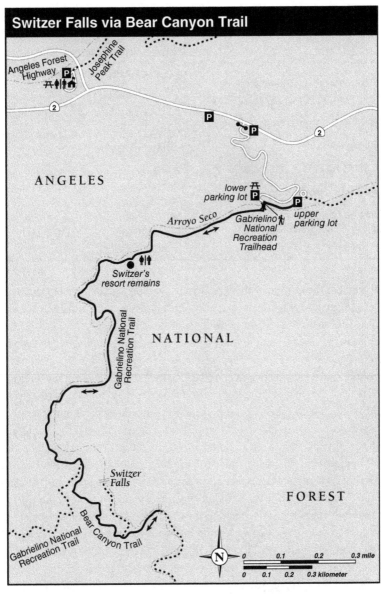

Switzer Falls via Bear Canyon Trail

Josephine Peak Trail

Angeles Forest Highway

P

2

P

P

2

ANGELES

lower parking lot

P

Arroyo Seco

Gabrielino National Recreation Trailhead

P

upper parking lot

Switzer's resort remains

Gabrielino National Recreation Trail

NATIONAL

Switzer Falls

Bear Canyon Trail

Gabrielino National Recreation Trail

FOREST

N

0   0.1   0.2   0.3 mile

0   0.1   0.2   0.3 kilometer

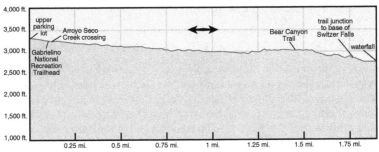

4,000 ft.

3,500 ft. — upper parking lot — Arroyo Seco Creek crossing

3,000 ft. — Gabrielino National Recreation Trailhead

2,500 ft.

2,000 ft.

1,500 ft.

1,000 ft.

Bear Canyon Trail

trail junction to base of Switzer Falls

waterfall

0.25 mi.   0.5 mi.   0.75 mi.   1 mi.   1.25 mi.   1.5 mi.   1.75 mi.

DISTANCE & CONFIGURATION: 3.9-mile out-and-back	**MAPS:** USGS *Condor Peak;* posted at Clear Creek Ranger Station just west of Switzer Falls parking lot
DIFFICULTY: Moderate–strenuous	
SCENERY: Waterfall, stream lined with oak and alder forest, chaparral hillsides	**WHEELCHAIR ACCESSIBLE:** First 0.25 mile
EXPOSURE: Mostly shade, some sun	**FACILITIES:** Picnic area, restrooms
TRAFFIC: Heavy	**CONTACT:** 626-574-1613; **www.fs.usda .gov/main/angeles**
TRAIL SURFACE: Dirt and rocks	**COMMENTS:** The weather at Switzer Falls can be quite different from the weather in the Los Angeles basin. Expect cooler temperatures in summer and occasional snow and muddy conditions in winter.
HIKING TIME: 2.25 hours	
ACCESS: Daily, 6 a.m.–10 p.m.; gate: daily, 6 a.m.–6 p.m.; Adventure Pass required to park	

you to proceed to the bottom of the falls at your own risk. As an added incentive, it cites a statistic: 118 accidental falls occurred at the falls between 1975 and 1977. A faded map gives you an idea of how close you are to the bottom of the falls.

After crossing the stream, the trail begins a steep uphill climb along the west wall of the canyon. The trail is completely exposed here, so be prepared to fish a hat out of your backpack and shed a layer or two of clothing. To the left are views of the 50-foot Switzer Falls. There is no clearing or stopping area to enjoy the view, so it's best to keep walking and avoid gridlock with other hikers. A chain-link fence lines parts of the trail here and serves as protection from a precipitous drop into the canyon. At about 1.3 miles from the picnic area, you will come to a trail junction. Follow the left fork downhill toward Bear Canyon. The right trail eventually ends up at the Mount Lowe Campground in Altadena.

After about 0.4 mile, the trail reunites with the Arroyo Seco creek and the shade that marked the first half of this hike. Turn left (upstream) and continue about 0.2 mile to a 15-foot waterfall running into a small pool surrounded by rock walls. Don't expect to have the pool to yourself; this area can be accessed via other Angeles National Forest trails and is often populated by mountain bikers and hiking groups on weekends. Find a vacant boulder and rest for a while before retracing your steps back to the picnic area. If you parked in the upper lot, you may want to stop again at the picnic area before the steep, shadeless climb back up the fire road.

GPS TRAILHEAD COORDINATES   N34° 15.976' W118° 8.747'

From the Foothill Freeway (I-210) in La Cañada–Flintridge, take Exit 20 (Angeles Crest Highway/CA 2), and drive 10 miles north on CA 2 to Switzer Falls picnic area on the right. Parking is available at pullouts at the top of the picnic area. There is also parking at the bottom of the picnic area, though this lot fills up quickly on weekends. The trail begins just beyond the footbridge on the west end of the bottom lot.

39 West Fork Trail

A cool place to rest along the West Fork Trail

In Brief

Once you get past the picnickers and graffiti-covered rocks at the river's edge, you'll find a quiet, flat trail that parallels a shaded, unspoiled stretch of the San Gabriel River. Strollers, bicycles, leashed dogs, and runners share the wide path with hikers, but it rarely seems crowded.

Description

CA 39 is one of the busiest entryways into the 650,000-acre Angeles National Forest. It snakes past the striking San Gabriel Dam and Cogswell Reservoir to the east and continues through to Wrightwood, a popular skiing destination (though passage is often closed due to repairs or rock- and mudslide dangers). The West Fork Trail of the San Gabriel River, which begins just off CA 39, is a terrific year-round hike flanked by a robust river on one side and steep canyon walls on the other. You will also find trout-fishing

DISTANCE & CONFIGURATION: 14-mile out-and-back

DIFFICULTY: Easy

SCENERY: Waterfalls, dense forest, canyon walls

EXPOSURE: Mostly shade

TRAFFIC: Moderate

TRAIL SURFACE: Paved fire road

HIKING TIME: 6 hours

ACCESS: Daily, sunrise–sunset; Adventure Pass required to park

MAPS: USGS *Azusa* and USGS *Glendora*

WHEELCHAIR ACCESSIBLE: Yes

FACILITIES: Portable bathrooms

CONTACT: 626-335-1251; **www.fs.usda .gov/main/angeles**

COMMENTS: The trailhead is near a popular tent-camping site and a designated off-road vehicle area; expect huge crowds on summer and holiday weekends, and arrive early. The U.S. Forest Service sometimes closes the access road to cars when traffic is heavy. For more information and road conditions, call the San Gabriel River Ranger District at 626-335-1251.

platforms, oak and pine forests, and a series of small but lovely year-round waterfalls, even in the dog days of summer. Fall brings the heady scent of pines and mellow brown and yellow foliage. Expect the river to flow high and mighty after winter and early spring rains; this is clearly the best time to witness the waterfalls. Glen Trail Camp is a good turnaround destination for cyclists and long-distance hikers, but you can make this hike shorter and turn around anywhere along the route without missing out on much.

Begin your hike by walking around the closed fire-road gate just before a small bridge on the west side of the road. The paved path descends briefly and heads west along the San Gabriel River, which lies to your right. The area near the gate is a favorite spot for picnickers and swimmers, especially on summer weekends. You will also see some graffiti on the rocks and bridge walls around here, but that soon disappears. After about 0.5 mile, the voices and boom box music also fade and you have the forest and river to yourself (along with maybe a handful of other nature lovers). At 1.1 miles, you'll pass a sign for Bear Creek, an unpaved trail that winds north into the forest; things start to get shadier and cooler at this point. Continue another 0.5 mile to a small bridge, where you'll find a few small clearings by the river that invite picnicking.

From here and for the next 5 miles, the road climbs a slow but steady 500 feet past groves of oak and cottonwood, year-round waterfalls, and inviting rock pools. As the trail winds deeper into the forest, it skirts a sheer rock wall on the left side for about 0.5 mile. Note the signs cautioning to watch for rockslides. A few other things to watch for: rattlesnakes and poison oak. Given the remoteness of your surroundings, it's not advisable to do this hike alone.

At 3 miles, you'll pass a sidewalk that leads to a trout-fishing platform on the right. From here, it's another 3-mile meander through a dense forest canopy and more small waterfalls to Glen Trail Camp, a flat, shady area perched along the river with picnic tables and 10 campsites. Most hikers turn around here, but the trail continues west another steep 0.5 mile to Cogswell Dam, and then hooks up with fire roads heading

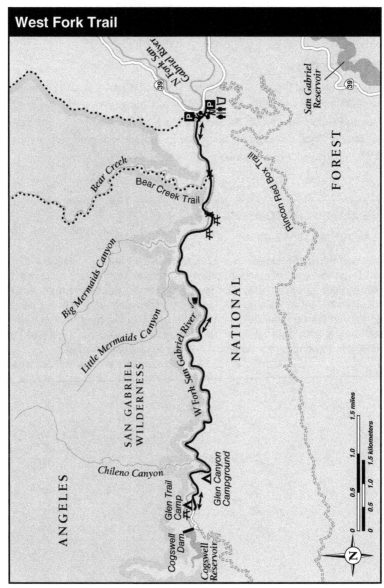

West Fork Trail

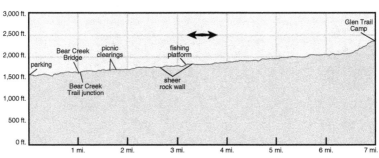

west toward Mount Wilson. After resting and rehydrating at Glen Trail Camp, retrace your steps to the parking lot.

Nearby Activities

For picnic supplies, you'll pass a few grocery stores and fast-food eateries along Azusa Avenue (CA 39) on the way to the trailhead. If you're hungry for a sit-down meal before or after your hike, try Canyon City Barbecue, a block off CA 39 at 347 N. San Gabriel Ave. in Azusa (**canyoncitybbq.com**). It's famous for its pulled-pork sandwiches and smoked brisket and is open Wednesday–Sunday.

GPS TRAILHEAD COORDINATES

N34° 14.522' W117° 52.201'

From the San Bernardino Freeway (I-210), take Exit 40 (Azusa Avenue/CA 39); head north 2.7 miles toward the mountains. Just before entering the forest, you will pass a green forest station (open Friday–Sunday starting at 8 a.m.) on the right, where you can pick up an Adventure Pass for the day for $5. Continue another 9 miles, paralleling the San Gabriel Dam to your left, until you reach a T in the road. Turn left (the East Fork section is to your right); then continue another 1.3 miles to a small parking pull-out on the left. Parking is also allowed along the road if the lot is full.

West Fork Trail begins near a busy camping site.

COAST

(INCLUDING MALIBU, PACIFIC PALISADES, PALOS VERDES)

Soaking in the view at Parker Mesa Overlook (see page 169)

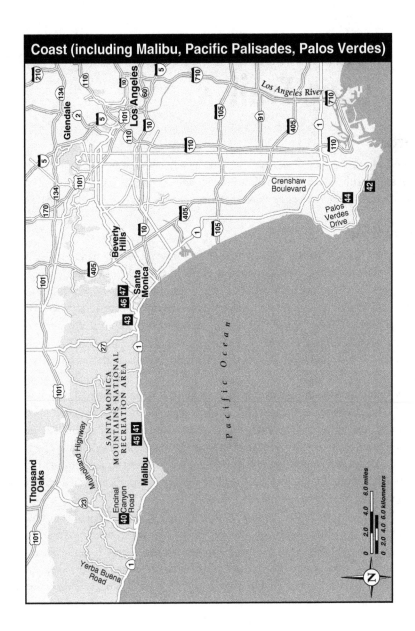

Coast (including Malibu, Pacific Palisades, Palos Verdes)

Los Angeles River

Los Angeles

Glendale

Crenshaw Boulevard

Palos Verdes Drive

Beverly Hills

Santa Monica

Pacific Ocean

SANTA MONICA MOUNTAINS NATIONAL RECREATION AREA

Mulholland Highway

Thousand Oaks

Encinal Canyon Road

Malibu

Yerba Buena Road

0   2.0   4.0   6.0 miles
0 2.0 4.0 6.0 kilometers

40 Charmlee Wilderness Park Loop Trail

In Brief

Despite a confusing lack of signage, this hike is a hassle-free trek past open meadows, coastal sage scrub, and seasonal wildflowers. Some of the unmarked trails lead to 1,300-foot bluffs and wonderful ocean views that extend as far as the Channel Islands.

Description

Once a cattle ranch, Charmlee Wilderness Park is now a 530-acre nature preserve operated by the city of Malibu. It includes an 8-mile network of trails and a shaded picnic area. Naturalists praise the park for its dozens of species of wildflowers, which include dove lupine, wild hyacinth, hummingbird sage, golden poppies, deerweed, sticky monkeyflower, and coastal lotus. On the other hand, the park is also home to many nonnative trees such as eucalyptus, Italian pine, Mediterranean palm, and New Zealand myoporum. Even in the fall and winter, this is a good place to hike because of the park's stellar clifftop ocean views.

It's a good idea to look at a map before starting out because the trail system is poorly marked. There is one posted at the trail kiosk near the picnic area. Pick up the loop trail at the southwest corner of the parking lot and follow the paved road uphill. The shadeless trail soon turns to dirt and curves around to the left, heading south toward a large water tank. If it's a clear day, you will be able to see the Pacific Ocean straight ahead of you. The loop trail skirts around the water tower, but you may detour up a small hill and walk around the tank for another good ocean view.

At 0.8 mile, the trail dips downhill and comes to a T. Head left and continue on the trail another 0.2 mile to a three-way intersection with a small wooden post marked 10. (A left turn brings you back to the parking lot and makes for an easy 1.5-mile hike.) A right turn extends the hike by about 1 mile and adds about 200 feet in elevation loss and gain. The right trail takes you past a wide-open meadow to an old concrete reservoir. From here, descend south to a stunning clifftop view of the Pacific. On a clear day, you can see as far as Catalina Island to the south and the Channel Islands to the north.

From here, you can head back up the hill and across the east side of the meadow, and pick up the unmarked Botany Trail at the northeast end. This will take you back to the picnic area near the parking lot. A big sign near the entrance to the picnic area warns visitors to refrain from picking the wildflowers. I encountered only one couple (having a picnic) on the Saturday afternoon I hiked this trail. Granted, it was a record-hot spring day, but I expected more people, given the park's proximity to Malibu and the San Fernando Valley.

Charmlee Wilderness Park Loop Trail

SANTA MONICA

CHARMLEE
WILDERNESS
PARK

MOUNTAINS

NATIONAL

RECREATION

AREA

Potrero Road

Encinal Canyon Road

Charmichael Road

pavement
ends

Nature
Center

water
tower

ranch house
ruins

meadow

Potrero Road

old
well

concrete
reservoir

BF Black Forest Trail
BT Botany Trail
CC Clyde Canyon Trail
EM East Meadow Trail
EC East Meadow Cutoff Trail
KT Kouba Trail
LL Lower Loop Trail
RT Russell Trail
WM West Meadow Trail

N

0   0.1   0.2   0.3 mile
0   0.1   0.2   0.3 kilometer

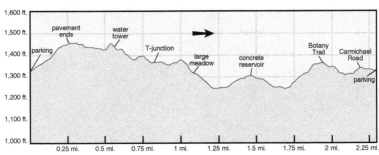

1,600 ft.
1,500 ft.
1,400 ft.
1,300 ft.
1,200 ft.
1,100 ft.
1,000 ft.

pavement
ends

water
tower

parking

T-junction

large
meadow

concrete
reservoir

Botany
Trail

Carmichael
Road

parking

0.25 mi.   0.5 mi.   0.75 mi.   1 mi.   1.25 mi.   1.5 mi.   1.75 mi.   2 mi.   2.25 mi.

DISTANCE & CONFIGURATION: 2.3-mile loop	MAPS: USGS *Triunfo Pass;* at kiosk near trailhead and **lamountains.com/parks .asp?parkid=95**
DIFFICULTY: Easy	
SCENERY: Wildflowers, ocean views	WHEELCHAIR ACCESSIBLE: No
EXPOSURE: Sunny	
TRAFFIC: Light	FACILITIES: Picnic tables
TRAIL SURFACE: Dirt	CONTACT: 310-457-7247; **lamountains .com/parks.asp?parkid=95**
HIKING TIME: 1 hour	COMMENTS: This dog-friendly park also attracts ticks, so long pants and socks are advised.
ACCESS: Daily, 8 a.m.–sunset; $4 fee at self-pay kiosk	

Nearby Activities

It's a steep, winding drive down Encinal Canyon Road to Pacific Coast Highway, but once you get there some of Malibu's best beaches are yours to enjoy. Robert H. Meyer Memorial State Beach, which includes the cliffside "pocket" beaches of El Matador, El Pescador, and La Piedra, is the closest. Neptune's Net, about 8 miles away at 42505 Pacific Coast Hwy., is an open-air fish-and-chips joint that attracts bikers and other PCH cruisers.

GPS TRAILHEAD COORDINATES

N34° 3.554' W118° 52.763'

From the Ventura Freeway (US 101), take Westlake Boulevard south until it turns into Mulholland Highway. In 8 miles, bear left onto Lechusa Road; then immediately turn right onto Encinal Canyon Road and go 1.2 miles to the park entrance.

Alternate directions: From Pacific Coast Highway/CA 1 in Santa Monica, head north and turn right onto Encinal Canyon Road; proceed 4 miles to the park entrance.

41 Corral Canyon Loop

The entrance to Corral Canyon is just off Pacific Coast Highway.

In Brief

This accessible 2.4-mile hike begins directly across the street from Dan Blocker State Beach in Malibu. It has a moderate elevation gain of 500 feet and wide-open views of the Pacific Ocean. Combine it with a visit to Malibu Seafood, a popular beachfront eatery next to the trailhead, and you have the perfect Southern California day trip.

Description

Once targeted for a luxury home development and golf course, Corral Canyon Park was acquired by the Santa Monica Mountains Conservancy in 1998 and is now billed as the last undeveloped coastal canyon in Los Angeles County to flow freely into the ocean. The loop trail opened in 2003 and is a well-maintained singletrack path that cuts through coastal sage scrub; native grassland; and a small forest of coast live oak, sycamore, and willow trees. The trail's location, across the street from a popular Malibu beach and next

DISTANCE & CONFIGURATION: 2.25-mile loop	ACCESS: Daily, sunrise–sunset; $4 fee at self-pay kiosk
DIFFICULTY: Moderate	MAPS: USGS *Malibu Beach;* at kiosk near trailhead and **tinyurl.com/corralcanyon map**
SCENERY: Chaparral, ocean and mountain views	
EXPOSURE: Mostly sun	WHEELCHAIR ACCESSIBLE: No
TRAFFIC: Light	FACILITIES: Bathroom, picnic tables
TRAIL SURFACE: Packed dirt	CONTACT: 805-370-2300; **nps.gov /samo/planyourvisit/corralcanyon.htm** or **lamountains.com/parks.asp?parkid=4**
HIKING TIME: 1 hour	

door to a popular outdoor seafood restaurant, makes it an ideal destination hike. After hitting the trail, you can indulge in a delicious lunch of fresh fish or take a cool dip in the ocean that you just admired from the hills.

Look for the trailhead at the southeast end of the parking lot, and follow the path as it descends into a thick forest of oak and willow trees. Soon you'll cross a pocket of coastal salt marsh and a seasonal river that flows into the ocean to your right. From here, the trail heads east toward the mountains and soon comes to an unmarked junction. Stay to the left and follow the (mostly flat) trail as it continues east. After about 0.4 mile, you will gain some elevation as the trail starts to zigzag east, then south, and gives way to some fine ocean and mountain views.

At about 0.75 mile, you will come to a small pullout with terrific views of the ocean and Pacific Coast Highway. From here, the path heads east briefly and then turns sharply and heads west toward the water. The final mile heads west, then south, and is accompanied by ocean views and a gradual descent back to the trailhead.

Nearby Activities

Lunch at Malibu Seafood (25653 Pacific Coast Hwy.; 310-456-3430) is the perfect way to cap a hike in Corral Canyon. It opens daily at 11 a.m. (call for closing times). Also nearby is Dan Blocker State Beach, a small stretch of public sand named for and once owned by the actor who played Hoss from TV's *Bonanza.*

GPS TRAILHEAD COORDINATES   N34° 2.060' W118° 44.062'

This trail is located along Pacific Coast Highway (PCH), between Malibu Canyon and Kanan Dume Roads. From the Santa Monica Freeway (I-10), take PCH north about 15 miles. After passing the Pepperdine University campus, look for signs for Corral Canyon and Malibu Seafood on the right, and park in the lot just before Malibu Seafood. There is a small lot near the trailhead; limited free parking is also available in pullouts on either side of the PCH. You can also access this trail via public transportation; for more information go to **metro.net**.

Corral Canyon Loop

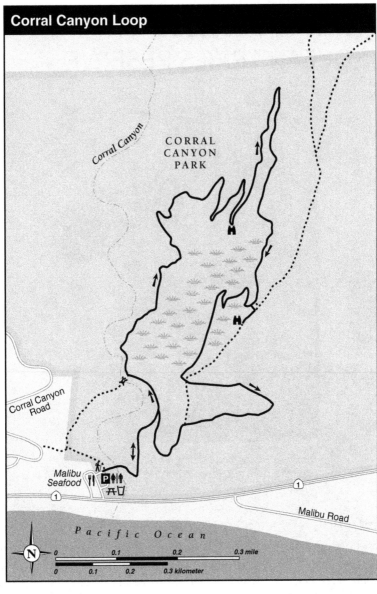

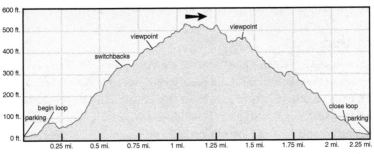

42 Palos Verdes:
OCEAN TRAILS RESERVE

*Signs at the beginning of the trail remind hikers
that Ocean Trails Reserve borders the exclusive
Trump National Golf Club.*

In Brief

A network of easy to difficult ocean trails begins at a swank golf course and leads to remote
rocky beaches and quiet benches with some of the best coastal views around. The trails
draw a wide range of recreational users, from parents with jogging strollers to equestrians
and runners in training who take advantage of the steep spurs down to the beach.

Description

Ocean Trails Reserve shares facilities with the most expensive golf course ever built. Pur-
ists will cringe at the fake waterfalls and neon-green lawns that flank the walkway leading
to the real trails on this hike, but I urge them to walk fast and focus instead on what lies
just beyond all that faux landscaping. Wildflower-covered bluffs and unfettered ocean
views are your companions for most of this California dreamin' hike. On a clear day, when

DISTANCE & CONFIGURATION: 4.6-mile out-and-back or balloon	ACCESS: Daily, sunrise–sunset; free
DIFFICULTY: Easy with some optional strenuous climbing	**MAPS:** USGS *San Pedro;* **rpvca.gov /DocumentCenter/View/150**
SCENERY: Ocean views	**WHEELCHAIR ACCESSIBLE:** Upper portions
EXPOSURE: Sunny	**FACILITIES:** Restrooms at La Rotonda parking lot
TRAFFIC: Moderate	**CONTACT:** 310-544-5252; **pvplc.org**
TRAIL SURFACE: Paved road with dirt trail spurs	**COMMENTS:** The spur trails off the main path leading down to the beaches can get very muddy and slippery after it rains.
HIKING TIME: 2 hours	

the water is an intoxicating mix of deep blue and aquamarine, and Catalina Island appears so close that you could throw a shell at it, it almost seems too good to be true.

I like to park in the lot at the end of La Rotonda Drive and start hiking from there. If you want to check out the glamorous clubhouse that comes with the golf course, there's also free parking available at Trump National Golf Club at 1 Ocean Trails Dr. (call ahead to make sure no special events are on tap).

From La Rotonda, look for the reserve sign at the north end of the parking lot and follow the paved path past a modern restroom facility. The manicured path essentially cuts right through the golf course (but the golfer's routes are clearly marked, so hikers don't wander onto the 13th hole). After about 0.5 mile the trail hits a T, with either side following the ocean. Turn right, ignoring the roaring faux waterfall to your right and focusing on the panoramic ocean views to your left. Soon you'll see a switchback trail leading down to the ocean on your left. I bypassed this turn and instead took the 0.5-mile Sunrise Trail down to the water for a brief detour. There's a brief spurt of shade; then the trail gives way to an ocean-view clearing anchored by two large boulders. With a sandwich and cold drink in hand, you may sit down and never want to leave this beautiful spot. If the tide is right, you can continue along the ocean and hook back up with the main trail via the Sunset Trail, or retrace your steps back to the main trail, which is what I did.

The paved path continues toward the golf clubhouse, eventually narrowing and turning to dirt. There will be some hitching posts and pristine picnic tables in this area. Continue on the dirt path as it curves around and meets up with the Sunset Trail. Those looking for a flat, easy hike will want to turn around here.

Beachcombers will want to take the Sunset Trail down to the rocky beach and add a brief shoreline stroll to their hike. The bluff-side beach is a treasure trove of rocks and shells. I found a lobster claw on my most recent visit. I ended my walk at the lifeguard stand (closed in the off-season) and PRIVATE PROPERTY signs and then headed back up the Sunset Trail to reconnect with the paved path.

Back at the trail split (near that faux waterfall), you can head left back to the parking lot or continue exploring the trail system. The dirt path continues to the Gnatcatcher

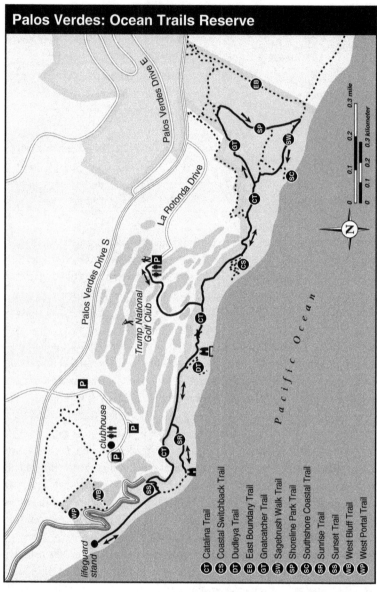

Palos Verdes: Ocean Trails Reserve

CT Catalina Trail
CS Coastal Switchback Trail
DT Dudleya Trail
EB East Boundary Trail
GT Gnatcatcher Trail
SW Sagebrush Walk Trail
SP Shoreline Park Trail
SC Southshore Coastal Trail
SR Sunrise Trail
SS Sunset Trail
WB West Bluff Trail
WP West Portal Trail

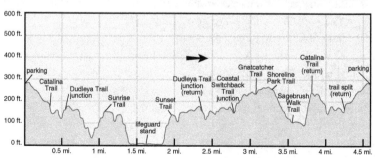

Trail, named for the endangered California gnatcatcher native to Palos Verdes. This trail leads east away from the ocean for about 0.5 mile and then curves back around to an ocean-view clearing with picnic tables and benches guaranteed to make you want to sit down and cancel all your plans for the rest of the day.

From here, either trail leads back up to the main trail and parking lot.

Nearby Activities

To extend your surreal coastal experience, consider staying or dining at Terranea Resort, a luxury Mediterranean-style resort just 4 miles up the road. Located on the site of Marineland of the Pacific, a sea-life amusement park that operated from 1954 to 1987, Terranea has a variety of eating options, from the upscale Mar'sel to Nelson's, a casual café with ocean-view fire pits. More info is available at **terranea.com.**

GPS TRAILHEAD COORDINATES

N33° 43.710' W118° 20.425'

Ocean Trails Reserve is in the heart of Rancho Palos Verdes. From Pacific Coast Highway, turn right onto Crenshaw Boulevard in Torrance, and go 1.3 miles. Turn left onto Palos Verdes Drive North, go 8.3 miles, and take La Rotonda Drive until it ends. Or turn right onto CA 213/Western Avenue in Lomita, and go 5 miles. Turn right onto West 25th Street, and go 1.3 miles. Then turn left onto La Rotonda Drive and take it until it ends.

43 Paseo Miramar Trail to Parker Mesa Overlook

Wildflowers along the way to Parker Mesa Overlook

In Brief

Coastal views and chaparral dominate the scenery for most of this popular Topanga State Park hike, which winds uphill along a wide, well-maintained fire road to a clearing with unbeatable views of the Pacific Ocean.

Description

To get to the Paseo Miramar Trail, you must pass through an upscale Pacific Palisades neighborhood. The road is narrow, so be wary of other cars and bicycles that might suddenly spring up on the other side of a curve. Except for one sign that points you in the direction of the trail as you head up the hill, this hike isn't well advertised. So it's all the more surprising to reach the trailhead and find a dozen or more cars parked on the street just south of it. Part of Topanga State Park's 26-mile coastal trail network, this hike is popular with mountain bikers, horseback riders, large chatty groups, UCLA students, solace seekers—you name it. If you don't mind the crowds and frequent whiz of mountain

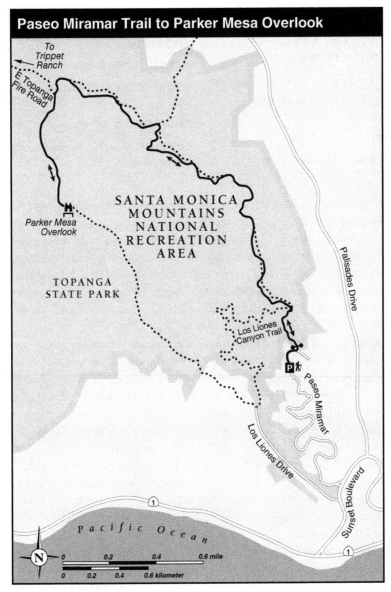

Paseo Miramar Trail to Parker Mesa Overlook

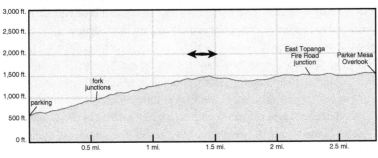

DISTANCE & CONFIGURATION: 5.5-mile out-and-back	**HIKING TIME:** 2 hours
	ACCESS: Daily, sunrise–sunset; free
DIFFICULTY: Moderate	**MAPS:** USGS *Topanga*
SCENERY: Wildflowers, chaparral, ocean and city views	**WHEELCHAIR ACCESSIBLE:** No
EXPOSURE: Sunny	**FACILITIES:** None
TRAFFIC: Heavy	**CONTACT:** 310-455-2465; **parks.ca.gov**
TRAIL SURFACE: Packed dirt	**/?page_id=629**

bikers flying past, it's an excellent way to introduce energetic out-of-towners to one of the more beautiful sides of L.A.

The limited number of parking spaces near the trailhead may force you to park nearby. Expect it to add as much as 0.5 mile of uphill climbing to the hike. When you get to the fire-road gate, follow the dirt path as it begins a gradual ascent past chaparral and views of the wealthy hillside neighborhoods of Pacific Palisades to the east. Soon you will be able to see the crescent-shaped coastline of Santa Monica to the south. It's just a small hint of the spectacular views to come.

Most of the trail is exposed from this point on, but salty ocean breezes help make it a comfortable year-round hike. Bring plenty of water and sunscreen, and don't expect to pass any rest areas on the way to the overlook. At about 0.25 mile, the Pacific Ocean comes into wide view on the left and pretty much stays with you for the rest of the hike. On a clear day, the deep-blue horizon is stunning.

At about 0.5 mile, you will truly begin to feel like you have left civilization far behind as the trail heads deeper into the mountains. The ocean weaves in and out of view on the left. To the east, you can see as far as downtown Los Angeles, fog permitting. After about a mile of nonstop climbing, the path levels for a bit, allowing for a chance to catch your breath and revel in the scenery. In the spring and early summer, mustard, California dodder (witch's hair), purple lupine, and other wildflowers stretch for what seems like miles on either side of the path.

The trail continues flat, winding along a mountain ridgeline, and then dips downhill into a rare patch of shade provided by a few coast live oak trees. Soon you will reach a wide grassy meadow and pass through another small cluster of oaks, manzanita, and chamise. At 1.8 miles, the trail begins another steep ascent as it heads northwest. You still have another 200 feet of elevation gain ahead of you, but the toughest climb is over.

At about 2 miles, you will come to a right turnoff for a dirt trail leading to Trippet Ranch, a popular Topanga State Park base for hikers and bikers (it's another 2.7 miles from here). Continue straight on the gently uphill path toward Parker Mesa Overlook as it heads due south toward the ocean. There are more nice views of the Santa Monica Mountains on the right. Savor the panoramic ocean-city-mountain views as you approach the final stretch of the hike to the overlook. After a brief final climb, the trail gives way to

Parker Mesa Overlook, a wide clearing with two large wooden benches with front-row views of the Pacific. If it's a clear, sunny day, don't expect to get a seat. These prime seats are often filled by hikers and bikers resting and soaking up the view. Take a break wherever you can and rehydrate before heading back to your car.

After a rest, head back to the trailhead the same way you came. The ocean and mountain views you get on the way back are just as excellent as those on the first half of the hike.

GPS TRAILHEAD COORDINATES

N34° 3.038' W118° 33.431'

From Santa Monica, head north on Pacific Coast Highway and turn right at Sunset Boulevard. In 0.4 mile make a left onto Paseo Miramar, and follow it about 1 mile uphill until it dead-ends at the trailhead. Make a U-turn at the trailhead and park on the west side of the street.

Alternate directions: Take I-405 to Exit 57 (Sunset Boulevard), and follow Sunset south 8 miles until just before it intersects with Pacific Coast Highway. Make a right onto Paseo Miramar, and follow it about 1 mile uphill until it dead-ends at the trailhead. Make a U-turn at the trailhead and park on the west side of the street.

This trailhead begins in a dense residential neighborhood high in the hills of Pacific Palisades. Parking is allowed on the street, but heed the restrictions, or your car may be towed.

44 Portuguese Bend Reserve:
BURMA ROAD TRAIL

In Brief

Gorgeous views of the Pacific Ocean dominate this well-tended Palos Verdes Peninsula trail frequented by hikers, mountain bikers, and horseback riders.

Description

The Palos Verdes Peninsula is a 26-square-mile area located in the southwest corner of Los Angeles County. Its name means "green sticks" in Spanish. The upscale community has managed to keep big hotels and industry at bay since limited residential development began in the 1920s, and the whole area has a peaceful, rural feel that vanished long ago from most other Southern California coastal areas.

There aren't many landmarks on this trail; its best feature by far is the ocean views that stay with you for most of the hike. On a clear day, you'll be able to spot Catalina Island and some of the northern Channel Islands. The Burma Road Trail begins at the end of Crenshaw Boulevard just beyond Burrell Lane. Walk around the gate to a packed-dirt fire road flanked by yellow wildflowers and coastal sage scrub. The backyards of several private homes are on your right beyond a chain-link fence; to the left and in front of you are sweeping views of the Palos Verdes coastline and rolling green hills dotted with distant houses. The trail descends gradually from an elevation of 1,200 feet to 500 feet. I did this hike on a weekday afternoon and saw more mountain bikers than hikers. I found out later that bikers love the many physically challenging singletrack paths that spin off the fire road near the trailhead. The main path is wide enough, though, that their presence isn't distracting. You also can expect to spot a good number of horseback riders, especially at the lower end of the path; the Portuguese Bend Riding Club is nearby, and its students and instructors use the trail for lessons and excursions.

At about 0.7 mile, the Burma Road Trail starts to level off and head away from the ocean, shrouded by dense foliage on the left and chaparral-covered hills on the right. The trail becomes smoother with fewer water drainage ruts at about 1.3 miles, and you'll be able to see Palos Verdes Drive, a relatively busy road that parallels the ocean, in the distance to your right. As you approach the 2-mile marker, the trail climbs upward another 0.5 mile to a small overlook with views of the Pacific. From here, you can retrace your steps for the uphill climb back to Del Cerro Park or continue on the path to a residential street that will eventually lead back to the trailhead. I prefer the out-and-back option for its ocean and hills scenery.

Cap this hike with one last spectacular view of the Pacific by walking up the grassy hill from the Del Cerro parking lot to a bench that overlooks portions of the path you just traversed.

Portuguese Bend Reserve: Burma Road Trail

Crenshaw Boulevard

Oceanaire Drive

Crest Road

P

DEL CERRO PARK

H

FILIORUM RESERVE

BR

FS

water tower

PP

IT

GR

RT

BR

AT

AT

BR

PORTUGUESE BEND RESERVE

EN

BR

IT

PA

KT

RT

VT

Narcissa Drive

WT water tower

GT

TT

PP

BR

RT

LS

PP

NS

PT

BR

IF

ST

PT

BO

KC

AT Ailor Trail
BO Barn Owl Trail
BR Burma Road Trail
EN Eagle's Nest Trail
FS Fire Station Trail
GT Garden Trail
GR Grapevine Trail
IF Ishibashi Farm Trail
IT Ishibashi Trail
KC Klondike Canyon Trail
KT Kubota Trail
LS Landslide Scarp Trail

NS North Sandbox Trail
PA Paintbrush Trail
PT Panorama Trail
PF Peacock Flats Trail
PP Peppertree Trail
RT Rim Trail
ST Sandbox Trail
TT Toyon Trail
VT Vanderlip Trail
WT Water Tank Trail

N

| 0 | 0.1 | 0.2 | 0.3 mile |
| 0 | 0.1 | 0.2 | 0.3 kilometer |

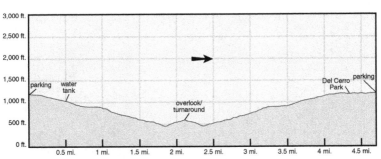

DISTANCE & CONFIGURATION: 4.6-mile out-and-back	**HIKING TIME:** 2 hours
	ACCESS: Daily, sunrise–sunset; free
DIFFICULTY: Strenuous	**MAPS:** USGS *Torrance;* **pvplc.org/_lands /portuguese_bend.asp**
SCENERY: Ocean views, chaparral-covered hills	
	WHEELCHAIR ACCESSIBLE: Upper portions
EXPOSURE: Sunny	
	FACILITIES: None
TRAFFIC: Moderate	
	CONTACT: 310-544-5252; **pvplc.org /_lands/portuguese_bend.asp**
TRAIL SURFACE: Dirt path	

Nearby Activities

Wayfarers Chapel, a glass church designed by architect Lloyd Wright (son of Frank), is an easy drive from Del Cerro Park. Surrounded by gardens and a small forest of redwood trees, the chapel is made of clear glass and framed by aged redwood timbers. Among the celebrities married here are Brian Wilson, Dennis Hopper, and Jayne Mansfield. The chapel and grounds are open daily, 9 a.m.–5 p.m. From Crenshaw Boulevard, turn left on Crest Road; then make another left on Hawthorne Boulevard and follow it to its end. Turn left on Palos Verdes Drive. Wayfarers Chapel is on the left at 5755 Palos Verdes Dr., across from Abalone Cove Shoreline Park.

GPS TRAILHEAD COORDINATES

N33° 45.459' W118° 22.033'

From the San Diego Freeway (I-405), take Exit 39 (Crenshaw Boulevard) in Torrance, and follow Crenshaw 9 miles to its end at Del Cerro Park. There is free parking in the park's lot sunrise–sunset or on the street just before the trailhead.

45 Solstice Canyon and Rising Sun Trails

The ruins of a historic ranch house in Solstice Canyon

In Brief

This hike has wide appeal and gets quite busy on weekends. It begins in a wooded valley on a flat trail that follows a creek to a year-round waterfall; it then winds up the hillside to a ridge offering canyon and ocean views. You'll also see the ruins of a historic ranch house and the remains of a space-research facility that tested satellite equipment in the 1960s and '70s.

Description

Solstice Canyon is an ideal hike to take on a summer day when triple-digit temperatures render most other Los Angeles trails oppressive. The area was once used by the Chumash Indians as a source of food, shelter, and water; later, ranchers grazed cattle in the wide-open meadows. The first leg of the trail is surrounded by trees, and the second half skirts a ridge that catches the ocean breezes that drift across Pacific Coast Highway. This hike can easily be altered to an out-and-back stroll that appeals to young children.

From the parking lot, look for the Solstice Canyon Trailhead and follow the wide dirt path through a wooded valley and alongside a stream. After about a mile, the trail reaches a year-round waterfall (expect more of a trickle in summer). On the other side of the

DISTANCE & CONFIGURATION: 3-mile loop	**MAPS:** USGS *Malibu Beach;* nps.gov /samo/planyourvisit/upload/Solstice-Canyon_v3.pdf
DIFFICULTY: Easy–moderate	
SCENERY: Seasonal stream and water-fall, foliage, ocean and canyon views	**WHEELCHAIR ACCESSIBLE:** Lower portions
EXPOSURE: Sun and shade	**FACILITIES:** Picnic tables
TRAFFIC: Busy on weekends	**CONTACT:** 805-370-2300; nps.gov/samo /planyourvisit/solsticecanyon.htm
TRAIL SURFACE: Dirt and gravel	**COMMENTS:** Solstice Canyon became a public park in 1988 and is now managed by the National Park Service. Wildfires severely damaged the area in 2007, but it has come back strongly and as green as ever.
HIKING TIME: 2 hours	
ACCESS: Daily, 8 a.m.–sunset; free parking in a small lot	

waterfall are the ruins of a home built in 1952 by the prominent African American architect Paul Williams. Known as Tropical Terrace, it was featured in *Architectural Digest* and praised for its integration of natural surroundings into the design. It was largely destroyed by fire in the 1980s, but the foundations, glittering glass walkways, and a large brick fireplace remain for visitors to explore and photograph.

From the waterfall, you can retrace your steps back to the parking lot or continue on the loop trail by taking the Rising Sun Trail up the hillside to the ridge. This part of the hike requires some effort, with a 400-foot elevation gain, singletrack path, and no shade. But it also yields some of the best ocean views around, along with gloriously cool breezes. After about a mile, the path starts to descend, and you'll come to the TRW Overlook. The quiet natural setting attracted aerospace giant TRW to rent the land to test satellite equipment for space missions in the 1960s and early 1970s. Destruction came in the form of another fire that swept through the area in 2007, and all that remains is the building foundations. From here, it's an easy hike back down to the parking area.

Nearby Activities

Lunch at Malibu Seafood (25653 Pacific Coast Hwy.; 310-456-3430) is the perfect way to cap any hike in Malibu. It opens daily at 11 a.m. (call for closing times).

GPS TRAILHEAD COORDINATES   N34° 2.329' W118° 44.998'

This trail is located along Pacific Coast Highway (PCH), between Malibu Canyon and Kanan Dume Roads. From the Santa Monica Freeway (I-10), take PCH north about 15 miles. After passing the Pepperdine University campus, look for signs for Corral Canyon and Malibu Seafood on the right, and park in the lot just before Malibu Seafood. There is a small lot near the trailhead; limited free parking is also available in pullouts on either side of the PCH. You can also access this trail via public transportation; for more information go to metro.net.

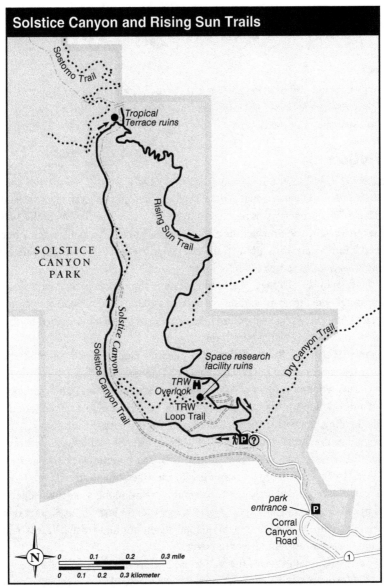

Solstice Canyon and Rising Sun Trails

Sostomo Trail

Tropical Terrace ruins

Rising Sun Trail

SOLSTICE CANYON PARK

Solstice Canyon

Solstice Canyon Trail

Dry Canyon Trail

Space research facility ruins

TRW Overlook

TRW Loop Trail

P **?**

park entrance

P

Corral Canyon Road

1

N

| 0 | 0.1 | 0.2 | 0.3 mile |
| 0 | 0.1 | 0.2 | 0.3 kilometer |

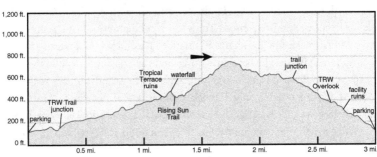

1,200 ft.

1,000 ft.

800 ft.

600 ft.

400 ft.

200 ft.

0 ft.

parking

TRW Trail junction

Tropical Terrace ruins

waterfall

Rising Sun Trail

trail junction

TRW Overlook

facility ruins

parking

0.5 mi.   1 mi.   1.5 mi.   2 mi.   2.5 mi.   3 mi.

46 Temescal Ridge Trail

In Brief

This heavily traveled trail near Pacific Coast Highway begins with a 1,000-foot ascent that gives way to panoramic ocean and city views, and then descends into a sycamore-shaded canyon to a seasonal waterfall.

Description

During the 1920s and 1930s, Temescal Canyon was the western headquarters for Chautauqua assemblies, the educational gatherings that featured concerts, lectures, and stage performances. The property was purchased by the Presbyterian Church in the 1940s and used as a retreat until 1995, when the Santa Monica Mountains Conservancy bought it and turned it into a park with hiking trails and picnic areas. The cabins and retreat facilities are now used as a summer camp for kids.

Do this hike on a weekday if you prefer solitude; the park is packed with a variety of people on weekends, from marathon trainers to extended families to fit parents with babies in tow. This is a great year-round hike because of the shade provided by the dense woodland that makes up a large part of the trail.

To get to Temescal Ridge, follow the signs for Sunset Trail, which begins just beyond the restrooms in the lower parking lot of Temescal Gateway Park. The dirt path descends into a wooded canyon of oak, maple, and sycamore trees and crosses a creek by way of a wooden footbridge. At about 0.5 mile, you'll come to a signed junction that marks the dividing line with Topanga State Park (this is where the no-dogs rule begins). Take the path to the left to get to Temescal Ridge. The trail to the right is an easier 0.5-mile hike to the waterfall. You can also hike this trail counterclockwise and take the waterfall trail to Temescal Ridge. I prefer to end the hike at the waterfall.

The ridge path immediately starts to climb upward along a narrow ridgeline surrounded by tall chaparral, gaining 1,000 feet in elevation in just 1 mile. Expect to see the usual variety of Santa Monica Mountains animal life on this hike: toads, lizards, squirrels, rabbits, and the occasional mule deer or coyote.

After a few twists and turns, the trail levels at a crest with spectacular views of the Southern California coastline: On a clear day, the views extend west to the ocean and Catalina Island, south to the Palos Verdes Peninsula, and east to downtown. Continue past the trailheads for Leacock and Bienveneda Trails to a signed junction with Temescal Canyon. From here, you can take the 0.5-mile trail uphill to Skull Rock, a lookout area with rock formations and even better views of downtown and the coastline, or follow the Temescal Canyon path as it begins a gradual descent through dense woodland back to the bottom of the canyon. At about 3 miles, you will reach a footbridge with a view of a small waterfall cascading over large boulders. After the winter rains, the water flow is pretty heavy; in the summer, it's not much more than a trickle. This is a good place to stop and rest or poke

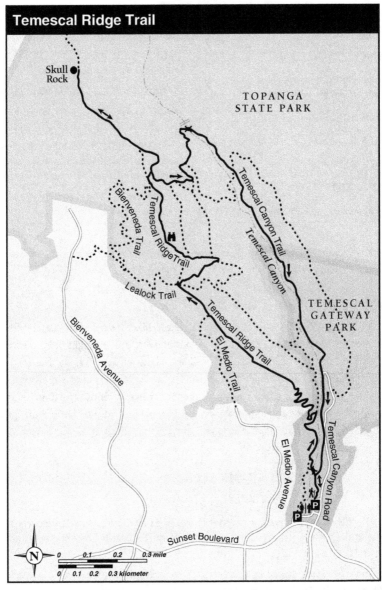

Temescal Ridge Trail

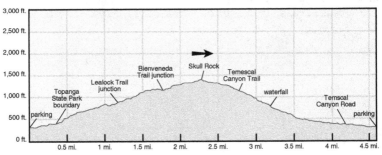

DISTANCE & CONFIGURATION: 4.6-mile balloon	fee at self-pay stations, or park along Sunset Boulevard or Temescal Canyon Road
DIFFICULTY: Strenuous	**MAPS:** USGS *Topanga;* at kiosks in parking lots and at supply store
SCENERY: Chaparral-covered hills, panoramic ocean and city views, waterfall	**WHEELCHAIR ACCESSIBLE:** No
EXPOSURE: Sun and shade	**FACILITIES:** Restrooms, water fountains, supply store with snacks and maps
TRAFFIC: Heavy	**CONTACT:** 310-454-1395; **nps.gov/samo**
TRAIL SURFACE: Dirt path	**/planyourvisit/temescalgateway.htm** or **lamountains.com/parks.asp?parkid=58**
HIKING TIME: 2 hours	**COMMENTS:** Dogs are only allowed on the lower half of this trail.
ACCESS: Daily, 5 a.m.–10 p.m.; parking	

around a bit amid the rocks (there are a couple of smaller waterfalls upstream) before continuing the gradual 1-mile descent back to the parking lot.

Nearby Activities

Consider hitting Will Rogers State Beach after the hike. It's a 2-mile stretch of sand, surf, playgrounds, and volleyball nets. From the parking lot, head straight on Temescal Canyon Boulevard to the intersection with Pacific Coast Highway. Turn left and then right into the day-use parking lot. If you're hungry, head north on Pacific Coast Highway a couple of miles to the Reel Inn for some fresh mahimahi or fish-and-chips. The ambience is surfer-casual, but the portions are ample, the prices reasonable, and the seafood top-quality. The restaurant is located at 18661 Pacific Coast Hwy., just north of Topanga Canyon Boulevard.

GPS TRAILHEAD COORDINATES

N34° 3.123' W118° 31.780'

From Pacific Coast Highway, turn east onto Temescal Canyon Road and drive 1.2 miles to the end. Parking is available in fee lots or on Temescal Canyon Road and Sunset Boulevard.

Alternate directions: Take I-405 to Exit 57 (Sunset Boulevard), and follow Sunset south 6 miles to Temescal Canyon Park. Turn right into the parking lot or park on the street.

47 Will Rogers State Historic Park: INSPIRATION POINT LOOP TRAIL

Enjoy 360-degree views from atop Inspiration Point.

In Brief

Cool coastal breezes, an easy-to-navigate path, and sweeping views of the Pacific make this trail popular with families, visitors, and UCLA students. The polo field and the intact 1920s ranch house that once belonged to Will Rogers lend a historical element to the hike.

Description

The park was originally the private ranch of movie star Will Rogers and his family. After Rogers died in a plane crash in 1935, his wife, Betty, willed the property to the state of California with the condition that it continue to be used for equestrian activities. On any given weekend between April and October, you'll find polo matches going on in the immaculate green field to the south of the hiking trails. The ranch also breeds and boards horses in the stables behind the main house.

In a way, this path represents the best and worst of Los Angeles. The panoramic views are unparalleled, and it's a great way for new transplants to convince their out-of-town

DISTANCE & CONFIGURATION:
2.2-mile loop

DIFFICULTY: Easy

SCENERY: Coastal sage, live oak trees, panoramic views of mountains and sea

EXPOSURE: Sunny

TRAFFIC: Heavy

TRAIL SURFACE: Dirt and gravel path

HIKING TIME: 1 hour

ACCESS: Daily, 8 a.m.–sunset;

$12 parking fee

MAPS: USGS *Topanga;* at visitor center, parking kiosk, and **parks.ca.gov /pages/626/files/WillRogersSHPFinal WebLayout2011.pdf**

WHEELCHAIR ACCESSIBLE: Visitor center area

FACILITIES: Restrooms, water, picnic area

CONTACT: 310-454-8212; **parks.ca.gov/?page_id=626**

friends and relatives that there's much more to L.A. than traffic and smog. But the trail to Inspiration Point is always crowded and tends to make me feel like I'm on a class field trip with an eclectic mix of people, from fit UCLA coeds and power walkers to parents pushing jogging strollers and older couples in golf pants and sun visors. If you prefer tranquility on your hikes, plan to go early in the morning or on a weekday, or consider exploring one of the several narrow paths that extend off this trail and link up with the 55-mile Backbone Trail or empty back into the parking lot. It's difficult to get lost within this 186-acre park, thanks to plenty of sign markers and the lack of heavy forest or brush.

From the lower parking area, follow the trail upward along switchbacks bordered by a white fence. Soon you'll come to a T where a sign directs you to the left. (The right path leads to the stables and back to the upper parking lot.) Even though you're only at an elevation of 550 feet here, there are great views of the Pacific Ocean and the nearby neighborhoods of Pacific Palisades and Santa Monica. At about 0.5 mile, you'll come to another turnoff on the right that leads back to the parking lot. Keep going straight toward Inspiration Point as the trail continues north, bordered by coastal sage and scrub brush. After another 0.25 mile, you'll come to a short out-and-back trail that leads to Inspiration Point, a wide, flat expanse with picnic tables, trash cans, hitching posts, and 360-degree views that include the Pacific Ocean, the snowcapped San Gabriels, and Catalina Island to the south. It's usually fairly crowded up here, but most people tend to snap a few photos and then leave.

From here, retrace your steps back down the short path and follow the main trail north. Soon you'll see a sign and trailhead for the Backbone Trail, a north–south trail that begins here and extends 55 miles to Point Mugu State Park in Malibu. This is also the border for the 11,000-acre Topanga State Park, another state park with an abundance of hiking trails. Continue on the Inspiration Point Loop Trail as it begins to dip east and then south back to the parking lot. You'll see chaparral-covered hills to your left and pass a right turn for Bone Canyon Trail, another narrow trail that leads back to the stables and parking lot. Continue southeast as the trail winds past the tony mansions of Brentwood in the distance. You can also glimpse the Getty Center from here, its

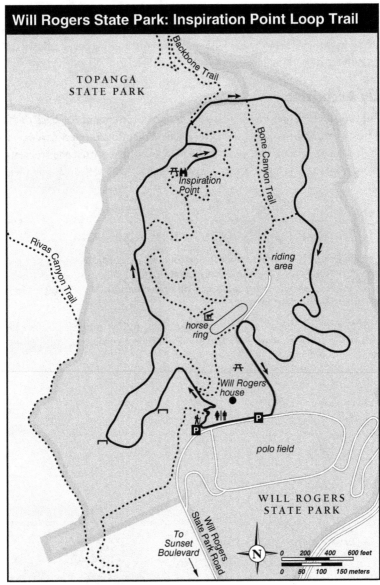

Will Rogers State Park: Inspiration Point Loop Trail

TOPANGA STATE PARK

Backbone Trail

Bone Canyon Trail

Inspiration Point

Rivas Canyon Trail

riding area

horse ring

Will Rogers house

polo field

WILL ROGERS STATE PARK

To Sunset Boulevard

Will Rogers State Park Road

N

| 0 | 200 | 400 | 600 feet |
| 0 | 50 | 100 | 150 meters |

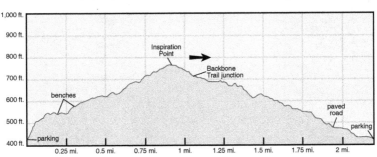

1,000 ft.
900 ft.
800 ft.
700 ft.
600 ft.
500 ft.
400 ft.

Inspiration Point

Backbone Trail junction

benches

parking

paved road

parking

0.25 mi.   0.5 mi.   0.75 mi.   1 mi.   1.25 mi.   1.5 mi.   1.75 mi.   2 mi.

glass-and-chrome walls perched on a hill to the east. As the trail continues downward, a string of gnarled live oak trees lends the only shade of the entire hike. Soon you'll see the stables and grassy picnic area to your left, as the trail turns into a paved service road. Follow this south to the parking lot.

Nearby Activities

If you find yourself here on a weekend between April and September, check out the polo matches held every Saturday and Sunday on the field that Rogers once played on with his pals Douglas Fairbanks and Tyrone Power. The field is the only outdoor regulation-size polo field in Los Angeles. For more information and a match schedule, go to **willrogers polo.org.**

GPS TRAILHEAD COORDINATES   N34° 3.280' W118° 30.792'

Take I-405 to Exit 57 (Sunset Boulevard), and follow Sunset south 4.5 miles to Will Rogers State Park Road. Turn right and follow Will Rogers 1 mile to the park's entrance. The lower lot is closest to the trailhead. The upper parking lot straddles the picnic grounds and the polo field to the south.

Alternate directions: From Pacific Coast Highway, follow Sunset Boulevard west 3.8 miles to Will Rogers State Park Road. Turn left and continue 1 mile to the park entrance.

A highlight of the Solstice Canyon trails is a large brick fireplace, pretty much all that remains of a manse built in 1952 and destroyed by fire (see page 173).

ORANGE COUNTY AND LA PUENTE HILLS

The Hsi Lai Buddhist Temple as seen from Hacienda Hills (see page 194)

Orange County and La Puente Hills

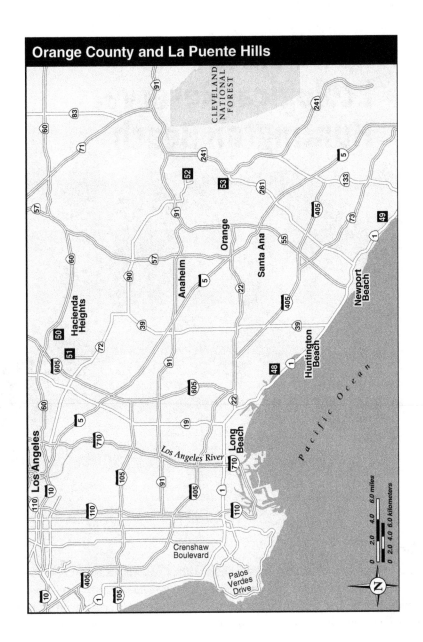

48 Bolsa Chica Ecological Reserve, Huntington Beach

Birds thrive within the Bolsa Chica wetlands.

In Brief

Despite being sandwiched between the busy Pacific Coast Highway and a field of active oil derricks, the Bolsa Chica Ecological Reserve is a valuable wetland that is considered one of the best birding spots in the state. Several miles of paved paths around a water inlet make this a haven not only for birders but also for power walkers and families.

Description

The Bolsa Chica marshland was once destined for a housing and commercial development with man-made marinas and canals, but environmental groups took the landowner to court and launched a Save Bolsa Chica grassroots campaign. The result: About 1,200 acres of the marsh have been set aside as open space and wildlife habitat, and a major rehabilitation project to remove defunct oil wells (Huntington Beach was once the

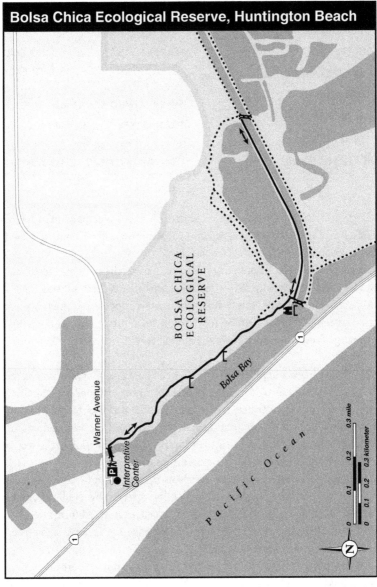

Bolsa Chica Ecological Reserve, Huntington Beach

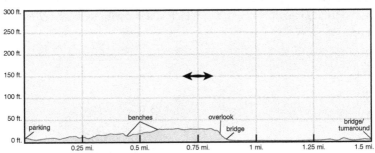

DISTANCE & CONFIGURATION: 3-mile out-and-back	**ACCESS:** Daily, sunrise–sunset; free
DIFFICULTY: Easy	**MAPS:** USGS *Seal Beach;* at the Bolsa Chica Wetlands Interpretive Center, 3842 Warner Ave.
SCENERY: Birds, marsh plants	
EXPOSURE: Sunny	**WHEELCHAIR ACCESSIBLE:** Yes
TRAFFIC: Moderate–heavy	**FACILITIES:** Portable toilets in parking lots
TRAIL SURFACE: Paved	
HIKING TIME: 1.5 hours	**CONTACT:** 714-846-1114; **bolsachica.org**

seventh-largest oil drilling area in the United States). The project, begun in 2004, was the largest coastal restoration ever undertaken in Southern California and returned nearly 600 acres of wetlands to their pre-1900 condition.

To access the trailhead from Warner Avenue, park in the interpretive center lot and walk east along Warner Avenue to a wood kiosk that marks the trailhead. The path follows a straight, exposed path south along the eastern side of the inlet. I recommend bringing sunscreen and binoculars on this hike. Even if you're not a serious birder, you may get the urge for a close-up view of the animal and plant activity taking place in and around the reserve.

At 0.6 mile, you will come to a wooden fence and a group of interpretive signs that detail the reserve's wildlife and history. The salt marsh was once a popular hunting ground for American Indian tribes. In the late 1800s, it was transformed into the Bolsa Chica Gun Club, a duck and fowl hunting club that dammed the original inlet, upsetting the tidal flow that brought marine life into the marsh. Later, a portion of the wetlands was used by World War II troops to watch for enemy attacks.

Today, despite its past, the reserve serves as a playground for 200 species of birds, including great blue herons, peregrine falcons, stilts, egrets, brown pelicans, and western sandpipers. Its plant life features cordgrass, prickly pear cactus, California buckwheat, tall eucalyptus, monkeyflowers, and black sage. Just past the interpretive signs, you'll come to an overlook with benches and more interpretive signs. This is a popular stopping point for birding. Just beyond this, you'll come to steps that lead to a footbridge dividing the two lagoons. It is a good place to spot ducks, geese, pelicans, egrets, common loons, and herons as they wait for a fish dinner. (The inlet is stocked with sea bass, halibut, and little-neck clams.)

From the footbridge, you can head east on a trail that straddles more marshland, or cross to the western side of the inlet and follow that south about a mile to a second parking lot. The latter option is the more popular one, especially for birders, although I found its proximity to the highway traffic distracting. The eastern trail is quieter and more pristine and just as abundant with birds and plant life, although some hikers may find the view of oil derricks in the distance just as distracting. At about 1.5 miles, you'll reach a bridge. From the bridge, you may turn back and retrace your steps or turn right or left to loop back to the footbridge. Before I did this hike, I thought of Huntington Beach as a traffic-choked Orange County suburb of surfer shops and tract homes. I came away with a newfound appreciation for its ability to keep development around this fragile coastal habitat at bay.

Nearby Activities

Bolsa Chica State Beach, directly across the street from the ecological reserve, is a popular place for swimming, sunning, and surf-fishing for perch, corbina, croaker, and sand shark. Also popular during the summer is bare-handed fishing for California grunion, a species that only spawns on Southern California beaches. The beach extends 3 miles from Seal Beach to Huntington Beach City Pier. A bikeway connects it with Huntington State Beach, 7 miles south.

GPS TRAILHEAD COORDINATES

N33° 42.693' W118° 3.598'

From I-405, take Exit 20 (Bolsa Chica Road), and follow Bolsa Chica 3.8 miles south to Warner Avenue. Turn right onto Warner Avenue, and follow it 1.4 miles west to Pacific Coast Highway. Just before the road ends, turn left into the interpretive center parking lot, or turn left on Pacific Coast Highway and follow it 1.5 miles to a second parking lot on the left.

---

49 Crystal Cove State Park:
EL MORO CANYON TRAIL

Spring wildflowers cover the hillsides of Crystal Cove Park.

In Brief

Bring lots of sunscreen for this tranquil, treeless hike through coastal sage scrub, grassland, and wildflower-covered hills.

Description

Crystal Cove State Park consists of 2,200 acres of campsites and hiking, bicycling, and horseback-riding trails. For years, it was used by the San Juan Capistrano Mission as grazing land for livestock. The land was sold to agriculture pioneer James Irvine in 1964.

DISTANCE & CONFIGURATION:
3.7-mile out-and-back

DIFFICULTY: Moderate

SCENERY: Spring wildflowers, ocean-view bluffs

EXPOSURE: Sunny

TRAFFIC: Moderate

TRAIL SURFACE: Dirt path

HIKING TIME: 2 hours

ACCESS: Gate: Daily, 6 a.m.–sunset; $15 fee for parking

MAPS: USGS *Laguna Beach;* at park office

and **crystalcovestatepark.org/map-of-hiking-trails**

WHEELCHAIR ACCESSIBLE:
No

FACILITIES: Restrooms, water fountains, campsites

CONTACT: 949-494-3539; **crystalcovestatepark.org**

COMMENTS: Crystal Cove has three campgrounds within its boundaries, though all are reached by a strenuous 3-mile hike; call 800-444-7275 for reservations and fees.

Irvine sold the land to the state in 1979, and it was incorporated into the California State Parks system. Its location, just off Pacific Coast Highway between the upscale towns of Newport Beach and Laguna Beach, is tough to beat—though some people may be annoyed by the newly built cluster developments that hover on either side of the park in stark contrast to the nature within it.

The trailhead for El Moro Canyon starts just beyond the stop sign at the park's entrance next to El Morro Elementary School. This is a good, mostly flat hike on its own, or you can use it to access other steeper trails within Crystal Cove State Park. There are helpful trail maps indicating "you are here" along the way, but I also recommend picking up a map from the park headquarters. A hat, sunscreen, and water are musts for this largely exposed hike. Dogs must be leashed and are not allowed on unpaved paths within the park.

Don't park in the school parking lot; you will likely get a ticket. Look for the fire-road gate near the entrance and take the dirt path beyond that. The path, flanked by coastal sage scrub year-round and yellow and purple wildflowers in the spring, starts out on a slight incline and then dips down, passing a baseball field and a well-kept mobile home park on the right. You'll catch occasional views of the ocean through the buildings. You can hear traffic noise from Pacific Coast Highway at first, but that soon fades away. A nice selection of native plants can be found within the park, including black sage, laurel sumac, lemonade berry, coastal wood fern, artichoke thistle, blue elderberry, and prickly pear cactus. Wildlife here includes deer, bobcats, roadrunners, quail, ravens, turkey vultures, and two kinds of rattlesnakes, the red diamond and the Western diamondback.

At about 0.3 mile, you'll come to a right turnoff for the BFI Trail. Continue straight on the flat El Moro Canyon path, which parallels a small stream. This path can get a little muddy in winter. When I hiked this trail in January, it was closed to mountain bikes because of muddy conditions caused by recent rains, but pedestrian traffic was fairly heavy. The path continues straight another mile or so to a turnoff for the East Cut Across

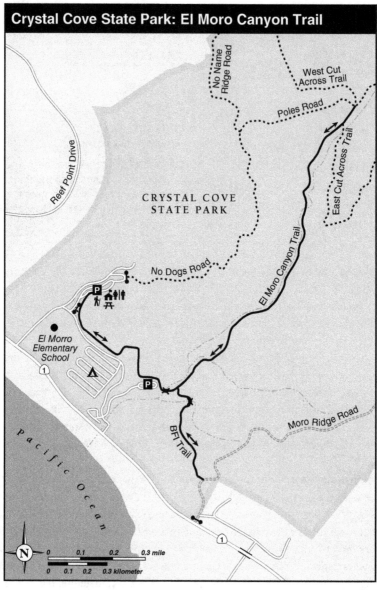

Crystal Cove State Park: El Moro Canyon Trail

No Name Ridge Road

West Cut Across Trail

Poles Road

East Cut Across Trail

Reef Point Drive

CRYSTAL COVE STATE PARK

El Moro Canyon Trail

No Dogs Road

El Morro Elementary School

Moro Ridge Road

BFI Trail

Pacific Ocean

N

0   0.1   0.2   0.3 mile

0   0.1   0.2   0.3 kilometer

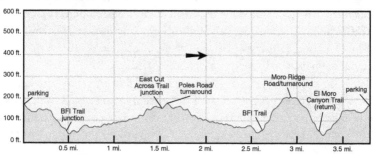

parking

BFI Trail junction

East Cut Across Trail junction

Poles Road/ turnaround

Moro Ridge Road/turnaround

BFI Trail

El Moro Canyon Trail (return)

parking

600 ft.
500 ft.
400 ft.
300 ft.
200 ft.
100 ft.
0 ft.

0.5 mi.   1 mi.   1.5 mi.   2 mi.   2.5 mi.   3 mi.   3.5 mi.

Trail, also known as I Think I Can. It's a steep dirt path that leads to Moro Ridge, where there are picnic tables and coastal views. Continue a little farther on Moro Canyon Road and you'll come to a turnoff on the left for Poles Road. This loops back via the No Dogs Road to the ranger station and parking lot.

Another option is to retrace your steps back down Moro Canyon Road to the trailhead for BFI Trail, a strenuous 0.5-mile climb that leads to good views of the Pacific Ocean and Moro Ridge Road. At Moro Ridge, the dirt trail ends and you'll reach a paved road that leads to picnic tables and a couple of campsites.

Nearby Activities

After your hike, walk across Pacific Coast Highway to the 3-mile stretch of beach that is also part of Crystal Cove State Park. Highlights include a broad bay that consistently ranks among the cleanest beaches in Southern California, a multiuse coastal trail, and a 1,140-acre protected underwater park that welcomes snorkelers and scuba divers. If you're in need of refreshment, don't miss the Shake Shack, a bright yellow roadside stand overlooking the cove that has served frothy drinks and sandwiches for 50 years (though it was acquired by Ruby's Diner in 2006).

GPS TRAILHEAD COORDINATES

N33° 33.936' W117° 49.393'

From I-5, take Exit 95 (CA 133 toward Laguna Beach), and head south about 10 miles until the road ends at Pacific Coast Highway. Make a right and proceed north about 3 miles to the park entrance on the right.

50 Hacienda Hills Trail

In Brief

This dirt-path loop is a gradual climb through cool forest and sunbaked switchbacks to 1,000-foot elevation and views of downtown Los Angeles, the coastal plains of Orange County, and the wooded community of La Habra Heights.

Description

The Hacienda Hills Trail is part of the Skyline Trail in the Puente–Chino Hills Wildlife Corridor, an unbroken chain of plant and wildlife habitat that extends about 30 miles from the Cleveland National Forest in Orange County to the west end of the Puente Hills in Los Angeles County. According to the Sierra Club, the area represents one of the largest intact native habitats in the urban Los Angeles basin. It is maintained by the Puente Hills Landfill Native Habitat Authority—a collaborative effort of Los Angeles County, the city of Whittier, and the Sanitation Districts of Los Angeles—which was created in 1984 to mitigate the effects of the nearby Puente Hills Landfill. The majority of hikers here seem to be residents of the Hacienda Heights area out for weekend exercise jaunts, but it never seems overcrowded. Dogs are allowed, and mountain bikes are permitted in parts of the preserve.

This trail begins just beyond the gate of a chain-link fence at the west end of Orange Grove Avenue in a residential neighborhood. The gate is usually locked, but hikers can pass through an opening on the left side. You can also access this trail from the small parking lot at the end of Seventh Avenue. The Habitat Authority spiffed up this area in 2005, adding benches, interpretive signs, and native-plant landscaping.

Begin by walking south along the chain-link fence past private homes. Wildflowers, cactus, and coastal sage scrub line the right side of the trail. There's also a piece of rusted-out farm equipment that looks like it hasn't been moved for half a century. Soon you'll come to a sign for the Habitat Authority Wilderness Preserve. Stay to your right and follow the dirt path as it dips west into shady forest before a series of uphill switchbacks. Look for the San Gabriel Mountains and inland urban sprawl to your right as you continue to ascend. Soon the flat, brown Puente Hills Landfill and a few radio towers will come into view to the north. Continue uphill on the path. Just beyond a sign that reads NO BIKES PAST THIS POINT, you'll come to a small, level area that offers panoramic views of the San Gabriels and downtown Los Angeles, as well as the landfill. To the east, you can also spot the red pagodas of the Fo Guang Shan Hsi Lai Buddhist Temple. Built in 1988, it is the largest Buddhist monastery in the United States.

This is a good spot to rest and drink some water before completing the loop. Despite the pockets of shade, much of this path is exposed to direct sunlight, so bring plenty of sunscreen and water. From here, the trail winds downhill to a barbed-wire fence and string of electric transmission towers. Bear left toward the water tower and follow the path south along the fence about 0.5 mile until you reach a Y. Head left (away from the

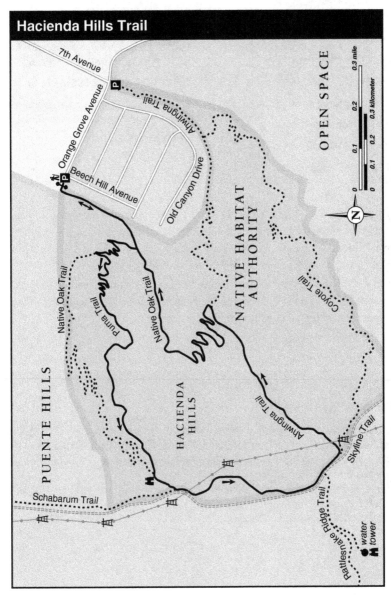

Hacienda Hills Trail

7th Avenue

Orange Grove Avenue

Ahwingna Trail

Beech Hill Avenue

Old Canyon Drive

OPEN SPACE

0.3 mile
0.3 kilometer
0.2
0.1 0.2
0.1
0 0

N

NATIVE HABITAT AUTHORITY

Coyote Trail

Native Oak Trail

Puma Trail

Native Oak Trail

PUENTE HILLS

HACIENDA HILLS

Ahwingna Trail

Skyline Trail

Schabarum Trail

Rattlesnake Ridge Trail

water tower

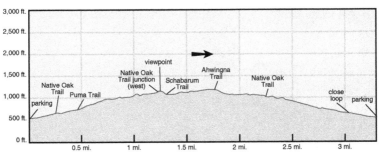

3,000 ft.
2,500 ft.
2,000 ft.
1,500 ft.
1,000 ft.
500 ft.
0 ft.

viewpoint

Native Oak Trail junction (west)

Ahwingna Trail

Native Oak Trail

Schabarum Trail

Native Oak Trail

Puma Trail

close loop

parking

parking

0.5 mi.   1 mi.   1.5 mi.   2 mi.   2.5 mi.   3 mi.

DISTANCE & CONFIGURATION: 3.4-mile loop	**ACCESS:** Daily, sunrise–sunset; free
DIFFICULTY: Moderate	**MAPS:** USGS *El Monte;* at Seventh Avenue kiosk or **habitatauthority.org/trails**
SCENERY: Mountains, trees	**WHEELCHAIR ACCESSIBLE:** No
EXPOSURE: Sun and shade	**FACILITIES:** Restroom at parking lot at Seventh and Orange Grove Avenues
TRAFFIC: Moderate	
TRAIL SURFACE: Gravel, dirt path	**CONTACT:** 562-945-9003, ext. 5; **habitatauthority.org/trails**
HIKING TIME: 2.25 hours	

brown sign marked MULTIPURPOSE TRAIL) as the trail winds back into the shady knoll that marked the beginning of the hike. At 2.5 miles, you'll come to a T in the path and a marker indicating that Orange Grove Avenue is to the left and Seventh Avenue is to the right. Head left (unless you parked in the Seventh Avenue lot) as the trail follows a few short switchbacks downhill and flattens into a wide dirt path leading back to Orange Grove Avenue. Urban noises like leaf blowers and horns honking will start to intrude as you reenter the residential neighborhood.

GPS TRAILHEAD COORDINATES

N34° 0.681' W117° 59.889'

From I-5, take Exit 134 (Pomona Freeway/CA 60), and follow CA 60 east 13.8 miles. Exit at Seventh Avenue/Hacienda Heights. Follow Seventh Avenue about a mile until it dead-ends at Orange Grove Avenue. Turn right and park at the end of the street. The trail begins on the other side of the chain-link fence.

Time your visit so it doesn't coincide with the evening rush hour; traffic heading east on the Pomona Freeway/CA 60 can be heavy.

51 Hellman Park:
PEPPERGRASS TRAIL TO RATTLESNAKE RIDGE TRAIL

The Buddhist Columbarium at Rose Hill Cemetery

In Brief

Peppered with a few muscle-burning uphill climbs, this trail is essentially an out-and-back fire road in a preserved open space that borders the cities of Whittier and Hacienda Heights. Several scenic singletrack detours loop back around to the main path. Its well-maintained trails and panoramic views draw big crowds on weekends.

Description

Located just off a Mayberry-like street in Whittier, Hellman Park is part of the Puente Hills Habitat Authority, a joint force that includes the city of Whittier and Los Angeles County and oversees more than 3,700 acres of public open space. It has several named trails that snake off the main fire road, but it's difficult to get lost, as all trails eventually hook back up with the main road. Mountain bikers use the trails too, but I've seen more hikers than cyclists during my visits to Hellman Park.

DISTANCE & CONFIGURATION: 5.5-mile out-and-back	ACCESS: Daily, sunrise–sunset; free parking in small lot or on street
DIFFICULTY: Moderate	MAPS: USGS *Whittier;* at kiosk near trail- head and **habitatauthority.org/trails**
SCENERY: City-to-ocean views, chaparral hillsides	
EXPOSURE: Mostly sun	WHEELCHAIR ACCESSIBLE: First mile
TRAFFIC: Heavy on weekends	FACILITIES: Restrooms, water
TRAIL SURFACE: Packed dirt	CONTACT: 562-945-9003, ext. 5; **habitatauthority.org/trails**
HIKING TIME: 2.5 hours	

The main trail begins just above a small parking lot off Greenleaf Avenue near a large sign with a map of the area. The elevation gain (and scenic payoff) starts immediately as you start walking uphill past the fire-road gate. On weekends, you will find yourself surrounded by lots of other exercise hounds in this early part of the hike. The diversity of people on this trail, from serious trail runners to families with toddlers, adds an interesting people-watching element to the experience and restores faith that people are seeking out nature as much as their local malls on any given weekend. This is also a good hiking option if you're looking to hit the trails alone but wary of the potential dangers of heading off into the wilderness by yourself. It's hard to get lost, and you'll rarely find yourself without company along the way.

At about 0.4 mile the trail splits; both paths merge back to the same trail, but most people opt for the wider Peppergrass Trail to the right. It's a tough uphill climb for about another 0.5 mile, but the views are already getting spectacular. At 1.1 miles, bear left as the trail hugs the canyon wall and gets briefly shady (a steeper fire road on the right eventually reconnects with the trail).

At about 1.4 miles, you'll come to a T intersection with a clearing that yields views to the north of Rose Hills Memorial Park, a century-old cemetery spanning 1,400 acres, as well as the striking orange pagodas of its Buddhist Columbarium. There's also a post marking the Rattlesnake Ridge Trail. Both paths lead to water towers that you can see in the distance. The water tower to the right is the more popular option. On my last visit, I hiked to both towers and enjoyed the contrasting vibes. Think of the bold graffiti-covered water tower to the right as rocker Adam Levine, while the more pristine one to the left, surrounded by a shaded lawn, is more in line with the ethereal sounds of Enya. Both offer spectacular views and flat surfaces (though no benches) to rest and refuel.

Once you've visited either or both water towers, head back to the clearing via the Rattlesnake Ridge Trail and retrace your steps on the fire road. After about 0.3 mile, you'll see a trail split with a sign that says MULTI-PURPOSE TRAIL. Take the path that descends to the right of the sign for a quieter singletrack experience and a different

Hellman Park: Peppergrass Trail to Rattlesnake Ridge Trail

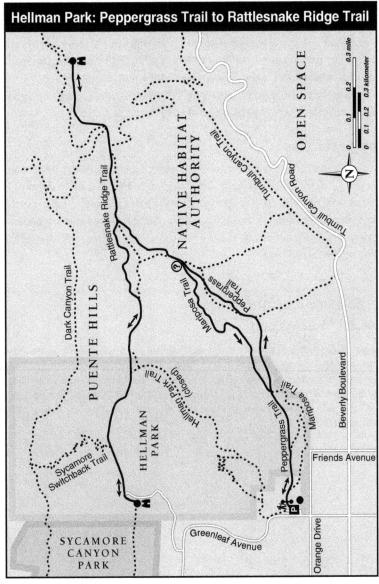

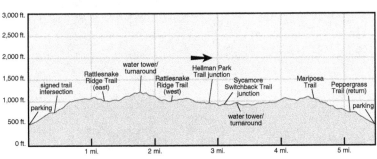

perspective on the way back down. This trail eventually meets up with the main fire road and kicks you back to the parking lot.

Hellman Park and its many modest-to-strenuous trail options pleasantly surprised me. Its location not far from the intersection of I-605 and CA 60 isn't convenient for many Angelenos, especially those living west of downtown. But I would encourage any semiserious SoCal hiker to make the drive and check it out. The views of ocean, mountains, and city are breathtaking and offer a unique perspective of Los Angeles and Orange counties.

Nearby Activities

After your hike, you can add a spiritual and culinary element to the day by driving 7 miles to the Fo Guang Shan Hsi Lai Temple (**hsilai.org**) in nearby Hacienda Heights. Its main shrine, manicured gardens, and conservatories are open to the public daily, 9 a.m.–5 p.m., and a vegetarian lunch buffet is served in a bright dining hall for a small donation. Just be sure to bring or wear a pair of pants or a skirt—no sleeveless shirts, tank tops, or shorts are allowed on the premises.

GPS TRAILHEAD COORDINATES

N33° 59.450' W118° 2.221'

From I-605, take Exit 16 (Beverly Boulevard) in Whittier. Head east on Beverly for 2 miles to Greenleaf Avenue. Turn left, and the park entrance is on your right. The small parking lot fills up fast on weekends; there's free parking on Greenleaf Avenue or Beverly Boulevard, but other streets around the trailhead allow permit parking only. The fire-road gate closes at sunset. Maps and more information are online at **habitat authority.org/trails**.

---

52 Oak Canyon Nature Center:
BLUEBIRD LANE AND WREN WAY

Thick stands of oak dominate the trails of Oak Canyon Nature Center.

In Brief

Shrouded by oak forest and serenaded by a small stream, this family-friendly hike offers a cool escape on a hot and cloudless day.

Description

Bordered by a golf course and several upscale gated communities, Oak Canyon Nature Center is a 58-acre park made up of three adjoining canyons that are tucked into the Anaheim Hills. Quails, scrub jays, raccoons, rabbits, and coyotes are among the wildlife that can be found here. Also located on-site is an amphitheater and the John J. Collier Interpretive Center, which houses wildlife and natural history exhibits. Don't hesitate to ask the friendly front desk staff to recommend a hike or go over the park's conditions before hitting the trails.

Start off by taking the dirt path uphill to the western hillsides behind the nature center. The path then heads south and is surrounded by coastal sage scrub, tall grass, and oak trees. There are a few small loop detours along this path, but they never wander very far from the main trail.

At about 0.3 mile, you will come to a sign for Wren Way. Follow the path up some rough steps to the right. At this point the trail turns to pavement and winds along a sunny

DISTANCE & CONFIGURATION: 2-mile out-and-back	Nature center: Saturday, 10 a.m.–4 p.m.; free
DIFFICULTY: Easy with a few difficult spots	**MAPS:** USGS *Orange*; at nature center
SCENERY: Oak forest, stream	**WHEELCHAIR ACCESSIBLE:** Portions at beginning
EXPOSURE: Shady	**FACILITIES:** Restrooms, water
TRAFFIC: Moderate	**CONTACT:** 714-998-8380; **anaheim.net /ocnc**
TRAIL SURFACE: Packed dirt and paved	
HIKING TIME: 1 hour	**COMMENTS:** No pets, horses, or bicycles are allowed in the park. Watch out for poison oak, especially after a heavy rain, which tends to leave the trails overgrown.
ACCESS: April–Oct.: Daily, 9 a.m.–5 p.m. November–March: Daily, 9 a.m.–3 p.m.	

ridge above the canyon. It also crosses a series of concrete gutters, which require some minor jumping (small children can be lifted across). If you look up, you will see the rooftops of homes that line the ridgetop surrounding the park. The trail quickly leads you back to nature, though, as you follow a short, steep flight of steps into the cool, leafy canyon and the path turns to dirt again.

At about 0.5 mile, you will come to a Y. Take the right turnoff for Bluebird Lane and head uphill. Then the path levels (again, I found it to be overgrown and tricky to navigate) before heading downhill and turning into pavement again. It is very shady here and you can see and hear the stream on your left. At about 1 mile, the trail ends at a primitive fence made out of discarded telephone poles. A desk volunteer told me that some visitors like to extend the hike by crossing over the fence and following a narrow path northwest to a reservoir. From here, you can access a 3-mile loop trail that winds around the water. The path is easy to find, but it is thick with poison oak. If you're not dressed appropriately, I don't recommend the extension. From the fence, you can retrace your steps back to the parking lot. Alternatively, you can access the Roadrunner Ridge Trail from here and loop back to the parking lot, instead of going out and back.

Nearby Activities

The nature center has all kinds of kid-friendly activities, such as Hikes for Tykes, crafts lessons, and storytelling hours.

GPS TRAILHEAD COORDINATES   N33° 50.311' W117° 45.425'

From downtown Los Angeles, take the Golden State Freeway (I-5) south to Exit 114B (CA 91 East toward Riverside). Follow CA 91 East for 10.9 miles, and exit at Imperial Highway/CA 90. Head south on CA 90 for 0.7 mile. Turn left onto East Nohl Ranch Road, and drive 1.7 miles. Make a left onto Walnut Canyon Road. The park entrance is 0.5 mile ahead.

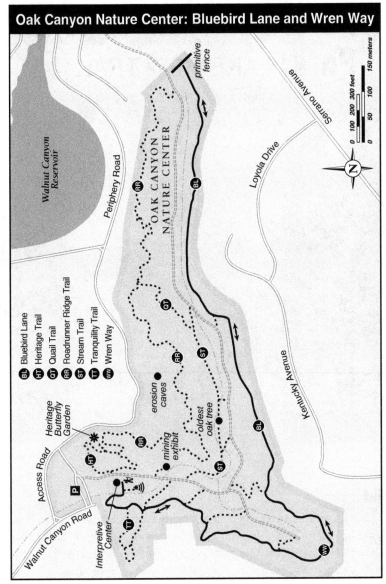

Oak Canyon Nature Center: Bluebird Lane and Wren Way

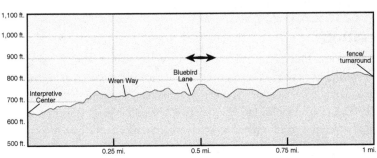

53 Peters Canyon Regional Park: LAKE VIEW TRAIL

The Lake View Trail skirts a 55-acre reservoir.

In Brief

This loop trail on the eastern edge of Orange County skirts a 55-acre reservoir past marshland; flowering cactus; and groves of willow, sycamore, and black cottonwood trees. Hundred-foot elevation gains at a couple of points make this a little harder than the average reservoir loop trail. The trail can be extended several more miles by taking one of the handful of moderate to difficult trails that wind through the southern portion of the park.

Description

James Peters was a 19th-century farmer who grew barley and beans in the upper part of the property and lived near a eucalyptus grove in the lower reaches of his namesake canyon. Once owned by agriculture pioneer James Irvine, it was purchased by the Orange County Parks Department in 1992 and turned into a public park. During World War II, it was used as a training area for the U.S. Army, which staged mock battles there.

DISTANCE & CONFIGURATION: 2.5-mile loop	**MAPS:** USGS *Orange;* at kiosk near trailhead and **ocparks.com/civicax/filebank/blobdload.aspx?BlobID=28645**
DIFFICULTY: Easy–moderate	**WHEELCHAIR ACCESSIBLE:** Yes
SCENERY: Freshwater marsh, grassland, coastal sage scrub	**FACILITIES:** Portable bathrooms in main lot, benches, water
EXPOSURE: Sunny	
TRAFFIC: Moderate	**CONTACT:** 714-973-6611; **ocparks.com/parks/peters**
TRAIL SURFACE: Paved	
HIKING TIME: 1.25 hours	**COMMENTS:** The park is open to hikers, joggers, mountain bikers, and equestrians. Pets are allowed but must be on a leash.
ACCESS: Daily, 7 a.m.–sunset; parking fee at self-pay kiosk	

This hike circles a reservoir that was built in 1931 to regulate the flow of water taken from nearby Irvine Lake to conserve rainwater runoff and irrigate crops to the south of the park. Waterfowl found here include mallards, snowy egrets, ospreys, double-crested cormorants, and belted kingfishers. Other birds spotted include gnatcatchers, Cooper's and red-tailed hawks, and cactus wrens. A second reservoir was built in the lower half of the park in 1940; it is now dry and serves as a flood-control basin.

Besides the reservoir, Peters Canyon has a running creek, a freshwater marsh, and a variety of trails used by mountain bikers, horseback riders, and exercise hounds from surrounding neighborhoods. It is meticulously maintained by the Orange County Department of Harbors, Beaches, and Parks.

The Lake View Trail begins beyond the information kiosk in the main parking lot. Follow the singletrack dirt path downhill and to the right as it parallels Canyon View Avenue and then hugs the reservoir. The first 0.5 mile of the trail is dominated by wildflowers, coastal sage scrub, and tall grass; the scenery then gives way to a freshwater marsh as the path moves closer to the water. The low-lying Anaheim hills surround you in the distance.

At just shy of a mile, the trail widens, and you will come to a turnoff for Cactus Point Trail on the left. Take the left turn and follow it past clusters of flowering cactus and a clear view of the reservoir and the parking lot from which you came. The path then rejoins the Lake View Trail. This is one of two points where the trail gains a little elevation. Continue past the dam on the left, and soon you will come to a T. This is Peters Canyon Trail, which runs north–south and covers the entire length of the park. From here, you can either turn left and follow the trail as it continues to skirt the reservoir back to the parking lot, or turn right to access the park's backcountry trails. If you choose the latter, expect to encounter a good number of mountain bikers, who favor the challenging up-and-down terrain of the East Ridge View Trail, which loops south past a grove of eucalyptus trees and rejoins Peters Canyon Trail at the park's southernmost end.

Peters Canyon Regional Park: Lake View Trail

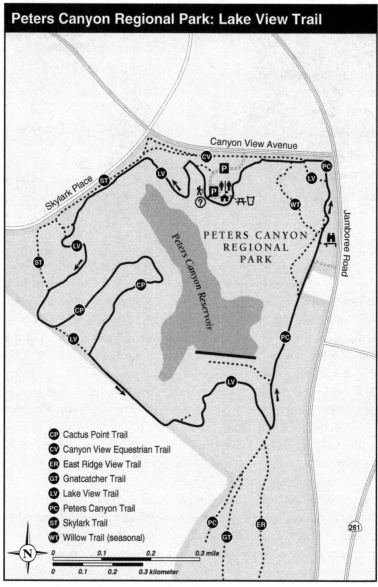

Canyon View Avenue

Skylark Place

Jamboree Road

Peters Canyon Reservoir

PETERS CANYON
REGIONAL
PARK

CP Cactus Point Trail
CV Canyon View Equestrian Trail
ER East Ridge View Trail
GT Gnatcatcher Trail
LV Lake View Trail
PC Peters Canyon Trail
ST Skylark Trail
WT Willow Trail (seasonal)

261

N

| 0 | 0.1 | 0.2 | 0.3 mile |

| 0 | 0.1 | 0.2 | 0.3 kilometer |

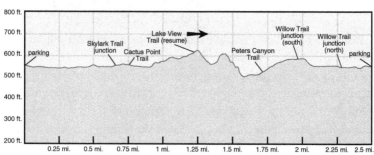

800 ft.										
700 ft.				Lake View Trail (resume)				Willow Trail junction (south)		
600 ft.	parking	Skylark Trail junction	Cactus Point Trail				Peters Canyon Trail		Willow Trail junction (north)	parking
500 ft.										
400 ft.										
300 ft.										
200 ft.										
	0.25 mi.	0.5 mi.	0.75 mi.	1 mi.	1.25 mi.	1.5 mi.	1.75 mi.	2 mi.	2.25 mi.	2.5 mi.

If you take a left turn at Peters Canyon Trail, you will find that the trail ascends again about 100 feet before winding past another viewpoint (with bench) at the 2-mile marker. After this, you will come to the least attractive part of the hike, as the trail edges away from the water and comes distractingly close to busy Jamboree Road on the right. At the junction with Canyon View Avenue, the path reverts briefly back to a singletrack before depositing you in the main parking lot.

Nearby Activities

After your hike, head to Old Towne Orange, a pedestrian-friendly square mile of restaurants and shops that bills itself as the antiques capital of California. To get there from Peters Canyon, turn left on Canyon View as you exit the park; then make a right on Newport and follow it to Chapman Avenue. Turn left on Chapman and follow it west until it runs right into the town center.

GPS TRAILHEAD COORDINATES

N33° 47.047' W117° 45.749'

From downtown Los Angeles, take the Golden State Freeway (I-5) south, and take Exit 107C (The City Drive) to Chapman Avenue in Orange. Follow Chapman east 7 miles through Old Towne Orange to Newport Boulevard. Turn right; then in 0.6 mile make a left onto Canyon View Avenue. The park entrance is 0.25 mile on the left.

SIMI AND ANTELOPE VALLEYS

The Pacific Crest Trail cuts through Vasquez Rocks, a natural area studded with ancient rock formations near Santa Clarita (see page 225).

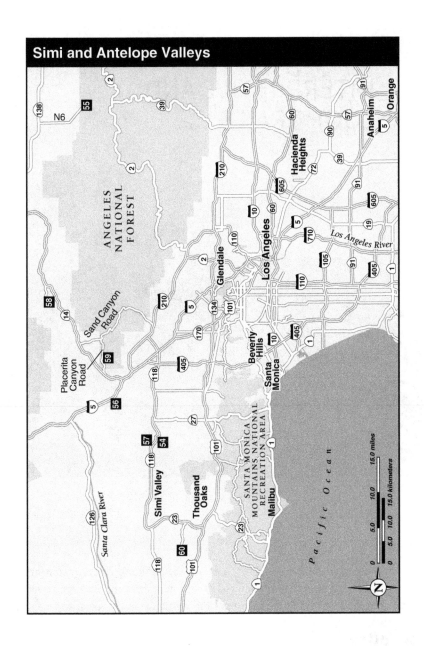

Simi and Antelope Valleys

54 Corriganville Park:
INTERPRETIVE AND LOOP TRAILS

Sandstone rock formations dominate the second half of this hike.

In Brief

This low-maintenance hike winds through an oak-shaded forest and the remnants of the park's heyday as a movie set, then follows a loop trail past dramatic sandstone rock formations. It's perfect for small children and out-of-town visitors who happen to be movie buffs.

Description

Founded by stuntman and B-movie actor Ray "Crash" Corrigan, Corriganville Park was one of the busiest movie sets in the country between the late 1930s and the 1950s. Among the hundreds of Westerns and adventure films that shot scenes here were *The Adventures of Rin Tin Tin, The Adventures of Robin Hood, The African Queen,* and *Fort Apache.*

In 1949 Corrigan opened the property to the public as an amusement park featuring stunt shows, stagecoach rides, pony rides, and a working Western town. It was quite

Corriganville Park: Interpretive and Loop Trails

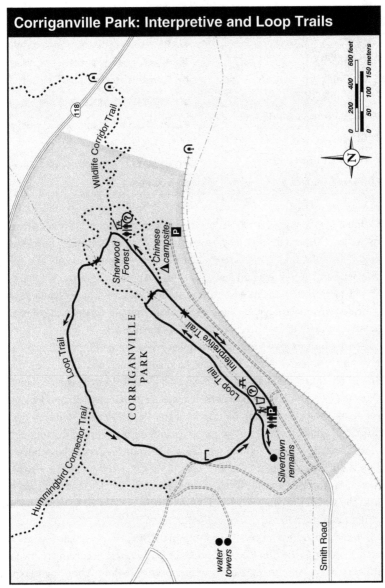

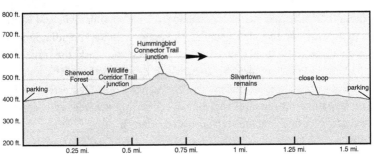

DISTANCE & CONFIGURATION: 1.7-mile loop	**ACCESS:** Daily, 6 a.m.–sunset; free
DIFFICULTY: Easy	**MAPS:** USGS *Simi Valley East;* **rsrpd.org** **/park/corrignavilleparkandtrail/two**
SCENERY: Oak forest, sandstone rock formations, Santa Susana Mountains	**corriganvillebrochures.pdf**
EXPOSURE: Mix of sun and shade	**WHEELCHAIR ACCESSIBLE:** Yes
TRAFFIC: Light	**FACILITIES:** Portable bathrooms, water, picnic tables
TRAIL SURFACE: Dirt path	**CONTACT:** 805-584-4400; **tinyurl.com**
HIKING TIME: 1 hour	**/corriganpark**

popular, attracting as many as 20,000 visitors on weekends. Major wildfires destroyed many of the sets in the 1970s, and the area languished until the city of Simi Valley purchased about 250 acres in 1988 and turned it into a regional park. Today it is used mainly as a hiking and jogging site, with an interpretive trail that chronicles the park's nature and wildlife as well as its former role as a movie set. The eastern side of the park is part of the Santa Susana Pass wildlife corridor, a tunnel designed to allow animals to migrate between the Simi Hills and the Santa Susana Mountains without having to cross the freeway.

To get to the Interpretive Trail, walk to the northeast end of the parking lot and look for the trail kiosk. There is a water fountain here and a current trail map on display, as well as an old brochure and map from the park's days as a Western-themed amusement park. Follow the packed-dirt trail past coast live oak trees, purple elderberry plants, and a handful of picnic tables on the left. Numbered signs along the trail point out the natural and historic highlights of the area. The path parallels an old railroad line dating back to the late 19th century. On the right across from a bench is a preserved mound of rock material used during construction of a railway tunnel that connected Chatsworth with Simi Valley. Soon you'll cross a footbridge and a small stream. The next sign, at about 0.2 mile, marks the site of the camp where Chinese laborers stayed in the early 1900s during the construction of the railroad tracks and tunnel.

Just past the campsite, you will come to a sign for Sherwood Forest. The oak trees on the left were featured in the film *The Adventures of Robin Hood,* according to the interpretive sign. This is also a good point to observe birds native to Simi Valley, such as sparrows, roadrunners, wrens, and thrashers.

At about 0.25 mile, you will pass a picnic pavilion on your right and another kiosk with a map and interpretive sign detailing the area's wildlife, including gray squirrels, coyotes, skunks, jackrabbits, and rattlesnakes. Just past the kiosk, the trail splits. To the right is the rugged Wildlife Corridor Trail, which heads north under the freeway via a tunnel and links up with other trails within the Rancho Simi Recreation and Park District. Take the path to the left and cross a small bridge that straddles what appears to be a dilapidated concrete drainage tunnel (more on this later).

The environment immediately changes from dense woodland to arid, sunny desert. Follow the trail uphill toward the large sandstone rock formations and distant views of the Santa Susana Mountains that dominate the second half of this hike. You can also see and hear the 118 freeway to the north, but I didn't find this to be overly distracting. In the spring, the boulders are attractively framed by colorful wildflowers. At about 0.6 mile, the still-shadeless path descends past rocky hills and more rock formations. There are few signs here, but the boulder caves surrounding the trail were apparently featured in many films and TV shows, including *The Fugitive* and *How the West Was Won.*

At about 0.75 mile, the path turns to pavement and there's a bench and hitching post on the left. Follow the road to the left as the pavement quickly turns back into dirt. To the right is a clearing below you. This is the remains of Silvertown, a cluster of building façades once used by filmmakers as a Western-style Main Street. At about a mile, turn right and walk 50 yards to get a closer look at Silvertown. Wildfires destroyed most of the set in the 1970s, and all that remains today are a few building foundations and low-lying rock walls.

Retrace your steps back to the main path, which soon turns shady again and resumes its role as an interpretive nature trail. At 1.3 miles, the path curves to the right past some picnic tables. At the wooden-fenced bridge, turn north and look at the empty concrete tunnel under you. This was built specifically to shoot water scenes at Corriganville for films such as *The Adventures of Robin Hood, The African Queen,* and *Jungle Jim.* Look for the square portholes on the sides of the walls; these were used as camera holes to capture the underwater shots. After the bridge, the path heads under more shade trees and toward picnic tables, and then curves back to the southwest to rejoin the Interpretative Trail and parking lot.

Nearby Activities

The Hummingbird Trail (page 221) can be accessed via a connector trail in Corriganville Park, though it requires crossing the freeway by way of an unattractive tunnel.

The Old Susana Cafe, at 1555 Kuehner Dr., just before the turnoff for Corriganville Park, is a good place to fuel up for breakfast or lunch after your hike. Its family-friendly menu includes burgers, omelets, and salads, and old photos of Simi Valley and Corriganville decorate the walls. Also not far is Underwood Family Farms in Moorpark (**underwoodfamilyfarms.com**), a large agriculture complex with pick-your-own produce, a petting zoo, and other kid-friendly activities.

GPS TRAILHEAD COORDINATES   N34° 15.875' W118° 39.155'

From downtown Los Angeles, take the Golden State Freeway (I-5) north to Exit 156A (CA 118) in Simi Valley. Merge onto CA 118 West, and go 12.7 miles. Just after crossing the Ventura County line, exit at Kuehner Drive, make a left, and drive about a mile to Smith Road. Turn left, following the signs for Corriganville Park. Park in the large lot.

55 Devil's Punchbowl Natural Area: DEVIL'S CHAIR TRAIL

In addition to the spectacular Devil's Punchbowl, hikers experience safety railings and barbed wire at the end of the trail.

In Brief

This out-and-back follows a moderate singletrack path to stunning views of a bowl-shaped gorge formed by the collision of three earthquake faults millions of years ago. Green and snowcapped in winter, the San Gabriel Mountains add a dramatic border to the park's stark white cliffs and tortured terrain. The 1.2-mile loop trail near the nature center is a gentler introduction to the area and great for small children and those in a hurry.

Description

This 1,300-acre park on the edge of the Mojave Desert gets its name from early American Indians who lived in the area and believed the land was inhabited by mountain lion demons. Now a part of the Los Angeles County park system, the park is located where the San Andreas, Pinyon, and Punchbowl Faults meet. The constant movement along the faults squeezes the underlying sandstone layers, pushing them upward, while wind and water erosion has sculpted the gorge into a breathtaking hodgepodge of peaks and

DISTANCE & CONFIGURATION: 7.4-mile out-and-back	**MAPS:** USGS *Valyermo;* at nature center, outdoor kiosk, and **devils-punchbowl .com/pages/map.pdf**
DIFFICULTY: Moderate–strenuous	
SCENERY: Rock formations, San Gabriel Mountains, juniper and pine trees	**WHEELCHAIR ACCESSIBLE:** First mile
EXPOSURE: Shade and sun	**FACILITIES:** Restrooms, water, picnic tables
TRAFFIC: Moderate	
TRAIL SURFACE: Fire road, singletrack dirt path	**CONTACT:** 661-944-2743; **devils-punchbowl.com**
HIKING TIME: 3 hours	**COMMENTS:** No camping is allowed at Devil's Punchbowl. Dogs are permitted on a leash. Call or check the website for weather conditions, especially in winter.
ACCESS: Gate: Daily, sunrise–sunset. Nature center: Tuesday–Sunday, 9 a.m.– 5 p.m.; free	

pinnacles at an elevation of 4,700 feet. It is only an hour's drive from Los Angeles, but you will feel like you are a world away from the city.

Below the Punchbowl rim, a juniper and piñon pine forest nourishes native mammals, reptiles, insects, and birds.

This hike begins off the parking lot across from the nature center. If you have time, stop by the center first and speak with the ranger on duty to get the lowdown on trail conditions (the path is sometimes blanketed by snow in winter). This is also the place to learn about the area's desert plants and wildlife, which include red manzanita, juniper, piñon pines, Pacific rattlers, geckos, and great horned owls.

Look for a sign for the Burkhart Trail and follow the fire road lined with red manzanita as it gradually ascends southward. The biggest elevation gains (and, lamentably, the least amount of shade) come during the first 0.9 mile of this hike; then it levels out to moderate ups and downs as you follow the rim to the overlook.

You'll pass a large sign with a map outlining Devil's Chair Trail, as well as a water tank and small shelter building. You'll have glimpses of the Punchbowl here, as well as views of the flat and sprawling Antelope Valley to your north. Continue on the fire road, and after about 1 mile, you will come to a sign and trail split with Burkhart Saddle. For Devil's Chair Trail, stay left as it narrows and becomes more shaded by large pines and firs. (Burkhart Trail heads west and then south to eventually hook up with the Pacific Crest Trail and Angeles Crest Highway.)

The trail descends moderately until it reaches a seasonal stream (though drought conditions have stemmed the water flow dramatically) and curves around to the left and heads uphill again. Now the views of the Punchbowl and San Gabriels become more prominent and stay with you pretty much the rest of the way to the lookout. After you reach the 1.5-mile marker, the trail narrows, and there are no guardrails or any other protection between you and a very steep canyon fall. Use extreme caution here and watch small children and dogs carefully. If you do this hike in winter and the conditions are

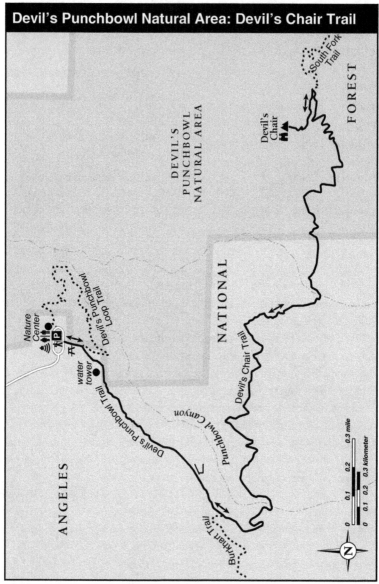

Devil's Punchbowl Natural Area: Devil's Chair Trail

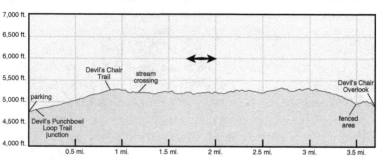

right, you may be treated to spectacular views of the mountains and rocks blanketed by snow. When I was here in mid-February, we only saw snow at the very peak of the mountains, but the air was cool and intoxicatingly fresh.

After another mile of gentle roller-coaster hiking, the trail begins to dip downward into the gorge to reach the Devil's Chair. It's a bit daunting to look down and realize that you're going to have to summon the energy to make it back up the path, but try not to let that put you off. You're about to witness an incredible, unobstructed view of the Punchbowl. For obvious safety reasons, the final trek down to the chair is completely protected by guardrails. There's room for plenty of people at the end to rest and regroup before heading the 3.6 miles back to the nature center.

The Punchbowl can be nearly deserted on weekdays, but Saturdays and Sundays bring lots of picnicking families and serious hikers and mountain bikers to the trails. My family hiked this trail on a busy three-day weekend and saw quite a few groups along the trail. My 9-year-old son completed the hike easily, while my 6-year-old stuck it out for about 2 miles. The 1.2-mile loop by the nature center would have been a better option for him.

Nearby Activities

The tiny town of Pearblossom, about 8 miles from Devil's Punchbowl, is a good place to stop for lunch or fresh produce. Valley Hungarian Sausage and Meat along CA 138 is renowned for its smoked-sausage sandwiches and bacon biscuits (open daily, 10 a.m.–5 p.m.). Charlie Brown Farms (**charliebrownfarms.com**) is another rest stop on CA 138 catering to tourists; it specializes in barbecue, shakes, candy, and all types of kitschy souvenirs. Another interesting side trip is Saint Andrew's Abbey, a Benedictine monastery in nearby Valyermo (**valyermo.com**). There is a tiny church with services every Sunday, a meditation pond, and a shop selling religious-themed ceramics.

GPS TRAILHEAD COORDINATES
N34° 24.843' W117° 51.494'

Take I-5 North to Exit 162 (Antelope Valley Freeway/CA 14). Follow CA 14 North for 28.9 miles. Get off at the Pearblossom Highway exit, turn left, and follow the signs to Pearblossom Highway (CA 138). Continue 14 miles to Longview Road (CR N6). Turn right, and drive 4.8 miles. Turn left onto Tumbleweed Road, which becomes Devil's Punchbowl Road, and continue 3 miles to the park.

56 Ed Davis Park in Towsley Canyon: CANYON VIEW LOOP TRAIL

In Brief

This hike begins with a gradual ascent past chaparral, coastal sage scrub, and seasonal wildflowers; peaks at a viewpoint with spectacular mountain and valley views; and then descends into a canyon past a small creek that still seeps natural oil from the park's days as an oil production facility. A steep 200-yard uphill detour to a viewpoint with panoramic vistas of the Santa Clarita Valley puts this in the strenuous category.

Description

Towsley Canyon is part of the 4,000-acre Santa Clarita Woodlands Park, just east of Santa Clarita. Fifteen million years ago this area was covered by deep ocean. Marine organisms built up in thick beds on the ocean floor, gradually covered with sand and gravel as the waters became shallow and receded. Subsequent uplift of the area caused the presence of oil- and gas-bearing fields on the land.

The Tataviam Indians, whose name means "dwellers of the sunny hill," were the first inhabitants of this 4,000-acre park. They used the area's naturally occurring asphalt for medicinal purposes and as a sealant for their baskets, according to a park brochure. Next came Darius Towsley, who arrived here at the end of the Civil War and began skimming and drilling for oil by way of a primitive spring pole method. Towsley eventually sold the property to Chevron (then called Pacific Coast Oil), which used the land for oil production for 120 years. It was later used for horse shows and film production, until the Santa Monica Mountains Conservancy turned it into public parkland in 1995. It is home to a wide variety of plants and wildlife, including red-tailed hawks, mule deer, coyotes, mountain quails, scrub jays, and California thrashers. Mountain lions have also been spotted in the hills, so use caution especially during early morning and evening hikes.

To get to the Canyon View Loop Trail, park in the first lot off The Old Road if you want to avoid the $5 fee required to park in the second (westernmost) lot. Turn right (west) from the parking lot and follow the paved road about 0.4 mile past the second parking lot and a small creek. Soon you will come to a bridge and see a large house and picnic area ahead of you to the left. This is the location of the ranger office, as well as the Towsley Canyon Lodge, a facility available for rent for meetings and other events.

The trailhead is past a small grassy area to the left of the lodge. If you follow Towsley Canyon Service Road, which continues west, it will take you to the Don Mullally Trail, a strenuous 5.5-mile hike with an elevation gain of about 1,000 feet.

The singletrack Canyon View Loop Trail immediately begins climbing uphill past tall grass, coastal sage scrub, wildflowers, and skeletal-looking oak trees that were burned in

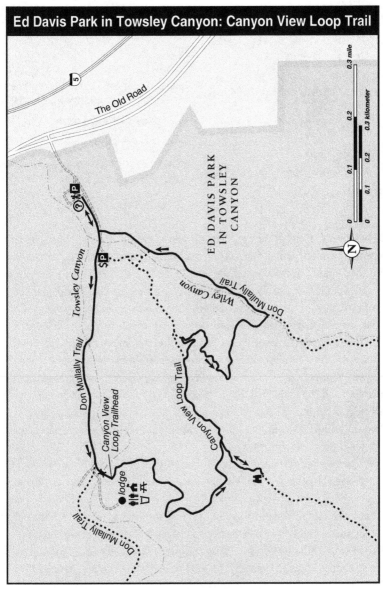

Ed Davis Park in Towsley Canyon: Canyon View Loop Trail

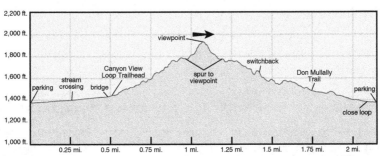

DISTANCE & CONFIGURATION: 2.2-mile loop	**ACCESS:** Daily, sunrise–sunset; free parking in lower lot; fee at self-pay kiosk in upper lot
DIFFICULTY: Strenuous	
SCENERY: Rugged mountains, coastal sage scrub, wildflowers (lupine, wild rose, monkeyflower)	**MAPS:** USGS *Oat Mountain;* at kiosk in lower parking lot and at ranger office and **lamountains.com/pdf/Towsley.Mullally.pdf**
EXPOSURE: Sunny	**WHEELCHAIR ACCESSIBLE:** No
TRAFFIC: Light	**FACILITIES:** Picnic area
TRAIL SURFACE: Packed and loose dirt	**CONTACT:** 661-255-3606; **lamountains .com/parks.asp?parkid=10**
HIKING TIME: 1.5 hours	

the 2003 wildfires that swept the area. The dirt path continues to switchback up a ridge for the next 0.5 mile or so, giving way to stellar views of chaparral-cloaked mountains on the right and the Santa Clarita Valley on the left. At 0.5 mile you will come to a turnoff for a steep singletrack path that leads to a viewpoint. It's a strenuous 200-yard climb to the top, but it's well worth the exertion for the 360-degree mountain and valley views. There is no place to sit, save for a single large rock, but you won't be able to keep yourself from staying a moment to revel in the fantastic views. Santa Clarita is home to many residential developments, and you can see their closely spaced orange rooftops from here, but the dramatic Santa Susana Mountains are by far the dominant scenery from this vantage point.

Once back on the main trail, the path levels and follows the mountain crest briefly, and then begins its gradual descent into the canyon. Soon the parking lots and Golden State Freeway come into view, though they are far enough away that you still feel as if you are in the wilderness. At about 1.2 miles, the trail passes under an old canyon oak tree— one of the few patches of shade—and then levels again at the bottom of a canyon. To the left you will see the hillside from which you descended. To the right is a fire-road gate that leads to Wiley Canyon Service Road. This takes you to the Don Mullally Trail.

To continue on the Canyon View Loop Trail, turn left at the old oak tree and follow the dirt trail north. You will cross what looks like a small stream, identified on the map as a ponded oil seep, and then continue past seasonal wildflowers and low-lying sage scrub. From the stream crossing, it's an easy 0.5-mile walk back to the first parking lot.

Nearby Activities

There are several good trails within Santa Clarita Woodlands Park. The East and Rice Canyon Trails, in the park's southern region, are also worth checking out for their views, diverse vegetation, and wildlife.

GPS TRAILHEAD COORDINATES   N34° 21.448' W118° 33.937'

Follow the Golden State Freeway (I-5) north to Exit 166 (Calgrove Boulevard) in Newhall. Turn left (west) onto Calgrove, drive back under I-5 to The Old Road, and head south less than 0.5 mile to the entrance for Towsley Canyon and Ed Davis Park on the right.

57 Hummingbird Trail

From the bottom of the Hummingbird Trail, you can see dozens of rock outcrops.

In Brief

Despite its proximity to a busy highway, this trail can be quite beautiful, combining dramatic rocky outcrops with delicate wildflowers. The consistent elevation gain of 500 feet makes for a good workout as well. This hike can also be extended by switchbacking another mile or so uphill to a junction with Rocky Peak Trail, a popular path leading to a viewpoint with an elevation of 2,700 feet and one of the highest points in Simi Valley.

This trail is best hiked in the spring, when the wildflowers are in glorious bloom and the weather hasn't yet reached the triple digits. It can also be accessed from a connector trail in Corriganville Park (see page 210), though it requires crossing the freeway by way of an unattractive tunnel.

DISTANCE & CONFIGURATION: 2-mile out-and-back	HIKING TIME: 1.25 hours
DIFFICULTY: Strenuous	ACCESS: Daily, sunrise–sunset; free
SCENERY: Simi Valley views, spring wild-flowers, sandstone rock formations	MAPS: USGS *Simi Valley East*
	WHEELCHAIR ACCESSIBLE: No
EXPOSURE: Sunny	FACILITIES: None
TRAFFIC: Light	CONTACT: 310-589-3200; **simitrail blazers.com/hikes/hummingbird.html**
TRAIL SURFACE: Dirt and gravel	

Description

Once the domain of the Chumash Indians, Simi Valley was discovered by eastern pioneers in the mid-19th century as an ideal farming site for sheep and cattle. The name Simi allegedly came from the Chumash word *shimiji,* which means "little white clouds." Settlement began in earnest in the late 1880s. Today, the area has grown to a city of 110,000 people that's known for its affluent gated communities and record low crime rate, though the wide-open spaces that attracted such residents as Ronald Reagan can still be found amid the suburban sprawl. This trail offers a window into both sides of the area—the dramatic rocky outcrops that date back to the Chumash and clear views of a major freeway and tightly packed residential developments with street names like Cowboy Court and Sasparilla Drive.

Don't let the nondescript trailhead stop you from exploring this trail. It's worth it to persevere, especially if you find yourself here in the spring. Yellow and purple wildflowers are in abundant bloom, and the hovering little birds that give the trail its name are guaranteed to dominate your hike.

To get to the trailhead, pass through the open gate of a nondescript chain-link fence that sits just north of CA 118. Follow the loose dirt path east as it heads downhill between a couple of oak trees; then take the first right back toward the highway. I had this trail all to myself on a weekday afternoon, though the freeway noise that accompanied most of the hike reminded me that I was never completely alone. Don't be surprised if you cross paths with mountain bikers headed down the trail toward the parking lot. They tend to take this trail one-way downhill, accessing it from the north–south Rocky Peak Fire Road.

At about 0.4 mile the trail makes a steep descent and then crosses over a concrete dam. At this point, the rocky outcrops you will soon be scaling are straight ahead and CA 118 is to the right. After crossing the dam, bear left past a sign for Rancho Simi Recreation District. The singletrack trail then begins a relentless ascent via switchbacks to the rock formations at the top of the canyon. There are several trails that branch off the main one along this route.

At about 0.75 mile, you will come to a signed trail marker and a green plastic fence. Continue straight up the hill. The path gets rocky here and a bit hard to navigate. Watch

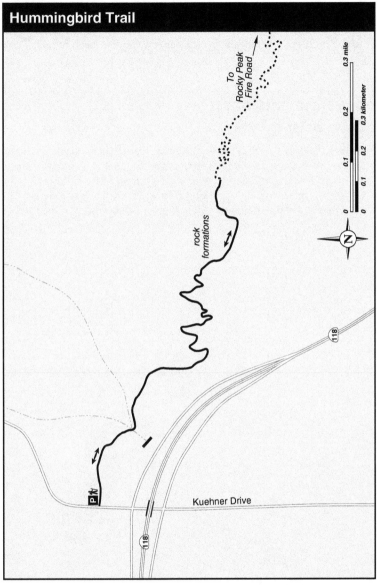

Hummingbird Trail

To
Rocky Peak
Fire Road

rock
formations

0.3 mile
0.3 kilometer
0.2
0.2
0.1
0.1
0
0

N

118

Kuehner Drive

118

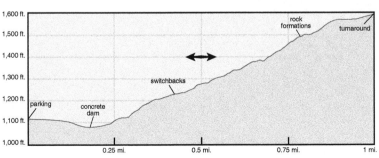

1,600 ft.
1,500 ft.
1,400 ft.
1,300 ft.
1,200 ft.
1,100 ft.
1,000 ft.

rock
formations
turnaround

switchbacks

parking
concrete
dam

0.25 mi.   0.5 mi.   0.75 mi.   1 mi.

out for loose boulders. At this point you will find yourself in the middle of the rock formations visible from the trailhead and freeway. From here, you can follow the path downhill and back to the trailhead or continue up the canyon another steep mile to Rocky Peak Fire Road.

GPS TRAILHEAD COORDINATES

N34° 16.819' W118° 39.710'

From downtown Los Angeles, take the Golden State Freeway (I-5) north to Exit 156A (CA 118) in Simi Valley. Merge onto CA 118 West, and go 12.7 miles. Just after crossing the Ventura County line, exit at Kuehner Drive, and turn right at the bottom of the ramp. Follow Kuehner 0.4 mile to a pullout parking area on the right side of the road. The trail begins at the opening in the chain-link fence. There is no sign marking the trail.

58 Pacific Crest Trail at Vasquez Rocks

Climbing around Vasquez Rocks is a fun activity to do before or after hiking a portion of the Pacific Crest Trail.

In Brief

This mostly flat hike is an easy way to experience a stretch of the Pacific Crest Trail (PCT) before it heads north toward harsher terrain. The trail winds past natural rock formations and a seasonal stream to a tunnel, then loops back on semi-rugged terrain along the west side of the rocks to the visitor/interpretive center. If you do the hike in late spring, you may encounter some PCT thru-hikers heading north on the 2,650-mile trail.

Description

Located in the northern corner of Los Angeles County, Vasquez Rocks is a 983-acre park marked by natural rock formations created centuries ago by geologic activity at the San Andreas Fault. Its craggy landscape has starred in episodes of *Star Trek, Bonanza,* and many other TV shows and films, and it was also once a trading crossroads for the Tataviam Indian tribe, who left behind petroglyphs that can be seen from the trail. In the

DISTANCE & CONFIGURATION: 5.5-mile balloon	**MAPS:** USGS *Agua Dulce;* at nature center
DIFFICULTY: Moderate	**WHEELCHAIR ACCESSIBLE:** No
SCENERY: Natural rock formations, desert landscape	**FACILITIES:** Restrooms, water, picnic area
EXPOSURE: Mostly sun, some shade	**CONTACT:** 661-268-0840; **parks.lacounty .gov/wps/portal/dpr/parks/vasquez_rocks _natural_area**
TRAFFIC: Moderate	
TRAIL SURFACE: Dirt and gravel	
HIKING TIME: 2 hours	**COMMENTS:** The maps at the interpretive center give you a general idea of the trail system, but they aren't comprehensive or to scale. Do your research before you set out, or check with a staffer if you have any questions.
ACCESS: Park: Daily, sunrise–sunset. Gate: September–March: Daily, 8 a.m.–5 p.m.; April–August: Daily, 8 a.m.–7 p.m. Nature center: Tuesday–Sunday, 8 a.m.–4 p.m.; free	

1870s the canyons and caves around here were a favorite hiding place for Tiburcio Vásquez, the 19th-century bandit and horse thief who eluded the law for decades before being captured and hanged.

This hike begins at the parking lot of the Vasquez Rocks Interpretive Center. The modern facility is a great before-and-after base for water, clean bathrooms, and maps, but you can also shorten the hike by about 0.5 mile by continuing on the gravel road to the lower parking area and pick up the trail there.

The PCT starts just inside the gate off Escondido Canyon Road. Follow the dusty path south about 0.5 mile as it skirts clumps of sagebrush and a few rock formations. Kids might be tempted to start climbing the rocks, but even better scrambling opportunities await down the road a mile.

After about 0.5 mile, you will see a dirt parking area on the right and a large pepper-tree in front of you. Continue past the tree toward the PCT marker, and follow the path in a southwest direction as it widens into a fire road skirting a low ridge. You'll see the Antelope Valley Freeway (CA 14) and hear some faint traffic noise in the distance. At about 1.75 miles, the fire road ends near a large wooden sign marking a major wildfire that swept through the area on July 7, 2007. Follow the singletrack trail to the right of the sign as it descends into the canyon. At the bottom, another sign for the PCT directs you left. (There are also some primo climbing/caving opportunities here for anyone looking for a water break or kid diversion.)

Follow the path left into the canyon as it crosses over a seasonal stream and skirts sheer rock canyons that create welcome pockets of shade and welcome blasts of natural air-conditioning. You may also see wild California rose, sagebrush, scrub oak, and Mexican elderberry (all identified by interpretive signs) along this stretch. The trail continues on a gentle roller-coaster path to the tunnel entrance, crossing and recrossing the stream a few more times. A few colorful graffiti markings and a fading PCT mural are on the

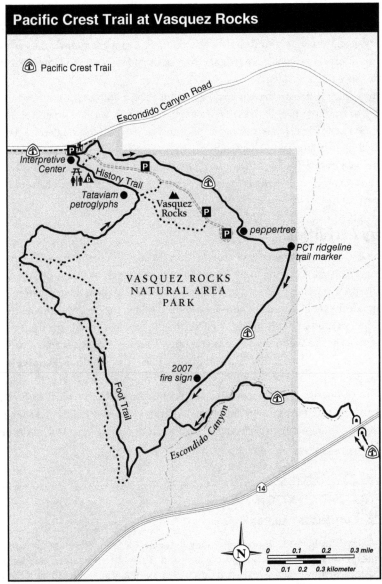

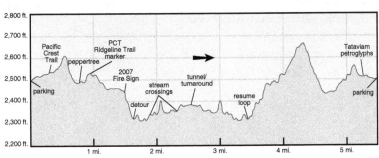

other side of the tunnel. We turned around here after refueling with snacks and water. Because you're under the CA 14 freeway, it's not exactly an idyllic spot to stop, but everyone in my group was ready to rest for a few minutes. From the tunnel, the easiest way back to the interpretive center is to retrace your steps and stop near the lower parking lot for a little more rock climbing.

If you'd like change up the scenery a bit and make it a balloon, you can retrace your steps back to the large Pacific Crest Trail sign and then follow the Foot and Horse Trail signs to the left (a right leads you back the way you came). The singletrack Foot and Horse Trail follows long switchbacks around the west side of Vasquez Rocks, eventually leading to the History Trail near the interpretive center. We stopped along this stretch to check out the American Indian petroglyphs. From there, it's a short walk back to the visitor center.

Nearby Activities

You won't find much commerce in or around Agua Dulce, so it's best to bring plenty of food and water. It's worth factoring in an extra half hour, however, to check out the Vasquez Rocks Interpretive Center. Opened in 2013, it's a welcoming place to stop before or after your hike to learn about the area. There are wildlife displays, posters from movies that were made in the area, and a fascinating rammed-earth sculpture just outside the front door that was created to change over time. The center is open Tuesday–Sunday, 8 a.m.–4 p.m.

Another nearby destination is the Halfway House Cafe (**halfwayhousecafe.com**), which has been featured in dozens of TV shows and movies, from *Heroes* to *Space Cowboys* to *Lost in America*. Open since 1931, it serves biscuits and gravy, chicken-fried steak, and other home-style meals for breakfast and lunch amid wood paneling and a long belly-up counter. As a bonus, diners can watch the planes from nearby Agua Dulce Airport take off and land.

GPS TRAILHEAD COORDINATES
N34° 29.334' W118° 19.298'

Take I-5 North to Exit 162 (Antelope Valley Freeway/CA 14). Follow CA 14 North for 14.3 miles, and exit at Agua Dulce Canyon Road. Turn left and follow the signs 1.9 miles toward Vasquez Rocks. Make a right onto Escondido Canyon Road, and the park will be on your right. There's parking at the interpretive center to your right, and the trailhead is to the left past the entrance gate.

59 **Placerita Canyon:**
WALKER RANCH

In Brief

This flat trail near Santa Clarita follows a seasonal stream past wildflowers and coastal sage scrub.

Description

At the western end of the San Gabriel Mountains, Placerita is an east–west canyon with a seasonal stream, chaparral- and manzanita-covered hills, and about 12 miles of hiking trails. Now run by the Los Angeles County Department of Parks and Recreation, much of the property once operated as a ranch belonging to a pioneer named Frank Walker and his family. Its picnic area and well-marked trails make it a popular weekend spot for families from the Antelope and Santa Clarita Valleys. Be sure to stop by the renovated nature center and pick up a map before setting off on the hike.

To get to Walker Ranch via Canyon Trail, cross the seasonal stream at the south end of the parking lot and walk up the dirt path to a brown trail sign. The trail is lined with small boulders and parallels the stream to the left. Besides the ranch grounds, this trail also links up with the Waterfall Trail, a 0.5-mile trek to a 25-foot cascade (if it's not a drought season), and Los Pinetos Trail, the park's toughest hike, with a 1,400-foot elevation gain.

You may still see traces of the damage left by the 2003 wildfires that swept through this area in the form of charred oak trees and manzanita along the hillside. Morning glories, wild cucumber, buckwheat, sage scrub, and other plants have grown in around the burned trees, but it was a startling sight when I first hiked this trail in 2005. Nature center officials estimate that it will be 15 years before the park's vegetation is restored to its pre-fire levels. In describing the devastation in a memo, the president of the not-for-profit Placerita Canyon Nature Associates wrote, "to say that the fires turned the park into an ashen wasteland would be an understatement."

Shortly after hitting this trail, you will pass a turnoff for Manzanita Mountain Trail, a mile-long uphill trek to a lookout at an elevation of 2,063 feet. Continue straight on Canyon Trail. After about 0.4 mile, you will pass beneath a grove of coast live oak and sycamore trees. The path is also lined with wooden signs that identify some of the park's native plants, including poison oak, hollyleaf, yerba santa, California buckwheat, and chamise.

The gurgling sound of the stream makes a pleasant companion as you meander along this easy stretch of the trail. At the 0.5-mile marker, you will come to the first of several stream crossings and another brown sign that tells you Walker Ranch is another 1.5 miles. Those with small kids or those looking for an easy jaunt may want to turn around here. The path narrows at this point and gets full sun exposure as it continues back and forth along the stream for about 0.5 mile.

DISTANCE & CONFIGURATION: 4.4-mile out-and-back	**HIKING TIME:** 2 hours
	ACCESS: Daily, sunrise–sunset. Nature center: Daily, 9 a.m.–5 p.m.; free
DIFFICULTY: Moderate	
SCENERY: Streambed, waterfalls, oak and sycamore groves	**MAPS:** USGS *Mint Canyon;* at nature center and **placerita.org/maps-brochure**
EXPOSURE: Mostly sun, some shade	**WHEELCHAIR ACCESSIBLE:** First mile
	FACILITIES: Restrooms, water, picnic area
TRAFFIC: Heavy on weekends	
TRAIL SURFACE: Dirt and gravel	**CONTACT:** 661-259-7721; **placerita.org**

At 0.75 mile, the trail briefly hugs the canyon wall and then turns shady before passing a series of small seasonal waterfalls on the left. Look to the right for more striking views of charred trees. Placerita Canyon is also home to plenty of wild animals, including coyotes, skunks, ornate shrews, California pocket mice, great horned owls, and 16 kinds of bats.

After crossing a dry streambed, the trail turns away from the stream briefly and is surrounded by shrubs and tall weeds. At about 1.8 miles, you will pass a rattlesnake warning sign on the left, then a cluster of picnic tables and an open fire pit. After passing beneath a big old California sycamore tree, the full-scale Walker Ranch picnic area comes into view. It's very shady here with a handful of picnic tables, a water fountain, and a trail kiosk with big maps of the park and the entire Angeles National Forest.

Just past the picnic area you will come to the turnoffs for a couple of other trails—Waterfall and Los Pinetos. It's another 0.6 mile and 300-foot elevation gain to a 25-foot waterfall and 2.3 miles to a fire road with scenic views of the San Fernando Valley.

From this intersection, Canyon Trail crosses another small streambed and then winds uphill past a grassy meadow on the right and the remains of Walker Ranch, a water cistern and a cluster of old wooden fences. The path ends at a small parking lot off Placerita Canyon Road. From here, you can follow the shady Oak Pass Trail back to the picnic area and retrace your steps back to the nature center.

Nearby Activities

The indoor-outdoor Placerita Canyon Nature Center (**placerita.org**) hosts family nature walks every Saturday and has exhibits on the area's natural history, plus displays of live animals such as rattlesnakes, turtles, and red-tailed hawks.

There's also an easy 1-mile hike highlighting Placerita Canyon's natural and cultural history that is great for families with small kids who might find the other trails challenging. It ends at a century-old oak tree, reputed to be the site of one of California's first gold discoveries.

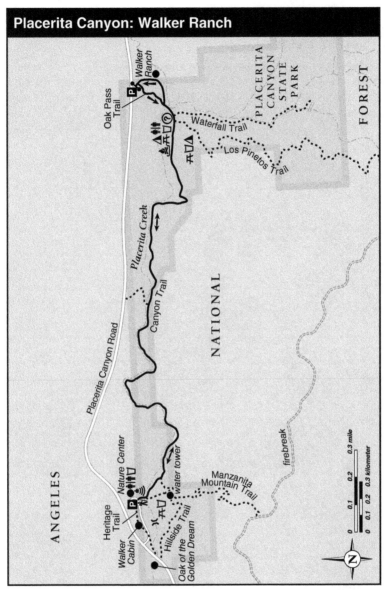

Placerita Canyon: Walker Ranch

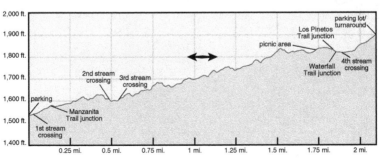

GPS TRAILHEAD COORDINATES

N34° 22.647' W118° 28.042'

Take I-5 North to Exit 162 (Antelope Valley Freeway/CA 14). Follow CA 14 North for 2.6 miles, and exit at Placerita Canyon Road. Turn right and drive about 1.5 miles to Placerita Canyon State Park. The entrance is on the right. There is plenty of parking in the upper and lower lots.

60 Wildwood Park:
LIZARD ROCK

The trail is named for this rock formation, which resembles a lizard.

In Brief

This hike begins as a straightforward stroll past grassy meadows and spring wildflowers, then gets steep as it climbs to Lizard Rock and panoramic views of the Conejo Valley and the Santa Susana Mountains. It is used by hikers, mountain bikers, joggers, dog walkers, and the occasional equestrian.

There isn't a stitch of shade on this hike, so plan it for early or late in the day, and be sure to bring hats and sunscreen. It can get scorching hot in summer, and the park tends to close after heavy storms. Call ahead to check conditions.

DISTANCE & CONFIGURATION: 2.7-mile balloon	**HIKING TIME:** 1 hour
DIFFICULTY: Moderate	**ACCESS:** Gate: Daily, sunrise–sunset; free
SCENERY: Grasslands, rocky outcrops, panoramic views of Simi Valley	**MAPS:** USGS *Newbury Park;* at trailhead kiosk and **tinyurl.com/wildwoodparkmap**
EXPOSURE: Sunny	**WHEELCHAIR ACCESSIBLE:** No
TRAFFIC: Light	**FACILITIES:** None
TRAIL SURFACE: Dirt and gravel	**CONTACT:** 805-495-6000; **cosf.org /wildwood**

Description

Like many of today's Southern California trail systems, Wildwood Park was once used by film crews as a substitute for the Old West. Films that shot scenes here include *The Grapes of Wrath, Spartacus,* and *Duel in the Sun.* Most of the cameras stopped rolling in the early 1970s, when bulldozers showed up to make room for tract home developments and a water treatment plant, though the park is still used for commercials and the occasional TV show. Today, the park is a 1,300-acre oasis amid urban sprawl and run by the Conejo Recreation and Park District. You can read about its history at the trailhead kiosk. There is also information about the park's wildlife, which includes mountain lions, rattlesnakes, and rabbits. Located in the city of Thousand Oaks, the park is bordered to the north by Mountclef Ridge, a volcanic-rock outcrop and wildlife corridor that can be seen from Mesa Trail. The area is also home to Conejo dudleya, a rare and endangered yellow-flower succulent that grows in a 10-mile radius around Mountclef Ridge, and yerba mansa, a white coneflower also known as lizard root, which thrives in moist soil.

Lizard Rock is a nice introduction to the park, but there are other well-marked trails from which to choose. Santa Rosa Trail is a 5-mile loop that leads to Mountclef Ridge. Paradise Falls Trail is a family-friendly 3-mile downhill jaunt to a 70-foot waterfall and picnic area. Moonridge Trail skirts a pretty creek and leads to a serene overlook marked by a large tepee. I followed Mesa Trail to Lizard Rock and then looped back on the Stagecoach Bluff Trail, which is a little more difficult than Mesa Trail.

To get to Lizard Rock, take the uphill path behind the trailhead kiosk and follow the signs for Mesa/Box Canyon. The first leg of this hike is pancake-flat and heads due west past grassy meadows and prickly pear cactus, with views of your final destination—Lizard Rock—in the distance. At about 0.3 mile, you will pass the turnoff for Santa Rosa Trail on the right, marked by a small sign. On the day I was here, the trail was closed due to disrepair.

Mesa Trail continues for about 0.75 mile and then meets up again with the Stagecoach Bluff Trail. To get to Lizard Rock, head straight as the path starts a gradual climb toward the rock formation that is now looming over the trail. At the top, take a moment to drink in the breathtaking views of valleys and mountains. I saw a handful of hikers along Mesa and Stagecoach Bluff Trails, but there wasn't a soul lingering at Lizard Rock.

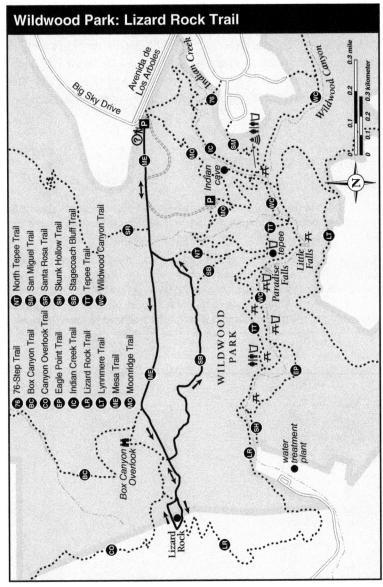

Wildwood Park: Lizard Rock Trail

76 76-Step Trail
BC Box Canyon Trail
CO Canyon Overlook Trail
EP Eagle Point Trail
IC Indian Creek Trail
LR Lizard Rock Trail
LT Lynnmere Trail
ME Mesa Trail
MO Moonridge Trail

NT North Tepee Trail
SM San Miguel Trail
SR Santa Rosa Trail
SH Skunk Hollow Trail
SB Stagecoach Bluff Trail
TT Tepee Trail
WC Wildwood Canyon Trail

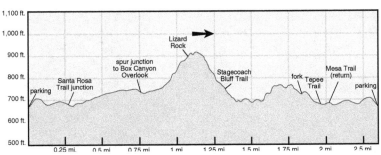

To get back, follow the trail along the back of the rock formation, and take it downhill to the right turnoff for Stagecoach Bluff. This trail is rockier and will give you more of an uphill/downhill workout (the elevation gain is 100 feet) as you head back to the parking lot. It also has views of the park's southern side, which includes the Hill Canyon water treatment plant and the tepee overlook that marks the end of Moonridge Trail. After about 2.5 miles, the trail rejoins Mesa Trail. Turn right and retrace your steps back to the parking lot.

GPS TRAILHEAD COORDINATES

N34° 13.187' W118° 54.184'

From US 101 headed north, take the Moorpark Freeway (CA 23) north about 2.5 miles to Avenida de los Arboles. Turn left and follow the road until it ends at Big Sky Drive. Turn left into the parking lot and look for the trailhead beyond the kiosk.

Alternate directions: From downtown Los Angeles, take the Golden State Freeway (I-5) north to Exit 156A (CA 118) in Simi Valley. Merge onto Ronald Reagan Freeway/CA 118 West, and go 25.8 miles. Continue onto Moorpark Freeway (CA 23), and go south 4.8 miles to Avenida de los Arboles. Turn right and follow it 3 miles until it ends at Big Sky Drive. Turn left into the parking lot and look for the trailhead beyond the kiosk.

Appendix A: Outdoor Shops

Adventure 16 Outdoor and Travel Outfitters

adventure16.com

11161 Pico Blvd.
Los Angeles, CA 90064
310-473-4574

5425 Reseda Blvd.
Tarzana, CA 91356
818-345-4266

REI

rei.com

214 N. Santa Anita Ave.
Arcadia, CA 91006
626-447-1062

7777 Edinger Ave.
Huntington Beach, CA 92647
714-379-1938

1800 Rosecrans Ave., Ste. E
Manhattan Beach, CA 90266
310-727-0728

18605 Devonshire St.
Northridge, CA 91324
818-831-5555

12218 Foothill Blvd.
Rancho Cucamonga, CA 91739
909-646-8360

402 Santa Monica Blvd.
Santa Monica, CA 90401
310-458-4370

Sport Chalet

sportchalet.com

400 S. Baldwin Ave., Ste. 910-L
Arcadia, CA 91007
626-446-8955

201 E. Magnolia Blvd., #145
Burbank, CA 91502
818-558-3500

2 Sport Chalet Dr.
La Cañada, CA 91011
818-790-9800

735 S. Figueroa St., Ste. 150
Los Angeles, CA 90017
213-542-5150

11801 W. Olympic Blvd.
Los Angeles, CA 90064
310-235-2847

13455 Maxella Ave.
Marina Del Rey, CA 90292
310-821-9400

Sports Authority

sportsauthority.com

1900 W. Empire Ave., Ste. R12
Burbank, CA 91504
818-260-0504

21301 Victory Blvd.
Canoga Park, CA 91303
818-715-1400

1531 W. Imperial Hwy.
La Habra, CA 90631
562-690-7900

1919 S. Sepulveda Blvd.
West Los Angeles, CA 90025
310-312-9600

Appendix B: Hiking Clubs & Organizations

La Cañada–Flintridge Trails Council
   lcftrails.org

LA Trail Hikers
   latrailhikers.com

The Los Angeles Hiking Group
   meetup.com/hiking-196

Mt. Lowe Volunteers
   503-624-8600
   mtlowe.net

Santa Monica Mountains Conservancy
   310-589-3200
   smmc.ca.gov

Sierra Club Los Angeles
   3435 Wilshire Blvd., #320
   Los Angeles, CA 90010
   213-387-4287
   angeles.sierraclub.org

Sierra Club Orange County
   angeles.sierraclub.org/orange

Index

About the Author

A NATIVE OF SUBURBAN PHILADELPHIA, Laura Randall lived in Washington, D.C., and San Juan, Puerto Rico, before moving to the Los Angeles area in 1999. Her byline can be found in a variety of newspapers and magazines, including the *Los Angeles Times*, *The Washington Post*, *Sunset* magazine, and *The Christian Science Monitor*. She is also the author of *Peaceful Places: Los Angeles* and *Five-Star Trails: Palm Springs*.

PHOTOGRAPHED BY JOHN KIMBLE

DEAR CUSTOMERS AND FRIENDS,

SUPPORTING YOUR INTEREST IN OUTDOOR ADVENTURE, travel, and an active lifestyle is central to our operations, from the authors we choose to the locations we detail to the way we design our books. Menasha Ridge Press was incorporated in 1982 by a group of veteran outdoorsmen and professional outfitters. For many years now, we've specialized in creating books that benefit the outdoors enthusiast.

Almost immediately, Menasha Ridge Press earned a reputation for revolutionizing outdoors- and travel-guidebook publishing. For such activities as canoeing, kayaking, hiking, backpacking, and mountain biking, we established new standards of quality that transformed the whole genre, resulting in outdoor-recreation guides of great sophistication and solid content. Menasha Ridge continues to be outdoor publishing's greatest innovator.

The folks at Menasha Ridge Press are as at home on a whitewater river or mountain trail as they are editing a manuscript. The books we build for you are the best they can be, because we're responding to your needs. Plus, we use and depend on them ourselves.

We look forward to seeing you on the river or the trail. If you'd like to contact us directly, join in at trekalong.com or visit us at menasharidge .com. We thank you for your interest in our books and the natural world around us all.

SAFE TRAVELS,

BOB SEHLINGER
PUBLISHER

Printed in the USA
CPSIA information can be obtained
at www.ICGtesting.com
JSHW011521130424
61126JS00002B/6

9 781634 040365